Probation

This book provides a comprehensive and accessible introduction to the work of the probation service. It brings together themes of policy, theory and practice to help students and practitioners better understand the work of probation, its limitations and potential, but above all its value.

Setting probation in the context of the criminal justice system, the book explores its history, purposes and contemporary significance. It explains what probation is, discusses emerging ideas around offender management, and the value of an approach that centres on the idea of desistance. It considers the practice realities of working with offenders in the community. The book also covers the governance of probation and how policy and practice are responding to contemporary concerns about crime and community safety, for example through the management of risk. Although the main focus is on England and Wales, there is some discussion of other UK jurisdictions and of contemporary trends in European probation practices.

This book will encourage readers to appreciate the practical and theoretical strengths and shortcomings of contemporary probation practice. Information and discussions are presented clearly, with guidance about further study and pointers towards more specialised re dings.

Probation: Working with offenders will be essential reading for trainee probation officers and students of probation and offender management.

Rob Canton is Professor and Head of Research in Community and Criminal Justice, De Montfort University, Leicester. As a former probation officer, he has done a great deal of international work, especially on behalf of the Council of Europe, and helped to draft the European Probation Rules.

Probation

Probation

Working with offenders

Rob Canton

Routledge
Taylor & Francis Group

LONDON AND NEW YORK

First published 2011
by Routledge
2 Park Square, Milton Park, Abingdon, Oxon, OX14 4RN

Simultaneously published in the USA and Canada
by Routledge
711 Third Avenue, New York, NY 10017

Routledge is an imprint of the Taylor & Francis Group, an informa business

British Library Cataloguing in Publication Data
A catalogue record for this book is available from the British Library

Library of Congress Cataloging in Publication Data
Canton, Robert.
   Probation : working with offenders / Rob Canton.
      p. cm.
   1. Probation—Great Britain. 2. Criminals—Rehabilitation—Great Britain.
   3. Corrections—Great Britain. I. Title.
   HV9345.A5C36 2011
   364.6′30941—dc22   2011000310

ISBN: 978–1–84392–374–9 hbk
ISBN: 978–1–84392–373–2 ppr
ISBN: 978–0–20380–916–7 ebook

Typeset in Times New Roman
by Keystroke, Station Road, Codsall, Wolverhampton

Printed and bound in Great Britain by
CPI Antony Rowe, Chippenham, Wiltshire

For Liz,
for lots of reasons

Contents

List of illustrations

Figures

Tables

Acknowledgements

Very many people helped in the writing of this book. I worked as a probation officer in Nottinghamshire for several years and my first debt is to the many service users with whom I worked, most of whom were ordinary people in circumstances of often overwhelming difficulty. The experience of working with them taught me most of what I think I know about probation and why it matters.

I learnt my trade alongside committed, conscientious and often inspirational colleagues. I have a lasting debt to them too.

I have gained an enormous amount from the writings of many distinguished scholars of probation and criminal justice, especially Anthony Bottoms, Nils Christie, David Faulkner, David Garland, Loraine Gelsthorpe, Hazel Kemshall, James McGuire, Gill McIvor, Fergus McNeill, George Mair, Mike Nellis, Peter Raynor and Gwen Robinson. Their influence will be apparent throughout the book.

Several people have helped and advised me by commenting on ideas and on draft chapters. I am most grateful to Bob Bearne, Alan Goode, Ann Gerty, Ian Fox, Beverley Radcliffe, Fergus McNeill and Philip Whitehead. Kathy Ferguson and Will Hughes went well beyond what might reasonably have been asked of them and gave me much well-judged feedback.

In the course of writing, I have received encouragement, advice and general support from many friends, including Aline Bauwens, Clare Canton, Mary Anne McFarlane, Ian Macnair, Alan Morrison, Leo Tigges and Jonathan Vickers.

Among my colleagues at De Montfort University, I am particularly grateful to Jane Dominey, Nick Flynn, Sarah Hilder, Jean Hine, Judy Hudson and Brian Stout. I have discussed the topics in this book so often and over so many years with Charlotte Knight and Tina Eadie that it is not always easy to disentangle my own ideas from theirs. Their comradeship and wisdom have been of inestimable value to me.

I have taught large numbers of trainee probation officers over many years and they have helped me to keep in touch with some of the realities of probation practice, as well as challenging me to clarify some of my odder ideas.

David Hancock, who co-edited the *Dictionary of Probation and Offender Management*, has been a great source of advice and support throughout. (Many readers will see, incidentally, that I have frequently referred to the *Dictionary* in this book. This is because, while it is not a final word on anything, it is often a useful first word.)

I am sure that I should have taken the advice of these friends and colleagues more often than I have.

This book was originally the idea of Brian Willan, whose work as a publisher did so much for the flourishing of criminology and criminal justice studies. His encouragement and advice were greatly appreciated. Julia Willan guided me in the later stages and to her and to Tom Sutton I am indebted.

To the leaders, helpers and cubs of Keyworth A Pack I say TAR. To my sons, Matt, Philip and Rich, I am really grateful for their support and for their patience when their father was distracted by the demands of writing. Liz has helped me in more ways than can be counted. To all of them my warmest thanks.

Rob Canton
Keyworth, Nottinghamshire
May 2011

Introduction

Probation in England and Wales celebrated a centenary in 2007. The Bishop of Worcester spoke in Westminster Abbey of a 'weight of glory down this hundred years' and 'a number beyond our counting whose lives have been changed by this great work' (Selby 2007). In his annual report for 2007–2008 (National Probation Service 2008a), the Director of the National Probation Service spoke of solid achievements in a challenging year (2008), demonstrating that many of the targets set for the service had been met or exceeded. English probation is respected internationally and seen by many countries as model to emulate.

Yet probation has been going through a turbulent time and, in a House of Lords Debate on 21 January 2010, many wise observers expressed deep concerns about developments and their implications for probation's future. The annual report for the centennial year turned out to have been the last one: the National Probation Service ceased to exist, subsumed into a National Offender Management Service, described as a 'monster bureaucracy' by Lord Ramsbotham who went on to say that probation had been 'virtually destroyed' in the process (Guardian 2010).

The very term *probation* had been becoming rare in the English criminal justice lexicon. Probation officers are now more commonly known as offender managers and there is no penalty now available to the court which includes the word probation. On the other hand, Probation Trusts have now been established across the country and are involved in the supervision of very large numbers of offenders. The government has announced a 'rehabilitation revolution' (Ministry of Justice 2010a) and in some interpretations of this ambition, probation's role, as both a provider and commissioner of services, will be crucial.

How are we to understand these developments and their importance? This book attempts to explain probation's policies and practices. As well as describing the work, the book critically explores influences on policy and the theoretical basis that informs practice. It discusses how policies work out in practice – not always, perhaps, in the manner expected by those who make these policies. After all, what an agency aspires to do and announces in its policies always bears an uncertain relationship to what it really does: the realities of the job to be done and the need to do it in a principled and ethical manner inevitably influence practitioners' interpretation and implementation of policy.

Three policy strategies

To make sense of the volatile politics that have buffeted criminal justice and probation in the past 30 years, three dominant policy 'strategies' have been identified (Cavadino and Dignan 2008; Cavadino, Crow and Dignan 1999, developing the work of Rutherford 1993).

The first of these is a *punitive* strategy that insists that punishment is what offenders deserve: it is the only way in which the distress of victims can be vindicated. And the practices of punishment protect us all, making us safer. There is a political imperative to be (and be seen to be) *tough on crime*.

This strategy has had a number of discernable direct and indirect influences on probation. For example:

- attempts by probation to present its interventions as punitive and demanding in the quest to present community sentences as 'credible alternatives to custody';
- the setting of the 'proper punishment of offenders' as among the aims of the National Probation Service;
- the prominence of punishment at all levels of the Offender Management Model (Chapter 7).

Second is a *management* strategy, which is concerned to 'dispose of the tasks in hand as smoothly and efficiently as possible' (Rutherford 1993: 13). This uses a different and cooler language than the punitive strategy, recognising that high levels of crime need to be dealt with in a systematic and rational manner. The purpose of criminal justice is the effective, efficient and economic management of cases. Manifestations of this strategy in probation include:

- an emphasis on evidence-led, effective practice ('what works');
- setting objectives and targets;
- performance management;
- inspections;
- area rankings;
- actuarial practices;
- national standards;
- structural changes to the organisation and governance of probation.

A third *ethical* strategy represents what Rutherford calls 'decency'. Rejecting the punitive strategy's assumption that their interests are always in opposition, this tries to find ways of valuing both offenders and victims. It is described here as an *ethical* strategy because its starting point is not *what works* but *what is right*. It has regard for fairness and justice, for human rights and the rule of law. This strategy is suspicious of the social, cultural and ethical consequences of political enthusiasm for punishment and sceptical of its efficacy in reducing crime. It believes that the social inclusion of offenders and an acceptance by the community of its responsibilities towards them is, both ethically and practically, the best way to reduce reoffending.

It has not been always been easy to affirm these principles politically, especially in circumstances where they offer an overt challenge to the other two strategies, but they persist – not so much as a strategy, perhaps, but as a 'liberal constraint' on the harsher manifestations of punitiveness and managerialism (compare Loader 2007). This strategy is especially stubborn in probation practice, arguably, because this decent regard for offenders and victims has been found by practitioners to be *what it takes to do the job* (Canton 2007).

Many recent policy developments in criminal justice and in probation can be seen as a working-out of these strategies and of the tensions among them. At different times, one or another is more openly asserted, but any modern criminal justice system will have to find ways of accommodating their competing claims.

The book's argument

We shall return to these strategies frequently. This book sets out to offer an accurate account and indeed aspires to equip readers to disagree with its main thesis. But I aim at more than a descriptive text. A central theme is that probation has often been pushed in wrong directions by punitivism and by managerialism. There will be no attempt to deny that punishment is a proper response to crimes, but it must be administered ethically and parsimoniously. A zeal for punishment leads to a level of social exclusion that produces more crime. Illiberal and callous attitudes begin to affect other aspects of our social interactions, not only changing the tone of crime control strategies, but through contagion of punishment, generating intolerance, mistrust and a corrosion of community. Punishment usually does not make us safer and excesses of punishment are not only morally corrupting for our relationships with one another, but can lead to more crimes.

Similarly, the management strategy rests on an unduly instrumental understanding of criminal justice: the idea that there is something(s) that a criminal justice system is 'for' and to which purposes it is reducible. Instrumentalism values outcomes over processes and elevates ends over means; managerialism favours auditable events and behavioural episodes, binary distinctions and clear-cut categories; it is suspicious of and devalues what it cannot comprehend and often distorts practice to fit its devices of measurement.

Within probation discourse, the dominance of effectiveness, efficiency and economy can suppress other intrinsic characteristics of criminal justice. It will be repeatedly insisted in this book that *how* things are done is not less important than the outcomes: for example, the manner in which a sentence is carried out is a critical part of the 'message' which punishment is intended to communicate (Duff 2001; Rex 2005). This is in no way to deprecate the importance of reliable and effective practice, which indeed is part of what an ethical approach requires. But probation is not reducible to the objectives that are set for it, to some of which (rehabilitation, public protection) its contribution is important but modest. Nor is it true that anything is acceptable so long as it 'works'.

David Faulkner wisely insists that:

> Criminal justice is not only about pursuing, convicting and punishing offenders: it is also about the exercise of the state's powers of interference, intrusion, control and ultimately of coercion, and correspondingly the limits which should be placed upon those powers.
>
> (Faulkner 2006: 349)

But this is not something that the state itself is always ready to acknowledge and has sometimes overlooked altogether as governments strive to establish their credentials in 'law and order'.

So while probation must set objectives, endeavour to achieve them and evaluate its work rigorously, it is not reducible to these objectives. It will be argued throughout that the value of probation consists above all in what it represents and stands for – especially the values of social inclusion and a belief in the possibility of personal change. If imprisonment vividly represents (at least temporary) exile, social exclusion and suspension from citizenship, probation betokens a determination to work with offenders in their communities – where they live their lives, have their relationships, have committed their offences and where one day they will accomplish desistance. This commitment to inclusion challenges the community as well as the individual. The idea that the community has responsibilities towards offenders as well as claims against them is unfashionable and requires political courage to affirm, but is central to what probation represents.

This book attempts to bring together themes of policy, theory and practice to help students and practitioners better to understand the work of probation, its limitations as well as its potential, but above all its value. A punitive approach starts on the basis that probation is intended to implement punishment; an instrumental approach sets objectives, mostly of public protection and reduced reoffending which are meant to guide practice; an ethical understanding insists that probation should be grounded in a view of the responsibilities and rights of offenders, victims and communities and that probation's organisation and practices should be guided by these principles. The implications of this understanding of probation are the subject of this book.

1 Probation and criminal justice

This chapter introduces the idea of probation, with a preliminary sketch of the probation service, its primary tasks and duties. The wider criminal justice system is then discussed and some models set out which offer different and complementary ways of understanding the character and significance of criminal justice and probation's place within it.

What is probation?

> If I were asked what was the most significant contribution made by this country to the new penological theory and practice which struck root in the twentieth century . . . my answer would be probation.
>
> (Sir Leon Radzinowicz (1958), quoted Haxby 1978: 148)

Probation is, originally and literally, a *proving* or *testing* and is used in this sense in contexts other than criminal justice (a new employee, for instance, may be taken on for a *probationary period*). This idea of *testing* will have been the most obvious connotation of the word when, in the late nineteenth century, it was adopted to describe a new penal measure. Offenders would be *on probation*: instead of being punished, and on their undertaking to be of good behaviour, they would be put to the test and given an opportunity to show they could lead good and industrious lives. Supervised by *probation officers*, who would 'advise, assist and befriend' them (Probation of Offenders Act 1907 s.4 [d]), if they neglected the requirements of the probation order, they might be returned to court and were then liable to be punished.

Max Grünhut accordingly found probation's strength to lie in 'a combination of two things, conditional suspension of punishment, and personal care and supervision by a court welfare officer' (quoted by Raynor 2006: 27). At different times and places, these two components have been given varying emphasis. In the Anglo-American tradition, probation's defining characteristic has been the *supervision of offenders in the community*; in other countries, especially those with a civil rather than common law tradition, the *conditional suspension of punishment* is emphasised (Harris 1995).

Many countries have probation agencies, but their tasks and responsibilities are diverse (see Chapter 16). Equally, many jurisdictions that do not have a probation service have organisations (state and non-governmental) that undertake what would be seen in England and Wales as 'probation tasks'.

As we shall see in more detail in later chapters, throughout its history, the Probation Service in England and Wales acquired new tasks and responsibilities (and lost a few besides), but for most of its history – and indeed now – probation's main tasks are:

- writing reports for the court to assist magistrates and judges to decide upon sentence;
- giving effect to the order of the court by supervising offenders who have been made subject to community punishments;
- working with serving prisoners;
- working with prisoners after release.

More will be said about all of these responsibilities in later chapters.

Probation in the criminal justice system

The character and work of the Probation Service have to be understood in the context of the wider criminal justice system. Yet even drawing the boundaries of that system is not at all straightforward (Lacey 1994). As well as the main criminal justice agencies, there are many departments, agencies, organisations and businesses in all sectors of the economy who are concerned with the reduction of crime, the detection, apprehension, conviction, punishment and rehabilitation of offenders, and working with victims.

Indeed there is a sense in which crime and criminal justice have become everybody's business. Not only are the formal agencies of criminal justice instructed to work effectively together (Home Office 2004a), but they need to liaise and often work in partnership with an indefinitely wide range of other organisations. Study of criminal careers (Farrington 2007) has led to a recognition of the critical contributions of (among others) education, health, employment and housing services. These are not 'criminal justice agencies', but their policies and practices can influence crime significantly and can make all the difference to offenders' prospects of rehabilitation and desistance. Accordingly, probation's engagement with these organisations is central to its contemporary work.

An account of the formal criminal justice system should cover at least the work of (and relations among) these agencies:

- Police – whose principal responsibilities include maintaining the peace and public order, prevention of crime, detection of crime and arrest of alleged offenders.
- Crown Prosecution Service (CPS) – responsible for prosecuting criminal cases investigated by the police, taking account of the likelihood of conviction and whether prosecution serves the public interest.

- Courts: Magistrates' and Crown Court – the authorities that determine a defendant's innocence or guilt and pass sentence on convicted offenders.
- Probation Service.
- Prison Service – holding prisoners securely, humanely, decently and lawfully; reducing the risk of their re-offending.

(The expression *the penal system* is often used for those agencies that give effect to the sentences of the court – the prison and probation services.)

There are several important associations between probation and the other principal agencies and some alliances have worked extremely well. Table 1.1 sets out some examples of probation working in partnership with the main criminal justice agencies.

Understanding the criminal justice system

It has been suggested then that probation must be understood in its context of the wider criminal justice system. But how is this system to be studied? King (1981) identifies a number of 'models' – vantage points or ways of looking at the criminal

Table 1.1 Some examples of probation in partnership with other agencies of criminal justice

Probation and police	Sharing a responsibility to prevent crime, police and probation work together – for example, in Multi-Agency Public Protection Arrangements (MAPPA) and Prolific and Persistent Offender Projects (Chapter 10)
Probation and CPS	The CPS considers *the public interest* when deciding about prosecution. Probation has sometimes participated in Public Interest Case Assessment schemes (probation staff making direct representation to CPS, who might otherwise be solely dependent on information from the police); there have also been Bail Information schemes (probation providing information and/or making arrangements to address CPS objections to bail). The CPS makes depositions available to probation staff preparing reports for Court (Chapter 5)
Probation and courts	Probation officers were officers of the court, although what this means has been altered by organisational changes in recent years. Magistrates were represented on Boards (less commonly on Trusts) as employers of probation staff. The courts receive reports and impose the sentences which probation implements. Courts have considerable influence on the amount and nature of probation work (Chapter 4 and 5)
Probation and prisons	Recent probation politics have been dominated by the question of probation's proper relationship with the Prison Service. Sound resettlement work requires close cooperation between prison and probation (Chapter 12). The creation of NOMS in 2004 was sometimes described as a merger while reorganisations in 2008 bind the agencies tighter (Chapter 14)

justice system. Some of these models (the 'practice models') presume a particular purpose for criminal justice and King proceeds to show what characteristics we might expect to find in a system that had such a purpose. Other ('theoretical') models are less concerned with the system's avowed purposes and explore broader influences on criminal justice as well as its wider significance and meanings. Together, these models offer the possibility of a rounded appreciation of the practices and institutions of criminal justice and punishment, which is indispensable to an understanding of probation.

Practice models

Due process

The *due process* model sets the *administration of justice* as the system's defining characteristic. This is a system of *justice* – not an ethically neutral way of dealing with crime – and in its procedures and practices the system should be manifestly just. Due process refers to those principles and procedures which should guide the state's behaviour towards those accused of criminal offences, those convicted and those punished. This model continues to exert a proper influence on sentencing (for example, proportionality – the idea that punishment must not be out of proportion to the crime – is a principle of justice). Due process discussion often focuses on the practices of arrest, prosecution, trial and sentence, but it remains very relevant to the implementation of punishment: for example, those subject to community orders have rights as well as responsibilities and are entitled to know what is expected of them and the consequences of non-compliance.

Crime control

This model begins with the assumption that the main reason for having an apparatus of criminal justice is to reduce the incidence of crime: this is what criminal justice is *for*. Sometimes this model appears to sit uncomfortably with the due process model: the safeguards of due process can look like obstacles to conviction and consequently undermine crime control. Due process safeguards – for example a suspect's right to silence, the right not to be tried more than once for the same offence – have been modified in recent years on this pretext. If due process tends to emphasise proportionality between crime and punishment, crime control will favour stern deterrent and incapacitative penalties (see Chapter 4).

The first two models share a common 'classical' understanding of offending (Newburn 2007: Chapter 5): offenders, as responsible and rational agents, chose to offend and so deserve to be punished and, since they are rational, they can respond to threats of punishment and refrain from offending. This is the presumption of the criminal law. But there are some people who are notably *not* rational agents: for example children and perhaps people who are mentally ill or with a learning disability. It seems wrong to punish people who in some sense are thought not to be (fully) responsible, perhaps because they do not (fully) understand the significance and effects of their actions. But if behaviour may be *caused* in some sense by influences beyond the person's control, perhaps *all* behaviour might be. Behaviour is, if not caused, at least strongly influenced by genetic inheritance and by environmental factors. This is a *positivist* understanding of human behaviour (Newburn 2007: Chapter 5): human actions are events in the world and, like all events, have causes that might be discoverable, even if not immediately apparent. Once you allow the social scientists into the courtroom, as it were, they threaten to take it over.

Treatment model

Thus we arrive at King's third model. (King calls this a *medical* model, but the term *treatment* is preferred here.) The treatment model supposes that behaviour is caused or compellingly influenced, so that stern punishment is both unfair and irrelevant: unfair because people should not be punished for matters beyond their control; irrelevant because only attention to these causes will stop their offending. To identify and change influences on offenders' behaviour, it is necessary to undertake individualised assessment and treatment. A criminal justice system that gave priority to treatment, then, would be characterised by assessment and individualisation, with wide discretion to allow for differences among people and their circumstances. The treatment model would prefer to regard sentencing as more a technical than a judicial matter – perhaps for psychologists to undertake rather than judges.

Restorative justice – a fourth practice model

A *restorative model* sets *making amends* as a purpose for the system. That responses to crime should endeavour to make good the harm that has been done appeals powerfully to many people's sense of justice (Wright 2008). This is not perhaps a prominent feature of most contemporary Western criminal justice systems, which tend to give a greater priority to punishment and crime reduction. At the same time, *reparation* is among the statutory purposes of sentencing (Chapter 4) and unpaid work/community service represents 'payback' for wrongs done (Chapter 11). In England and Wales, such approaches are more prominent in youth justice, but there is much innovative and valuable work being done to develop restorative justice and there are some visions of probation practice in which restorative approaches would be at the centre (Duff 2001). This will be considered further in Chapter 13.

Relations among the practice models

Sometimes these models fit together. For example, to the extent that treatment 'works', it contributes to a reduction in reoffending and thus to crime control. Again, it is hoped that offenders' experiences of restorative approaches will tend to reduce their offending. But there are also tensions among the models that are more than differences of emphasis. For example, due process advocates are suspicious of treatment's impatience with the 'constraints' of due process and the idea that interventions should be determined not by proportionality, but by the needs or risks of the offender. Crime control proponents suspect that finding 'causes' is too much like making excuses and that treatment is an inadequate substitute for punishment.

In practice, each model must allow for the claims of others. It is legitimate to expect that criminal justice should contribute to a reduction in crime, yet crime control without regard for justice can lead to cruel and excessive punishment. Treatment can be positive and constructive, but the model needs the checks and balances required by respect for due process. Thus, in practice systems have to find a way of reconciling diverse and sometimes competing claims.

Each model has implications for probation, as Table 1.2 summarises:

Table 1.2 Probation and the practice models

Practice Model	Purpose and characteristics	Examples of how this applies to probation
Due process	Criminal justice is 'for' justice, which should shape practice and procedure	Fair, consistent and scrupulous determination of punishment; court's orders must be implemented in a principled manner respecting the rights of offenders; accessible and effective complaints procedures
Crime control	Criminal justice practice should reduce crime	Crime reduction and public protection as prominent objectives; probation's outcomes and successes assessed through reduced reconviction; contemporary priority of public protection through thorough assessment and management of risk
Treatment	Broadly encompassing all modes of intervention that seek to change the offender's behaviour other than principally through fear or physical restraint	Rigorous assessment of risk and offending-related need; interventions following from assessment; principles of risk, need and responsivity; effectiveness gauged in terms of reduced reconviction or associated indicators
Restorative justice	Emphasis on making amends	Restorative approaches; mediation, conferencing; unpaid work/ community payback as making amends; increasing victim awareness

Theoretical models

These practice models are ways in which policy makers and practitioners articulate the meaning and purpose of what they do: they are part of the system's self-awareness. Yet King further elaborates three 'theoretical models', which, while they do not usually form part of the official discourse of the system, illuminate some of criminal justice's broader functions, meanings and significance, as well as exposing influences upon the forms that criminal justice and punishment practices take.

Expressive (Durkheimian) model

This model emphasises criminal justice's function in *denouncing crime and affirming social values*. Criminal justice practices – and perhaps especially the practices of punishment – are expressive and communicative: criminal justice not only *does* but *says*. The idea of the *messages* of punishment is readily understood and recognised to be important by offenders, sentencers, victims and the general public (Rex 2005).

The origins of this understanding are to be found in the work of Emile Durkheim (Garland 1990). The criminal law is an expression of the values that the community shares – and which indeed, in a significant sense, make a group of people into a community. Criminal justice ought not to be morally neutral: its practices should affirm the values of society – in a liberal democracy *our* values (Duff 2001). People affirm and thus strengthen these shared values and the solidarity of their community in and through their response to the violations that crimes represent. Crime is, to an extent, socially useful because it occasions this reaffirmation.

Punishment is above all a practice of *blaming* or censure (von Hirsch 1996). At earlier times, many punishments took place in public – in the presence of those who knew the offender – and constituted a vivid and dramatic communication, often through shame and ridicule (Sharpe 1990). Although the character of modern punishment has been transformed, these expressive and communicative features are much more than residual.

King calls this the 'status passage' model, drawing attention to the different statuses at stages in the criminal justice process – suspect, defendant, convict, probationer, prisoner, parolee. Each status attracts different entitlements and invites different social reactions. The rituals of trial and punishment *tell us how we should feel and think* about wrongdoing. Thus, in and through these ritualised practices, communal sentiments are evoked and vindicated. Since communal values are held sacred, Durkheim argues, responses to crime typically evoke powerful emotions:

> Emotions pervade penal law and the criminal justice system. Offenders, victims and witnesses bring their emotions to the courtroom, criminal courts deal with crimes of passion, and their decisions can occasion public outrage and anger, or feelings of vengeance among victims. Offenders feel shame and

remorse when they have transgressed the laws, and offences provoke feelings of moral disgust. At the same time, victims as well as offenders elicit our compassion and sympathy.

(Karstedt 2002: 300)

This helps to explain how the punitive strategy achieves its political resonance, chiming with the outrage and frustration that crime often evokes and which demands vindication. Yet the emotions evoked by crime and punishment are complex and ambivalent (Canton 2007) and the emotive character of criminal justice – the empathy that may be felt towards victims and (at least in some circumstances) towards offenders – is a potential resource to proponents of an ethical approach (Loader 2005).

Some effects of the emotional power of crime and punishment are, perhaps, especially acute for probation because what probation represents – social inclusion, a belief in change, moderation in punishment – conflicts with the emotions that we are called upon to feel towards offenders. All this has profound implications for probation's legitimacy and standing. In recent years, probation has tried to challenge punitiveness in the language of reason (a management strategy). But perhaps the dispassionate language of evidence, effectiveness and efficiency fails to connect with these powerful and deep-rooted emotions: it may be simply in the wrong register.

This model, then, is a reminder that the practices of punishment are not merely instrumental – not just ways of bringing about certain ends – but reflect our values, cultural commitments and sensibilities. More than this, the institutions and practices of criminal justice influence – indeed partly constitute – the character of a society (Garland 1990).

Bureaucratic model

While notions of degradation, ritual and the affirmation of shared values may be one reading of criminal justice, those who attend a busy modern criminal court are more likely to be struck by the sheer procedural routine. As a series of 'cases' are dealt with, the complex and messy realities of each defendant's situation must be interpreted, redefined and transformed into manageable cases to be processed efficiently.

This bureaucratic model recognises that in modern societies responses to crime are managed through established procedures, institutions and offices. These developments *transform the character* and the cultural meaning of punishment (Garland 1990). A formal system stands between the offender and the expression of public sentiment, so that punishment ceases to be social and becomes technical and professional instead. Moral judgements, which the expressive model saw as the very essence of the response to crime, are set aside – indeed may be disavowed as 'unprofessional' – and displaced by technical assessments.

Many of these tendencies have accelerated recently in response to the recognition that 'high' crime rates are probably normal. Criminals must then be managed routinely and smoothly by agencies with limited resources (Garland 2001). Managerial goals are set for agencies with measures – typically measures of economy and efficiency (sometimes too of effectiveness, although this can be harder to capture) – against which their performance is evaluated in terms of throughput, outputs and unit costs.

As such work has become ever more tightly prescribed, management, audit and inspection processes have been extensively deployed. Central government must ensure that local areas are performing as required and local agencies in turn must make sure that staff advance these objectives. While these disciplines are common to many public agencies, a particular stimulus in the criminal justice sector towards more assertive management has been the increasing politicisation of crime and punishment (Downes and Morgan 2007). The more that crime and punishment are regarded as (party) political issues, the more government has to be seen to deal with them; and the more, therefore, must government seek to direct and monitor the activities of the agencies, putting itself in a position to demonstrate their successes and be seen to be responding assertively to their failures.

From the early 1980s, new styles of management, imported from the private sector, were applied to probation (Brownlee 1998), including:

- hands-on professional management;
- explicit standards and measures of performance;
- greater emphasis on output;
- stress on greater discipline and parsimony in use of resources.

(Raine and Willson 1993: 68)

These developments (sometimes known as New Public Management) have had considerable consequences for the organisation and practices of probation (Raine 2007), as well as for how it understands, presents and evaluates its work. One effect is that probation has had to reinterpret (perhaps *reduce*) its practice to *measurable* episodes and outcomes. Tightly specified practice is much more readily amenable to inspection and audit.

These developments have led to changes in the boundaries of professional discretion (Chapter 15). The need for the organisation to manage an ever-increasing workload, as well as a proper and demonstrable commitment to rigour and consistency, requires the use of systematic 'instruments' to determine the content and sequence of assessment and enable its outcomes to be precisely specified (see Chapter 7). At the same time, structured decision-taking, assigning individuals to categories that determine the nature and intensity of subsequent intervention, alter practitioners' understanding of their work and the place of professional judgement.

The aspiration to provide efficient, effective and economic services is unimpeachable. The influences of bureaucratic rationality also constrain the excesses of punitiveness. At the same time, bureaucracies and their arrangements can become inflated and self-serving. Some performance measures fail to capture quality, introduce perverse incentives and can lead to inappropriate practice in pursuit of a target. It has been suggested that 'what works' was marred and 'dehumanised' by the manner of its implementation and evaluation (Raynor 2006). Again, some modes of performance management misunderstand and even distort the practice they purport to evaluate, for instance around the complex questions of compliance and enforcement (Canton 2008b). Others have warned how the political and moral character of responses to crime can be suppressed by the 'actuarial dimension of modern managerialism [so that] it may become difficult to counterpoise the traditional language of, for example, "justice", against the aggregative and instrumental assumptions of an actuarial approach' (Bottoms 1995: 33).

Whatever the merits of these developments, however, this model illuminates contemporary characteristics of criminal justice and of probation more specifically. The 'bureaucratized rationalism, necessary to meet the social control needs and legitimacy conditions of modern societies' (Hudson 1996: 91) moulds, constrains and sometimes even determines the character of policy and practice and no understanding of criminal justice can be complete without an appreciation of this dimension.

Power model

The most familiar criticism of Durkheim is that he failed to give an adequate account of power. It is not that the criminal law represents a consensual, collective sentiment; rather it reflects the ruling class's perception of its own interests. Specifically, 'Law is made by men, representing special interests, who have the power to translate their interests into public policy' (Quinney and Trevino 2001: 35). The final model, then, draws attention to the way in which the criminal justice system is implicated in the wider social order, reflecting, reproducing and legitimating the social structure, its power relationships and inequalities.

These ideas have been most fully worked out in the Marxist tradition (Garland 1990: chapters 4 and 5). Crime is understood as a response to the injustices of the social order, to capitalism and its contradictions. The criminal justice system, upholding that social order, is necessarily implicated in capitalism's exploitations and oppression. This model envisages:

- criminal laws that favour some groups rather than others;
- enforcement, detection and prosecution procedures that target some types of wrongdoing and/or some groups rather than others;
- levels of punishment that censure some kinds of conduct more severely than others that are 'objectively' at least as harmful;
- weightier punishments for some groups compared to others.

There are critiques of this type levelled against many contemporary criminal justice systems (for example Reiman 1990; Dorling *et al.* 2008; Drake *et al.* 2010). A rejoinder that evolved into the position known as 'left realism', however, objected that crimes are most commonly *intra*-class, the powerless offending against one another rather than against the powerful, and that a robust policing and criminal justice system benefits the weak more than the strong – who can mostly look after themselves (see Newburn 2007: Chapters 12 and 13). It remains the case that the crimes of the powerful attract neither the same political attention nor rigours of enforcement as the 'crimes of the streets'.

Disadvantaged and discriminated-against groups are significantly over-represented among arrested offenders and in prison populations the world over (Reiman 1990; Drake *et al.* 2010). Such groups are also heavily over-represented as victims: there are some kinds of crime that are (and/or have been) taken less seriously than they should be – violence against women and children in their own homes, human trafficking for sexual and other forms of exploitation, hate crimes – and this seems plainly related to victims' difficulties in establishing them as crimes that merit robust and effective responses, arising from their lack of political power.

While overt repression is manifest at certain times and places, the more general mode of social control to which criminal justice contributes is *ideological*, denouncing certain kinds of conduct and affirming the legitimacy of the institutions of the state – transforming power into accepted authority. On this analysis, law is seen as a powerful ideology which helps legitimise (capitalist) relations 'by phrasing particular economic interests in a vocabulary of universal rights' (Garland 1990: 112). Systems avow that they are systems of justice, not (or not merely) of control, and through their response to transgressions against the social order ('crimes') bestow legitimacy upon that order. The authoritative pronouncements of sentencing denounce certain kinds of behaviour, but also, more subtly but no less effectively, some kinds of people or ways of living by accepting or denying considerations in mitigation.

Gelsthorpe (2001) found that magistrates distinguished between 'troublesome' and 'troubled' women, often sentencing the troublesome more severely while mitigating punishment for the troubled. This can have the effect of legitimating ways of living that are taken to be acceptable while denouncing those that are not. Unconventional people and lifestyles are thus censured – part of what is meant by structural discrimination. When a court accepts mitigation that presents the offender as a responsible parent or as a hard-working employee it clarifies a standard and an expectation, implying that other defendants, who could not be so described, should not merit such compassion.

These normalising and legitimating functions of criminal justice are illuminated by the work of Michel Foucault (Foucault 1977; Garland 1990: Chapters 6 and 7). At the heart of Foucault's work is an examination of how the human sciences – for example, medicine, psychiatry, criminology – and the social institutions with which they are deeply interdependent (hospitals, asylums, prisons) contribute to the control and 'discipline' of modern societies. This is achieved by stipulating and inculcating standards of *normality*.

The normal child, the healthy body, the stable mind, the good citizen, the perfect wife and the proper man – such concepts haunt our ideas about ourselves, and are reproduced and legitimated through the practices of teachers, social workers, doctors, judges, policemen and administrators.

(Philp 1985: 67)

At the same time, necessarily, the area of *deviance* is demarcated and becomes a subject for 'investigation, surveillance and treatment' (*ibid.*).

When probation insists on *pro-social* ways of behaving and tries to influence the ways in which people think and behave, helping them to overcome 'cognitive deficits' (Chapter 6), it is involved in these controlling processes of normalisation. There is no necessary implication that such control is somehow a 'bad thing': all human communities deploy mechanisms of this type. But to the extent that a social order is unjust, its criminal justice system can be accused of lending authoritative support to its injustices.

While these critiques were originally developed in relation to class, many of the arguments are quite as applicable to other dimensions of difference – for example, gender, race, sexuality. There is a radical tradition in probation (Walker and Beaumont 1981), which considers how working probation officers might practise in a way that avoids collusion with oppression and injustice, recognise the socio-economic origins of offending and develop a way of practising 'in and against the state'.

This model can no more constitute a complete characterisation of criminal justice than any other, but probation should never lose sight of it. The offenders with whom probation works are often massively disadvantaged, with troubled personal biographies associated with considerable structural disadvantage. Economic marginalisation, poverty and social exclusion are among the most persistent characteristics of offenders at all times and in all places. Punitive approaches to punishment regard this, if they acknowledge it at all, as excusing crime; instrumental strategies see it as substantially irrelevant. But the power model outlines the structural dimensions of unfair discrimination which persist even when efforts have been made to address personal and cultural discrimination (see Chapter 3). Unless probation and the other agencies of criminal justice work actively to redress injustice, then the accusation that the pretensions to justice avowed by the criminal justice system are merely ideological has considerable force.

The value of the models

Together these models offer a rounded understanding of criminal justice and probation's place within it. Garland (1990) concludes that each tends to a reductive (and thus incomplete) understanding of criminal justice. Rejecting any single approach, he argues (1990: 279) that these analyses are best seen as 'reciprocal commentaries, mutually deepening'. Moreover, while King describes his models as *vantage points*, they also represent immanent tensions within criminal justice: there are perhaps many different things that criminal justice practices ought to do and express and often tensions among these objectives and meanings. Table 1.3 summarises the ways in which these models illuminate the work of probation.

Table 1.3 Probation and the theoretical models

Theoretical model	Understanding of criminal justice	Examples of how this applies to probation
Expressive	Criminal justice and punishment as vindication of shared community values; CJS is expressive – it *says* as well as does	Probation should articulate the right values, in how it undertakes and explains its work and in *the kind of organisation that it is.* Challenges of communicating at emotional level. Different 'audiences' with different expectations
Bureaucratic	Modern institutions processing types of event and people against a background of expected high rates of crime	Disciplines of effectiveness, efficiency and economy. Targets linked to funding. Performance management. Emphasis on outcomes can change the character and meaning of sanctions
Power	Criminal justice reflecting, reproducing and legitimating an unjust social order. Disadvantaged groups over-represented in penal populations and as victims	Characteristics of offenders under supervision. Structural dimensions of anti-discrimination. Probation's advocacy for social justice. Intrinsic value of just practice, irrespective of its contingent effects on reoffending

Practices and developments become clearer through the lens of the theoretical models. The power model explains, for instance, political outrage at street violence, while gaze is averted from the violence of the powerful – robust punishment for assaults, but mostly regulatory responses to workplace injury and fatality (Tombs and Whyte 2008). The expressive model explains how punitive approaches have such resonance in political debate and how arguments in the different register of evidence and reason often fail to persuade. The bureaucratic model illuminates how performance management and targets, even when generating irrelevant or perverse outcomes, retain their grip on practice and transform its character.

Summary

In this chapter, probation has been introduced. It has been argued that probation must be understood in the broader context of the criminal justice system. Some examples have been given of probation's work in partnership with other agencies. The criminal justice system has been presented as a complex social institution which is not reducible to a single purpose. Moreover, the several purposes that may be set for it do not always readily harmonise and indeed may sometimes be in tension. A failure to recognise this can lead to frustration and disappointment, not least because of an exaggerated expectation about what the criminal justice system can in fact achieve by way of crime reduction and victim redress.

The practices of criminal justice and punishment not only reflect but also reproduce and indeed partly constitute the structure and culture of society. This is part of the reason why no instrumental account is adequate. Punitive approaches to crime make for a punitive society; insistence on justice in and through the work of the authoritative institutions of criminal justice goes to make a society a just one.

Questions

- Is crime control more important than due process?
- In what ways have the influences of the bureaucratic model changed the work of probation?
- Should probation, as an agency of the state, seek to challenge social injustice? If so, how it can it avoid being politicised? If not, must it ignore or collude with such injustice?

Further reading

David Garland's work is indispensable, especially Garland (1990). See also Christie (2000, 2004). Excellent accounts of criminal justice are Zedner (2004) and Cavadino and Dignan (2007). Whitehead (2010) demonstrates the value of many of the main sociological traditions in illuminating developments in probation.

2   Probation's histories

This chapter looks at the history of probation. A very 'broad brush' is taken to the task and some of the detail will be included in later chapters. This chapter sets a context, showing that current arrangements and practices, as well as contemporary policy debates, can often only be understood once their history is appreciated. History also reminds us of *change* – that things were not always as they are now and that dominant ways of thinking about and practising probation will not necessarily continue in future.

After looking at one way of telling probation's story, as a series of phases characterised by different ideas and practices, another way of approaching the subject is considered. There are some themes and indeed some tensions in policy and practice that are near-constant throughout probation's history – continuities that are at risk of getting lost in a narrative that focuses on change.

Phases in probation's history

> Offence after offence and sentence after sentence appeared to be the inevitable lot of him whose foot has once slipped. Can nothing be done to stop this downward career? I hope that some practical work could be organised in the police courts . . .
>
> From a letter by Frederic Rainer, a Hertfordshire printer, to the Church of England Temperance Society, which, with his 5 shilling donation, is thought to have encouraged the Society to appoint a 'missionary' to the Police Court at Southwark.
>
> (quoted in Vanstone 2004b: 1)

As the last chapter should have led us to expect, the origins of probation are complex, with discernible social, moral, economic and political influences working sometimes together, but sometimes against each other (Garland 1985; 1990; Vanstone 2004b). Like most criminal justice agencies, probation has no determinable date of birth. From the middle years of the nineteenth century, local and often informal practices were developing of releasing offenders from court on their promise of good behaviour or under the supervision of a responsible person (Bochel 1976; Raynor and Vanstone 2002; Vanstone 2004a). The Probation of

Offenders Act 1907 consolidated and regulated these practices, enjoining probation officers to 'advise, assist and befriend' those under their supervision and,
through a period of uneven and gradual implementation, began to establish probation throughout England and Wales.

In its subsequent developments, a usual (and useful) approach has been to
identify a number of *phases*. One such framework (following Whitehead and
Statham 2006) structures our initial account.

Saving souls by divine grace

> I have been treated with the greatest respect, and afforded every facility for
> doing good, by the police court officials. I am glad to report that hundreds of
> men and women have listened to that one Divine instrument, the Gospel, in its
> simplicity, from my lips, as well as advice to shun strong drink.
>
> Mr. Nelson, missionary to the Southwark and
> Lambeth districts, *c*.1878, (quoted in Bochel 1976: 21)

Early probation was a confidently moral enterprise, originating in the work of
the Police Court missionaries, with their strong Christian convictions and
opposition to alcohol. While other motivations – notably the defence of the social
order against crime, indolence and intemperance – were influential too (Vanstone
2004b), probation articulated its mission as helping deserving wrongdoers to find
redemption. Yet theirs was a hard-headed and practical Christianity. Thomas
Holmes, Police Court Missionary, wrote 'I wonder how it is that folk undoubtedly
good think that poor humanity can be warmed, fed and comforted with tracts, or be
saved with goody stories' (quoted in McCulloch 2004: 148) and urged practical
forms of assistance: to walk the path to salvation you need a pair of stout boots.

The missionaries, and those who welcomed their involvement, were also
prompted by the same sentiment that had affected Rainer – a dismay at the futility,
if not cruelty, of successive punishments without any attempt to help or indeed to
deflect offenders from crime in any way other than through the threat of punishment. To this extent, probation was a rejection of punishment; the 1907 Act (s. 1
[2]) said that a Probation Order might be imposed where it was considered
inexpedient to inflict any punishment. This point should be emphasised: towards
the end of the twentieth century, probation was asked to implement *punishment
in the community* and the contemporary offender management model (NOMS
2006) insists that punishment is one component of every community sentence. It
is worth recalling, then, that the original probation order was not meant to *be*
punishment, but *instead* of it.

The instrument of change was principally the character of the probation officers
through their *relationship* with probationers (Bochel 1976). If probationers failed
to take advantage of the opportunities during this period of testing, their time 'on
probation', they could be taken back to court for punishment.

Casework, diagnosis, rehabilitation and positivism

> [Probation in England] was transformed from a service devoted to the saving of souls through divine grace to an agency concerned with the scientific assessment and treatment of offenders.
>
> (McWilliams 1986: 241)

Probation gradually became more secular and 'scientific'. If human conduct has its causes, the probation officer's task must be to identify and address them. Psychological understandings of the mainsprings of human behaviour now informed the officer's work and skilled method, more than the influence of personal character, came to be seen as the principal means of effecting change. The predominant technique was social casework, involving investigation, diagnosis and treatment. Officers needed to recognise and work with:

> all the major experiences and relationships which go into making [the client] the person he is, with conflicts of whose origins he may be unaware, with problems whose solution may be less in external circumstances than in his own attitudes, with tensions, faulty relationships, inabilities to face reality, hardened into forms he cannot alter unaided.
>
> (Younghusband, quoted in Bochel 1976: 180)

This 'treatment model' was the dominant paradigm for most of the middle years of the twentieth century and loss of faith in it precipitated probation's next 'phase'.

Collapse of the rehabilitative ideal and 'alternatives to custody'

The model, however, increasingly came under attack:

- from the political left for its neglect of the role of social injustice in the causes of crime through seeking explanation only in terms of personal shortcoming – and indeed responding to it only at that level;
- from the political right for its erosion of individual responsibility in claiming to find reasons for misbehaviour that were too readily seen as excuses;
- and from research that seemed to show that probation interventions did not 'work'.

> It has seemed . . . that longer sentences are no more effective than short ones, that different types of institutions work about equally as well, that probationers on the whole do no better than if they were sent to prison, and that rehabilitative programmes . . . have no predictably beneficial effects.
>
> (Brody 1976: 37)

Still, if probation treatment did not (could not be shown to) work, neither did anything else and probation could at least claim was that it was no less effective than prison, that it was more humane and that it was cheaper. Probation's primary objective became providing alternatives to custody.

The expanding prison population dominated policy and throughout the 1970s probation extended its repertoire of alternatives, adding community service, hostels, day centres and supervising offenders released under the parole system (introduced by the Criminal Justice Act 1967). While it is hard to show that any of these measures had much discernible impact on the numbers of people in prison, the innovations of this period changed the character of probation and formed the basis of many of its subsequent developments.

For much of the 1980s, the Conservative government's dilemma was how to limit prison expansion without compromising its claims to be the party of law and order in an increasingly politicised debate (Downes and Morgan 2007). *Punishment in the community* was the chosen solution: punishment should be demanding, but could take place outside of prison so long as community penalties were demanding and rigorously enforced. Probation was the agency to give this effect and directed to move 'centre stage' in the implementation of the new sentencing framework introduced by the Criminal Justice Act 1991 (Dunbar and Langdon 1998).

Penal pessimism and punishment

The 1991 Act emphasised just and proportionate punishment: rehabilitation and other reductive strategies (see Chapter 4) were not rejected, but punishment to match the seriousness of the crime was the guiding rationale. Although this was explained in terms of the requirements of justice, it is not a coincidence that this was a time of pessimism (or scepticism) about the capacity of the criminal justice system to make more than a modest contribution to crime control (Garland 2001). Rising crime rates had confounded the hope that crime would diminish with the increasing prosperity assured by the welfare state and there was no evidence that changes to criminal justice practice could do much to influence these trends.

The principles of the 1991 Act were compromised as penal politics became increasingly punitive in tone while Michael Howard was Home Secretary (Dunbar and Langdon 1998). Probation had been placed in a precarious position: if the main purpose of sentencing is to impose punishment, could probation credibly present itself as adequately punitive? Better, perhaps, to affirm its contribution to the reduction of reoffending (Canton 1993), but the evidence that it was effective in this way was not yet apparent.

Renaissance of rehabilitation: evidence-based practice

The best of probation practice can substantially reduce reconviction. Effectiveness will bring with it confidence about the way the service works but also increase the public's confidence in the supervision of offenders.

(Chapman and Hough 1998: 4)

The aspiration that intervention could lead to change and reduce offending was reinvigorated by research findings from Canada and USA, that appeared to show that if programmes were implemented as designed and targeted at the right offenders, a measurable reduction in reconvictions could be demonstrated (Raynor and Vanstone 2002). Guiding principles and methods, many of them cognitive behavioural in character (Chapter 6), were identified and were to be applied consistently and systematically to reduce reconviction (Chui 2003). A panel was established to assess the quality of programmes of intervention and to accredit formally those that met the criteria (Chapter 8); accredited programmes would then be 'rolled out' and delivered across the country. Many new concepts and terms entered the probation vocabulary at that time, including the *risk principle*, *criminogenic needs*, *responsivity* and *programme integrity* (Chapter 6). Probation found new confidence in its ability to effect change.

Further phases?

Some would propose still more recent phases. Public protection has, arguably, displaced or at least qualified the priority of rehabilitation through effective practice and the assessment and management of risk is now the single most important of probation's objectives (Chapter 10). Offender management (Chapter 7) could be seen as a new phase, especially with the creation of the National Offender Management Service, although this is perhaps better seen as an organisational and practice development to deliver effective rehabilitation and public protection, rather than a 'phase' in its own right.

Other approaches to probation's history

The conventional account, then, is of a journey from 'advise, assist and befriend' to 'enforcement, rehabilitation and public protection' (Worrall and Hoy 2005) – a journey with discernible steps, identifiable milestones and turning points.

This schematic account provides a serviceable framework within which to locate developments in probation, but it has its limitations. An episodic history emphasises change and risks suppressing continuities. A new phase never completely displaces its predecessor: 'History is not the replacement of the old by the new, but the more or less extensive modification of one by the other' (Garland 2001: 168). Features of earlier phases typically remain, exerting a continuing influence on practice. Thus, probation's original overtly moral mission, more usually framed nowadays in secular language, has an abiding importance and an identifiable contemporary echo in the profession's affirmation of 'probation values' (Chapter 3). Again, the recognition of the value of consistency, reliability and encouragement by the first officers is close to what is now called 'pro-social modelling' (Cherry 2005), while the importance of *relationship* in enabling change has been reaffirmed by contemporary research (Chapter 9).

The attempt to demarcate phases can distort the history too. At a time (roughly late 1970s to mid 1980s) when the phased history would have it that probation had repudiated treatment and was content to offer alternatives to custody, there was a great deal of innovative practice – much of it inspired by the approach of McGuire and Priestley (Priestley *et al.* 1978; McGuire and Priestley 1985) – and indeed significantly 'evidence-led', even though that 'phase' had apparently yet to arrive. Less obviously, phases sometimes *anticipate* their successors, with characteristics adumbrating more radical transformations. For example, psychology, alongside eugenics and other 'social sciences', was an influence on probation's development well before the 'phase' of treatment (Garland 1985; Vanstone 2004). Again, the attempt to establish probation as an 'alternative to prison' is not something that can sensibly be confined to a single phase, but has been a near constant.

Moreover, histories are often dependent on documents, including policy and legislation. Cohen (1985) refers to such accounts as 'stories' – not to question their veracity so much as to draw attention to their uncertain relationship to the realities of practice. A policy history, for example, is a history of aspiration, but some (perhaps many) of probation's aspirations have, notoriously, been frustrated. Bluntly, what an organisation says is not always a reliable account of what it does.

Some historians (notably McWilliams and Vanstone) have therefore tried to get closer to the practitioner experience – through court reports, case records and personal accounts. Even here there is room for caution – not only because practitioners' accounts are themselves stories with a consequently uncertain relationship with what actually took place, but because there are other stories to be told besides.

If the voice of the practitioner is often barely audible in these histories, the voice of the probationer/client/service user is usually silent. To a significant extent, their experiences are lost and unrecoverable, but they are a central part of probation's history and a reminder that the histories recounted by policymakers, researchers or even practitioners are not the only possible accounts. Appreciation of this limitation can reframe reflections on probation's past – and present. For example, for many years, a vexed question was whether probation's purpose was 'care' or 'control' (Harris 1980), but this was debated almost entirely at the level of intention and aspiration. Few people asked service users: when probation strove to 'care' was it experienced as caring? When it tried to 'control' was it felt to be controlling?

We need, then, to understand the 'offender perception' (Bailey 2007). The desistance literature in particular (Chapter 9) recognises that it is not just life events and opportunities that conduce to (or delay) desistance, but the *meaning* and significance that (ex-)offenders attach to such experiences – on which they have a privileged insight. Again, as punishment gives messages, in its pronouncement and in the manner of its implementation, then whether and how this message is 'received' and interpreted must be critically important (Duff 2001; Rex 2005). So while offenders' perceptions may be hard to get, their absence is a serious gap in probation's history and recent attempts to address this are greatly to be welcomed. (Bailey 1995; Rex 1999, 2005; Maruna 2000; Farrall and Calverley 2006.)

All these experiences of probation, however multifarious and elusive, are quite as much a part of its history as the more formal accounts and a sensitivity to these dimensions and possibilities suggests much about probation's past – and indeed its contemporary significance and possible futures.

Some constant tensions in probation's history

> Having developed as a means of managing tensions, arbitrating between conflicting forces, and getting certain necessary things done, social institutions typically contain within themselves traces of the contradictions and pluralities of interest which they seek to regulate.
>
> (Garland 1990: 282)

There are a number of tensions with which probation has had to engage throughout its history – tensions that are often constructive, giving an impetus for innovation and development. Exploring probation's history in this way does justice to its continuities, complementing the focus on change that is a premise of a history of phases.

Local and national

For most of its history, probation has been organised locally. Policy and direction were formally determined by local probation committees (Probation Boards), independent bodies corporate, constituted mainly by Justices of the Peace (magistrates). At the same time, there have always been influences towards (national) uniformity – for example, through the Home Office which, from the beginning, encouraged, advised, regulated and inspected. More recently, there have been centralising trends, ostensibly to promote consistency as well as efficiency, culminating in the creation of a National Probation Service for England and Wales and subsequently the National Offender Management Service.

Her Majesty's Inspectorate of Probation (HMIP)

At the centre of mechanisms to ensure probation's accountability to government, HMIP has always been an influence towards uniformity. Nowadays it reports to the Secretary of State on the effectiveness of work undertaken by the Probation Service, NOMS and the Youth Justice Board. It also assesses the effectiveness of arrangements for this work, working as necessary with other inspecting authorities. Through its scrutiny of areas and its 'thematic' (topic-based) inspections and by disseminating good practice, it contributes to improved performance, policy development and effective implementation (Ramell 2007; H M Inspectorate of Probation 2010). In the late 1990s, HMIP took initiatives in commissioning and publishing research and guidance on effective practice and contributed enormously to the development of *what works* (see Chapter 6). When probation lacked adequate central authority, HMIP led on policy development. The changes in governance in the last decade have important implications for HMIP (Morgan 2007). HMIP had functioned as a surrogate for a National Directorate, but

> the creation of the National Probation Service entailed a different focus and methodology for HMIP. It has been argued (Morgan 2007) that NPS/NOMS should take charge of routine performance management, enabling HMIP to be less an arm of government and more an independent inspectorate.

Chapter 14 will show there are still contentious debates about the extent to which local areas should have the latitude to develop their services as they think fit – a question raised sharply with the arrival of Trust status. But whatever opinion is held on the proper apportioning of authority and policy between local and national levels, the tension between them has been a persistent and dynamic feature of probation's history.

Judicial and executive

Overlapping (but not co-extensive) with the first dynamic is the tension between probation as 'officers of the court' or as an instrument of the executive. Originally, as we have seen, probation officers were seen as officers of the court, but as crime and justice have become increasingly politicised (Downes and Morgan 2007), government has had to try to direct probation practice to deliver its policies of law and order.

The extent to which sentencing and the institutions of punishment 'belong' to courts or to the legislative is a live debate with constitutional implications. Should probation's primary accountability be to the court as it gives effect to its orders? Or to central government to implement penal policy? This tension has been a significant feature of probation's history, its present and no doubt its future.

'Inside' and 'outside'

Much of probation's work throughout its history has been with serving and former prisoners (Chapter 12). Probation officers nowadays, as offender managers, are increasingly involved in the management of a prison sentence. The idea that work with offenders after release should build upon the experience in custody in a 'seamless sentence' was a primary rationale for the amalgamation of the two services in a National Offender Management Service.

The aspiration that providing 'alternatives to custody' is the way to reduce the prison population also yokes probation firmly to prison, its problems and its volatile politics. Others have questioned whether this organisational arrangement jeopardises connections with the community where probation officers have sometimes seen themselves as advocates of offenders to the rest of society and whence it derives much of its legitimacy (see Chapter 14; Faulkner 2006; Harding 2003; Nellis 2007a). Community engagement can be in tension with the priorities of prison and this too has been a dynamic in the service's history.

Social and psychological

Ideas of personal redemption, social casework and cognitive behavioural approaches focus on the individual. Even as their more sophisticated versions recognise the need to understand the individual in social context, this individualised focus can obscure or suppress an awareness of the significance of the social, economic and political context of offending. Yet working probation officers have always recognised the social context of their work and noticed the common predicaments of poverty, deprivation and local economic and social conditions (Harding 1987). This is the origin of community development work and attention to concepts like social capital, with its identifiable connection with desistance (Chapters 8 and 9).

Many offenders have biographies of neglect, trauma and distress, with insufficiently developed abilities to manage their problems effectively. Yet behaviour is a function not only of personal motivation and abilities, but also of opportunities – including opportunities that are presented or constrained by economic and structural factors. In reality, both social and psychological factors influence offending behaviour and usually both must be addressed in response.

Care and control

Reflecting its historical relationship with social work, probation has often emphasised its responsibility to provide care for those under its supervision. Yet this understanding of probation was vehemently repudiated in the late 1980s. People were under supervision because they had committed crimes and the role of probation was to reduce their reoffending and to administer punishment, not attend to their welfare. They were to be seen as offenders, not clients (Chapter 3).

If control was an uncomfortable conception of their work for some officers, others were quite as uneasy with the idea of providing 'care' compulsorily, that offenders on probation were 'sentenced to social work' (Bryant *et al.* 1978). Some argued that the functions of care and control were irreconcilable (Harris 1980). Yet while at different times probation has found it expedient to emphasise one role or the other, both have been and remain an irreducible part of its work and the tension between them has been an influential driver of policy and practice.

Individuals and families

Until the creation of the Children and Family Court Advisory Support Service in 2001, when separating parents unable to agree about residence or contact with their children took their dispute to court, the agency with the responsibility to offer impartial advice was the Family Court Welfare Service, a part of the probation service. While this had become a specialist unit within the service, many probation officers had undertaken at least some family court work in the course of their career. The participation of probation officers in these activities enriched their understanding and broadened their repertoire of skills – for example in conciliation and mediation that could be applied to other aspects of 'conflict resolution' (Chapter 13; Skidmore 2007a; Mantle 2007).

Most obviously, this 'civil work' enabled officers to acquire an appreciation of the significance of family and upbringing. Contemporary probation is very much an adult service, but probation officers often used to attempt family work, recognising that a young person's well-being is often decisively influenced by experiences at home (Raynor and Vanstone 2007). The desistance literature recognises that people typically come to refrain from offending in a context of a life made meaningful in and through personal relationships (McNeill 2003).

Whether considering offenders as 'children' or as parents, then, the family is a critical influence on people's behaviour and potentially a decisive resource in achieving and sustaining desistance (Wedge 2007). This perspective also offers an holistic appreciation of people in their personal lives, rather than seeing them solely in terms of their offending – a counter to the tendency to regard offenders as carriers of risks and needs.

Sameness and difference

Undue discretion allows for idiosyncrasy, inconsistency and scope for prejudice and favouritism (Chapter 15). The disciplines of working in an organisation call for consistent and systematic practice in the implementation of policy. If practitioners assume too much latitude, the organisation's achievement of its objectives will be jeopardised.

Yet while there are compelling arguments for consistency, people and circumstances differ in so many ways that there will always be a need for sound professional judgement to take complex decisions. Chapter 3 will explore some of the ethical consequences of the requirement to respect diversity. The tension between 'consistency' and respect for diversity, doing justice to relevant differences among people without this collapsing into arbitrariness or capriciousness, constitute another dynamic in probation's story.

Inclusion and exclusion

> Concepts such as 'social exclusion', and the related ideas of community and social responsibility, can be interpreted in different ways. They can be interpreted openly, in the spirit of a liberal, tolerant and compassionate society; or restrictively as a way of demanding social conformity and of insisting on compliance with norms and expectations as a condition of social acceptance. Failure to comply then brings punishment, and leads to further exclusion. The balance which a government, a society or a community finds between the two sets of attitudes and approaches will change over time, but the balance is one of the features which defines its character.
>
> (Faulkner 2007: 298)

As an agency of the state, probation has always exercised a function of discipline and control. Probation may affirm its belief in the possibility of change, but in practice has to qualify this optimism with other considerations. Thus, the first officers, in making a case for the deserving defendant, either explicitly or by implication rejected or abandoned the undeserving. In this sense, probation from the beginning was 'contributing to the exclusion and severe treatment of the undeserving' (Vanstone 2004a: 37). Social diagnosis tried to differentiate the treatable from the intractable; alternatives to custody urged community sentences for some – in contrast to those for whom custody was 'inevitable'; risk assessment is an influential consideration in determining sentence at court and the subsequent management of the sentence imposed.

While the language changes – redeemable or damned, treatable or recalcitrant, safe or risky, motivated or unmotivated – it is at least possible that it is much the same people who find themselves on the wrong side of this divide. For that matter, the acceptance that probation offers is conditional – on being of good behaviour, leading an industrious life and otherwise conforming to the requirements of supervision. This is part of the *normalising* function of probation that the power model illuminates and questions (Chapter 1).

Other tensions could be elaborated: offenders and clients; consent and compulsion; relationship and professional method. The point is that these tensions are the very stuff of probation and it is neither possible nor in any case desirable to seek to reconcile them. At times, having tried to reject one 'pull' in each of these tensions, probation has soon been made to rediscover it in the realities of practice. And consequently, in any foreseeable future that includes probation in a recognisable form, it will continue to work with these tensions.

Continuities and the realities of practice

Among the most significant continuities in probation's history is what probation *represents* – what it says and stands for, the values to which it strives to give expression (Chapter 3). Prominent among these values are *a belief in the possibility of change* and *social inclusion* (though the term is quite new, the ideal is enduring). These values are related: probation has typically emphasised that change depends not only on attitude and motivation, but on opportunities, the social as well as the individual. Rehabilitation and reintegration imply not only offenders willing to attempt to change, but a society prepared to accept them and to support them in this endeavour.

> Some things do not change. The world in which the probation service operates is the real world of social change and conflict, crime and human frailty. Structures, laws, expectations and organisational requirements do change at often bewildering speed but people . . . are the threads which are constant.
>
> (Whitfield 2001: 8)

A neglected possibility is that the realities of probation work circumscribe the extent to which policy initiatives can change things. These realities continue to insist themselves upon probation practice and constitute another mediating factor when policy is implemented. This explains how an ethical approach can function as a constraint upon penal strategies. For example, a punitive strategy may call for condemnation and hard treatment, but the reality of having to engage with people and gain their compliance calls for fairness, respect, encouragement and personal interest.

The history of probation, then, has sometimes been described as a journey from 'advise, assist and befriend' to 'enforcement, rehabilitation and public protection' (Worrall and Hoy 2005). But while this may be the story, it may not adequately represent the realities of practice. Despite the sharp rhetorical contrast, in each of its phases, probation has sooner or later made the discovery that the best way to enforce, rehabilitate and protect the public is *by advising, assisting and befriending*.

Summary

This chapter presented a brief conventional account of the 'phases' in probation's history. While this approach provides a useful structure for locating trends and events, any such framework must be recognised as artificial and contestable. Probation histories are inevitably partial and in particular fail to represent the perspectives of service users or indeed those who (like the victims of crime, perhaps) may have felt that probation neglected them. It was next suggested that there are some persistent themes in probation's history that were presented as a number of 'tensions' that are intrinsic to probation practice and perhaps irresolvable. It was concluded that probation's history should attend also to what it has represented and the distinctive values that have been constant throughout much of the change in 'story' and in practice.

Inquiry into probation's history is an illuminating and instructive endeavour – for its own sake, but also in the attempt to understand the dynamics of change; to appreciate (or to criticise) probation's contemporary position and significance; and to anticipate (and even, perhaps, to influence) its future.

Questions

- The experience of offenders/clients/probationers is said to be absent from most histories. How might they have experienced probation supervision in its different 'phases'? Do you think that the experience of being supervised is different now from what it might have been in 1999? What might these differences be?
- The author suggests "While the language changes – redeemable or damned, treatable or recalcitrant, safe or risky, motivated or unmotivated – it is at least possible that it is much the same people who find themselves on the wrong side of this divide." Are these distinctions just different ways of justifying favouring some groups while rejecting others? And do you agree that those rejected are perhaps 'much the same people' all the time?

- The author refers to 'the realities of practice', but what are these and to what extent do they limit what can be achieved through changes of policy?

Further reading

Start with the two chapters in the *Handbook of Probation* (2007) – Nellis (2007a) and Raynor and Vanstone (2007). Students of probation's history should then consult Bochel (1976); Garland (1985); McWilliams (1983, 1985, 1986, 1987); Radzinowicz and Hood (1990); Brownlee (1998); Oldfield (2002); Raynor and Vanstone (2002); Vanstone (2004a, 2004b); Whitehead and Statham (2006).

3 Probation values, justice and diversity

Justice is the first virtue of social institutions, as truth is of systems of thought. A theory however elegant and economical must be rejected or revised if it is untrue; likewise laws and institutions no matter how efficient and well-arranged must be reformed or abolished if they are unjust.

(Rawls 1972: 3)

This chapter considers the values that probation should stand for. After some initial thoughts about how to approach these questions, we discuss some of the ways in which probation has tried to give expression to its values. The government's rejection of social work values and the emergence of community justice are considered. Anti-discrimination and diversity, often at the centre of these discussions, are then explored. The chapter concludes with a proposal to try to ground probation values in human rights.

Values

Values are more than moral beliefs or ideas. They are prescriptive: they say how people should behave. We may not always live up to our values, but their purpose is to prescribe certain kinds of conduct – and to rule out other kinds. When any value is affirmed, then, the first question must be: what would count as accomplishing it in practice (and what would constitute a violation of it)? Unless this can be answered, the value is at best incomplete and possibly vacuous (Canton 2007).

There is an important sense, moreover, in which someone's values are not so much what they *say* as what they *do*. As Clark (2000: 31) puts it: 'values . . . should always be understood as the ongoing accomplishments of skilled and knowledgeable persons imbued with a moral sense'. Values accordingly may not reliably be read off from mission statements and business plans, but must be inferred from the practices of organisations.

Since values are intimately connected with actions in this way, practice and processes – *how* things are done – are no less important than outcomes and 'ends'. Instrumental and managerial strategies – with their preference for outputs, outcomes and auditable episodes – can be indifferent to this and this is among the ways in which this conception of criminal justice may lose sight of its moral character.

A profession's values should emerge from its experience of trying to deal with morally complex states of affairs in principled and decent ways. Some traditional probation values may be hard to change precisely because they are the product of reflective and ethical responses to the demands of practice. Rather than framing an abstract series of values, which we then strive to apply to practice, perhaps the requirements of practice ought to be allowed to influence these values (Canton 2007: 245).

Probation and the values of social work

Probation has often explicitly affirmed the ethical significance of its work (Nellis 2007b). Many of the earliest probation officers found inspiration in Christianity, understanding their work as a distinctively moral endeavour (Chapter 2). Even as the service became more secular, this ethical self-awareness was expressed in different ways, but continued to be prominent.

For many of the middle years of the twentieth century, the values that probation espoused were said to be *social work values* and it was this especially that the government was rejecting when, in the 1990s, it repudiated social work as an appropriate characterisation of probation. The *skills* of social work and probation, after all, are in many respects very similar: case management, working in part-nership, the assessment and management of risk are prominent skills in both professions. Much (not all) of the *knowledge* required to work in probation and in social work – sociology, social policy, psychology – is common to both.

What the government was emphatically rejecting were the *values* of social work. Such values include respect for persons, confidentiality and self-determination (Biestek 1961). What place should such values have in working with offenders or in the implementation of *punishment in the community*?

> Probation officers now routinely talk of the criminals they are dealing with as 'offenders' – which is what they are – instead of the euphemistic language of 'clients' which I encountered as Home Secretary.
>
> (Straw 2009)

The term client was especially deprecated. To refer to someone as an offender is to take (and invite others to take) a particular attitude towards them – perhaps an attitude of punishment or discipline – and the notion that offenders were 'clients' undermined the idea of punishment in the community. The term remained important to many probation officers precisely because 'client' connotes respect, dignity and entitlement to service – as well as connecting probation with the traditions of social work which many still valued.

> 'Clients' have become 'offenders' it seems; and 'offender' slides easily from being a statement of fact – that a person has committed an offence or some offences – into an assertion of identity; they like the publicans and sinners of the gospel reading become a social class, a 'them'.
>
> (Selby 2007)

Nevertheless, as Smith (2005: 634) insists:

> for all the rhetoric of punishment and public protection, risk management and enforcement, when practitioners decide what they are actually going to do to engage and motivate clients, help them access resources and convey a sense of hope in the possibility of constructive change, they will find themselves using ideas and skills that have emerged from social work theory and research.

And since values are expressed in practice and are not somehow separate from it, the values of social work, even if articulated in a different language, persist in probation – in part, because this is what it has been found it takes to do the job well.

The emergence of community justice

But if probation was not to be social work what was it? Mike Nellis (1995) had suggested that the values of social work were (ethically and politically) an inadequate characterisation of probation values and he was among the most persuasive proponents in this country of an emerging concept of *community justice*. After the election of the New Labour government in 1997, probation became part of an emerging community justice sector and while many practitioners were reluctant to lose the values of social work, others recognised an opportunity to influence the character of probation's future. Community justice was a resonant even inspirational term, but its denotation was unclear, and the values that were to guide it were yet to be determined (Nellis 2000).

So what is community justice and what might it be? This will be discussed in Chapter 14. Here it is enough to say that community justice calls for the community's active participation in preventing and in responding to crime. It focuses on solving the problems which crime causes, but also the social problems of which crime itself is often a symptom. Among its guiding principles are *making good* the wrongs of crime and processes of *reintegration*, drawing attention to the responsibilities that communities have towards those of their members who have committed offences, as well as offenders' responsibilities to do what they can to offer real or symbolic reparation and to strive to desist from further offending. It is an inclusive approach to justice that recognises victims, communities and the wider society, whose rights and interests must also be part of any ethical account of probation's work (Nellis 1995).

Anti-discrimination, diversity and power

Anti-discrimination and diversity have rightly been prominent in almost all recent discussions of probation values. A system that tolerates and perpetuates unfairness cannot be described as a system of justice and probation's commitment to opposing unfair discrimination is grounded in principles of justice, equality and inclusiveness. As the following discussion reflects, the value of anti-discrimination cannot sensibly be considered separately from its realisation in practice: notoriously, this is an aspect of probation where practice has failed to achieve its aspirations.

Discrimination and anti-discrimination

Awareness that the criminal justice system discriminates unfairly against certain groups has stimulated a great deal of research and analysis (see Further Reading). *Discrimination* involves treating some person or people differently and to their disadvantage on unfair grounds – for example, their race, gender or sexuality. (It should be noticed that unfair discrimination can also take the form of favouring some in comparison with others – not just disadvantaging those others.) Laws against discrimination on the basis of race, gender and disability have progressively been extended to give formal protection against discrimination on other grounds – for example, religion or belief, or sexual orientation. *Anti-discrimination* opposes the ways in which people are unfairly dealt with on the basis of one or more aspects of their personal identity.

The National Audit Office (2004) focuses on six key 'strands of diversity':

- 'race';
- disability;
- gender;
- sexual orientation;
- age;
- religion/belief.

though we could also add:

- ethnicity;
- culture;
- social class;
- physical or mental health;
- employment status;
- language;
- educational attainment.

Some of these characteristics can be immediately obvious – gender, perhaps age, sometimes 'race' or ethnicity; other characteristics are not readily apparent – sexual orientation, religious beliefs, some kinds of disability. For these reasons and others, some of these attributes are much more readily monitored. Since monitoring – the identification of 'groups' and comparisons among them – is the main way of ascertaining discrimination, shortcomings in monitoring processes can fail to recognise (and thus conceal) unfairness. Examples of this include sexual orientation and learning difficulties which, in the nature of the case, are less readily monitored, so that discrimination, however real, is consequently less easy to demonstrate.

Monitoring can point to over- (or under-) representation (for example, young black men are more likely to be stopped than young white men). But this kind of analysis is often contested and inconclusive (Phillips and Bowling 2007). These inquiries are of value as markers or pointers for investigation, but:

- they do not in themselves demonstrate unfairness (perhaps there are defensible reasons for over-representation);
- even if we are confident that the analysis exposes unfairness, it cannot reveal the origins of this . . .
- . . . or the remedy;
- broad statistical categories can conceal as much as they expose – for instance, an average aggregate finding about 'women' could obscure very different experiences of black women, lesbian women and indeed black lesbian women (Hedderman and Gelsthorpe 1997; Hudson and Bramhall 2005 on the category 'Asian').

It takes much longer for some kinds of discrimination to be recognised and to arouse concern. Racism and sexism have long been recognised – which is by no means to say that they have been adequately redressed – while discrimination on grounds of sexuality and disability have struggled to gain political attention. This may be attributable to the relative political power and assertiveness of those challenging such discrimination and/or to the willingness of agencies to contemplate the need for changes in their practices. Fear and denial make some forms of discrimination much more readily discussable than other forms.

A sustained and effective attempt to change unfairness needs an understanding of the origins of unfair discrimination. A familiar explanation is *racism, sexism* (or other '-isms'), suggesting that the origin of discrimination is to be found in the views of practitioners and their power to give expression to their prejudicial attitudes. But while (for instance) racism and sexism must not be denied, the *explanatory* power of such terms is limited and attempts to redress this are consequently often disappointing. It is plainly important that policy makers and practitioners be encouraged to examine and change their own attitudes. At the same time, many years of commitment to opposing discrimination have only gone some of the way towards changing the position.

Nellis and Gelsthorpe (2003) make this point about *gender*. Academic criminology, at least since Carol Smart's influential work (1976), has incorporated many rich feminist perspectives and insights, some of which have been taken up by the probation service. Meanwhile, the practitioner workforce in probation has shifted and more women than men – many more among the more newly qualified – are employed as probation officers. Yet during and despite all this, the number of women in prison was markedly increasing (Gelsthorpe and Morris 2002) while community provision for women remained inadequate (Gelsthorpe *et al.* 2007).

Indirect and institutional discrimination

While the 'Probation Service has a long-established commitment to equal opportunity and social justice' (Hilder 2007: 9), unfair outcomes seem to persist, surviving recruitment and training initiatives, as well as changes in policy and personnel. Plainly there is a need for an analysis that goes beyond direct discrimination.

The law too recognises that discrimination can take different forms. *Indirect discrimination* is often of particular relevance in scrutinising criminal justice. This occurs when, irrespective of intention, 'a provision, criterion or practice' puts people at a particular disadvantage, where it cannot be shown that the provision, criterion or practice is a proportionate means of achieving a legitimate aim. (See Equality and Human Rights Commission (http://www.equalityhumanrights.com/) for the legal framework and guidance.)

Table 3.1 sets out Thompson's (2006) useful and influential model and applies it to probation.

The ways in which unfairness may be embodied in policy and practice are often subtle and complex. Hood (1992) studied the over-representation of black people in prison by investigating the sentencing decision. He directed attention to custodial remand and to *plea* as significant factors in the explanation. These influences were far from obvious and addressing them is not straightforward. Among other examples, the theoretical basis, design and implementation of accredited programmes and assessment instruments in probation have been argued to be *gendered* (Shaw and Hannah-Moffat 2004) – their significance, application and consequences impacting differently on women and men. The criminogenic needs of women, again, cannot be assumed to be the same as those of men (Gelsthorpe 2001; Kemshall *et al.* 2004) nor are the 'pathways to desistance' necessarily the same for women and girls as for men (McIvor *et al.* 2004; Rumgay 2004). The Corston Report (2007) is a powerful political statement of the distinctive needs and vulnerabilities of some women within the criminal justice system. A failure to acknowledge these differences could lead to services that are irrelevant (or worse) to women. Traditions and practices may 'carry' discrimination in an organisation's work.

Sensitivity to the personal level of discrimination has led people to be cautious about *discretion*. Phillips and Bowling (2007), Hudson and Bramhall (2005) and others recognise that where decision-makers have too much discretion, there is an increased possibility that their personal prejudices will influence them, to the detriment of some groups and individuals. While there is much truth in this, an awareness of cultural and structural aspects of discrimination should alert us to the possibility that a removal of discretion can lead to quite as much unfairness. The search for 'consistency' can lead to a denial of difference (Canton and Eadie 2004, 2008). The development and dissemination of a tightly prescribed best practice may not always do justice to the many ways in which people are different from one another. Policy is unavoidably generalised, assuming a 'standard case', a generic 'offender', who often turns out to be, if only by assumption, a young

Table 3.1 Three levels of discrimination

Thompson's model	Probation context
Structural	
Discrimination reflects (and reproduces) the power structures of a society. Social, economic and political conditions enable certain groups to have power over others, to establish their own advantage in access to resources and opportunities and to sustain these inequalities	The dimensions of discrimination perceived in probation and in the wider criminal justice system correspond to these social divisions (as the power model – Chapter 1 – emphasises). Nor may it be assumed that criminal justice legislation never embodies unfairness. Moreover, penal policy has often had unexpected and perverse consequences. Policy innovations are regularly assessed against an 'equality impact assessment',[1] recognising the importance of vigilance against such possibilities. Poor policy and practice are likely to impact differentially upon those with the least power in an inevitable *gradient of disadvantage*
Cultural	
Shaped by (and shaping) the structural level, this recognises that group norms sustain discrimination. Language, patterns of behaviour, assumptions and stereotypes are shared among dominant groups (and can be 'internalised' by those discriminated against)	As well as the wider social culture, the 'occupational culture' – how practitioners collectively understand their work and influence one another – can be a 'carrier' of discrimination, enabling it to persist despite turnovers of staff. Law and policy are mediated and interpreted collectively as practitioners establish conventions about *how things should be done*. Office dynamics and politics, allocation practices (who is assigned what type of work and why) are examples
Personal	
Influenced by (and influencing) the other two levels, this refers to prejudicial personal attitudes which find expression in behaviour and language	It is because unexamined attitudes can lead to unfair treatment – and because structural and cultural legacies are likely to instil prejudice – that probation personnel must continue to reflect and to explore the origins of their own views and the effects on practice. The personal level continues to be very important – but not the only level at which discrimination must be identified and changed

white man. Hudson (2001: 166) puts it well: 'Once the subject of justice is given back his/her social context and flesh and blood reality, it is clear that difference is the standard case, and that differences are routinely irreducible.'

Combating unfair discrimination

Our discussion suggests that there are three principal components to anti-discrimination, as Figure 3.1 illustrates.

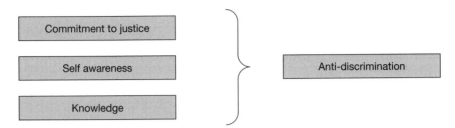

Figure 3.1 Three requirements in challenging discrimination

1   Since discriminatory practice is unjust, there must be an *ethical commitment to justice*.

2   Anti-discrimination calls for *self-awareness* and undefensive personal reflection. The Macpherson Report (1999: 6.34) includes in its definition of *institutional racism* the 'unwitting prejudice, ignorance thoughtlessness and racist stereotyping which disadvantage minority ethnic people'. If discrimination can be unwitting (or unconscious or unintentional) (*ibid.*), then plainly people should strive to become more aware of their own attitudes, some deep-rooted and unacknowledged, to ensure that they do not find unfair expression in practice. So anti-discrimination is never just a detached intellectual endeavour inquiry. We have to be prepared to think about others and ourselves in quite different ways and be willing to question some of our most basic assumptions – not only about others but about ourselves and ourselves in relation to those others. This calls for courage as well as emotional maturity.

3   Effective anti-discrimination further calls for a deep and detailed *knowledge* and understanding of the practices of criminal justice. The way in which systematic disadvantage operates requires investigation and understanding, as does the implementation of measures to redress unfairness. As Bhui insists (2006: 185) 'anti-discriminatory practice is not something that can be taught separately from its professional and organisational context'. Commitment to justice and enhanced self-awareness are invaluable, but not enough.

Discrimination often takes the form either of denying difference or of exaggerating difference. You may be unfair and ineffective if in your work you treat everyone as if they are just the same. But you should not think that people are so different that you cannot understand or relate to them at all. To do so is to deprive oneself of the empathy that is at the heart of the capacity to respect other people.

Gelsthorpe (2007) notes that there have been accusations of *too much* disparity between black and white offenders (exaggeration of difference) and *not enough* differentiation between men and women (denial of difference). Similarly probation has sometimes disavowed its responsibilities to people who are mentally unwell by saying that their needs are so distinctive that they cannot benefit from the standard interventions of probation (Canton 1995). This, like many such claims, is over-generalised and stereotypical; but equally to deny that there are any relevant differences can also let down people who are mentally unwell. Both these forms of discrimination can be found to operate in the criminal justice system (Canton 2008a).

Diversity

Talk of discrimination has been substantially superseded in official discourse by the language of diversity (Stout 2007). If discrimination attends to difference as problematic, diversity is to be celebrated. It is certainly true that the differences among people enrich us all: diversity offers a discourse within which this can be recognised.

> *Everyone* is in certain respects
> a   like everyone else
> b   like some other people
> c   like nobody else
>
> (adapted from Murray and Kluckhohn 1953)

The earlier list of 'dimensions of difference' makes it immediately apparent that *all* of us have *all* the characteristics listed (everyone has a gender, age, ethnicity etc.). It is possible for people to remain comfortably unaware of at least some aspects of their identity, just because they are so taken for granted and not called into question. People can grow up without reflecting on their own race, gender and sexuality – though only if they are white, male and heterosexual: in England, people who are black or from minority ethnic groups, women, gay men and lesbian women will never be unaware of these aspects of their identity. Without self-awareness and reflection, this taken-for-grantedness can be consolidated as a complacent sense, endorsed by many aspects of culture, that this is what it is to be 'normal' and that those with differences of identity are 'other'. The assumption of normality is among the most powerful modes of oppression and marginalisation (Knight *et al.* 2008).

> They behave this way not because I'm black but because they are white.
>
> (Alice Walker 1993: 38)

Since all of us have all of these characteristics, there is an indefinite number of variations in the way in which these characteristics combine in each individual: the constellation of difference is distinctive – perhaps unique – for everyone. For example, someone may be a woman *and* young *and* black *and* lesbian *and* atheist and so on. So while it is possible and often useful to assign people to groups for certain purposes, any 'group' we construct on the basis of a single common characteristic will still be very diverse in all other respects.

It is, moreover, precisely at the intersections, overlaps and indeed *interactions* among these groupings that people are most vulnerable to discrimination.

Gelsthorpe (2006: 100) observes 'within the broad realm of Criminology, we find that "race" and "gender" have been given exclusive attention. What has been conspicuously absent from analyses is an investigation of their various intersections'. It is as if criminology assumes that 'All the women are white, all the blacks are men' (Hull *et al.* 2003; Rice 1990).

While the discourses of discrimination and diversity draw attention to difference, there are many things that all people have in common. It is probably not too reckless to claim that we all have common biological needs and common basic emotions; that we need to feel respected and valued; we need the liberty to pursue our own interests and projects. To say this is not to deny that *how* these needs are to be met may well be different from person to person, but it is to insist that the indispensable human and professional attribute of empathy – to attempt to imagine what it may be like to be another – is often at the heart of good anti-discriminatory practice and is not made unachievable because of differences among us.

The discourse of diversity brings difficulties of its own (Knight *et al.* 2008). In particular, it sometimes risks losing the insight that differences among people are systematically associated with differences of power and it is this that often leads to unfairness and difference of treatment. Before diversity can be truly celebrated, unfairness must be opposed. We need a way of talking and thinking about these matters that does justice *both* to the consideration that discrimination operates to the systematic disadvantage of some groups *and* to the fact that the configuration of personal attributes that make up our identity is distinctive, if not unique, for everyone. The language of diversity illuminates this second consideration; the language of discrimination connects much more effectively with issues of power and the many levels at which it can lead to unfairness.

Probation values and human rights

How might a positive ethics of probation be constructed? Anti-discrimination and working well with diversity are best understood as a commitment to making sure that everyone is treated as fairly and as well as possible. But the discourse tends to focus on relational questions – how some people are dealt with *compared to others*. But what kind of treatment should this be? We need a clearer understanding of the *substantial* question of what is due to offenders and victims, what it is to treat them fairly and well. An ethics of probation must therefore engage with the complex and contested matter of the rights of victims and offenders, as well as working to ensure that these are accorded to everyone.

Human rights – rights we have in virtue of our common humanity and that are not contingent upon gender, race, sexuality, abilities or beliefs – are the most sound foundation for this construction. (This already looks like a promising beginning in opposing unfair discrimination.) It encompasses *everyone's* rights – victims as well as offenders, for example, and the families and dependants of offenders, who are often profoundly affected by punishments imposed. Nor do these rights have to be *deserved* – sole and sufficient credentials are to be human.

At the centre of human rights is the principle of *personhood*. To be a person is to be an agent and this requires:

- autonomy;
- choice (genuine choice must be informed, requiring adequate information)
- ability to act (which requires a minimum provision of resources and capabilities);
- liberty (against anyone blocking this) (Griffin 2008: 33).

In other words, *with due regard to the requirement to respect the rights of others*, the values of personhood entail rights to act freely on our own informed choices, without impediment and with genuine opportunity. Punishment involves some limitations of these rights, but such limitations should not go beyond the requirements of a legitimate penal purpose (Chapter 4).

A familiar distinction is between liberties and claims. Liberty rights affirm that, as governments pursue the general welfare, certain rights may challenge and sometimes constrain their projects. But citizens also call upon their governments to create conditions in which they may thrive (claims). For people to have real chances to pursue their interests and projects calls not only for others' forbearance from interference, but also propitious circumstances and meaningful opportunities. Both these kinds of rights are central to the work of probation. Punishment, perhaps by definition, involves the withdrawal, suspension or limitation of certain rights, but this must be undertaken in a principled manner. At the same time, as we shall find repeatedly in this book, pathways out of crime require meaningful opportunities to find and develop law-abiding ways of living – conditions in which people may thrive.

There are three particular advantages in articulating probation values in the language of rights (compare Cavadino and Dignan 2007).

First, this would make probation values *mainstream*. The values of probation ought to be accessible to everyone and expressed in the common language of contemporary ethical discourse. A problem with affirming the values of social work was that it confined probation to a narrow account of professional ethics that lacked resonance and was probably of little interest to people outside the profession.

Second, human rights is an *international* discourse. Among the reasons why this matters is that some key human rights concepts are intrinsically *comparative*. The idea that a response to an offence should be proportionate, for example, is central to several conventions and recommendations (van Zyl Smit and Ashworth 2004), but how are we to know whether a sanction or measure is proportionate without some kind of comparison with other countries? How can we get any purchase on such questions without seeing our practices in an international and comparative context? And where there is a conflict between individuals' rights and the common good, it is not clear that the state is an even-handed judge in its own cause. Accountability to the international community is an important safeguard.

Third, the Human Rights Act 1998 incorporated the European Convention for the Protection of Human Rights and Fundamental Freedoms into UK law. If probation values could be articulated in these terms, they would acquire the strength and legitimacy of law. They also become justiciable – matters that can be put to test in court.

A rights-based statement of the values of probation

Some ethical principles for probation can be inferred from this conception of human rights. Among the most important are:

1   Believing in the possibility of personal change, probation should help to: create opportunities for people to lead fulfilling and crime-free lives; enable them to acquire the skills needed to avail themselves of those opportunities; and motivate them to do so.
2   Recognising people's responsibilities and rights, probation should address offenders as responsible, self-determining people.
3   As far as possible, offenders should be fully involved in (informed and consulted about) any decisions that affect them. They should be actively involved in assessment, planning, interventions and evaluation.
4   Probation seeks to gain the consent of offenders. Even when staff are obliged to take action against someone's wishes, they should always try to secure the offender's understanding of and, so far as possible, consent to any decisions that affect them.

Although these principles derive from the values of personhood, they also recognise effective practice. People must be actively involved in identifying and working with their own problems. Further, the most effective form of control is self-control. External controls are sometimes necessary, as punishment or to increase public protection, but the attempt to command the offender's under-standing and consent should always be an objective of probation's work:

5   The purpose of intervention is to reduce the likelihood of reoffending. Inter-ventions must accordingly be constructive and not punitive in character.
6   Probation should countenance no imposition or limitation of rights unless this can be justified by some legitimate penal purpose.
7   Probation must always have regard to the rights and interests of offenders, even when the rights and interests of others must take priority.
8   Some limitation of rights is a necessary consequence of punishment but any such limitation of rights should be *either* lawful and deliberate punishment *or* minimised. Any restrictions on offenders' rights must be proportionate to the offence.
9   Offenders are members of the community some of whose rights have, for the duration of the penalty, been taken away or compromised. Once the penalty has been served, these rights should be fully reinstated. In this respect,

communities have responsibilities towards those of their members who have committed crimes.

Some punishments (notably imprisonment) curtail opportunities and, once the sentence has been completed, the state should assume a responsibility to create opportunities (for example, for employment). This principle argues that rehabilitation through resettlement and after-care is a *right* – not just a continuation of a custodial sentence (Chapter 12; see also Rotman 1994; Lewis 2005; Ward and Maruna 2006):

10   Social inclusion is a requirement of social justice and a key guiding principle in probation practice. Since people who do not have fair and reasonable access to the services and institutions of civil society (social exclusion) are more likely to offend, this principle also helps to reduce offending.
11   To achieve the social inclusion of offenders, probation must work in close partnership with the agencies of civil society. Meeting the complex needs of many offenders call for co-ordinated and complementary inter-agency work. Probation should use its expertise to help other agencies to make their services genuinely accessible to offenders.

These principles attempt to connect the work of probation to the wider society. They go beyond organisational claims about the advantages of working in partnership to say that the services and institutions of civil society should be genuinely available to offenders as a matter of social justice:

12   All probation practices must respect the interests and rights of victims of crime, in work with them or on their behalf, as well as working with offenders to help them to recognise the harm that they have caused.
13   Probation should explain its work and its significance to the public. Its values, policies and practices must be open and must command the confidence and trust of the community. (This is a requirement of legitimacy.)
14   Probation policy and practice should be evidence-led. Rigorous research and evaluation should guide the work of probation agencies.

This is not just an organisational virtue, but an ethical one: to evaluate is a mark of sincerity of purpose. If probation's objectives are worth achieving, the extent to which they are indeed being achieved must be appraised.

There may be circumstances in which these principles may be in conflict with each other or with other ethical principles. This is in the nature of rights-claims: few rights, if any, are absolute. For example, while interventions should be constructive and not punitive, there are interventions – for instance, necessary constraints on some sex offenders – that will indeed be experienced as punitive and restrictive because they safeguard the rights of others. Again, while completion of the lawful sanction ought normally to restore people to their full rights, the continuing risk posed by some means that their rights may have to continue to be circumscribed. These principles, then, are best understood as morally relevant considerations that ought always to be marked and allowed for when decisions are to be taken. Even where they must give way to other moral considerations, infringement should take place with a sense of regret, an impetus to seek other solutions and an attempt to mitigate the implications for the offender.

Task

European Probation Rules attempt to apply the European Convention to the work of probation trying to specify what human rights really entail (Council of Europe 2010).

Download the European Probation Rules and compare these with the list above. Do you share these values? (Why or why not?) Is there something that you feel should be added (or subtracted)? What practices follow from this set of principles – how can they be 'brought to life'? How do the practices of the probation service measure up to these principles? Are some of them insufficiently respected?

Summary

In this chapter, the importance and the meaning of values have been discussed; the idea of community justice has been briefly introduced; questions of diversity and anti-discrimination have been raised and considered. The chapter has concluded with the proposal that human rights may be the best way to articulate the values of probation and an attempt has been made to generate some policy- and practice-guiding principles.

A premise throughout has been that probation is best seen not as way of reducing the prison population nor as a means of enhancing public safety, but as the institutional expression of some of the values that ought to characterise a decent society – that there may be other ways of responding to offending than imprisonment, that people can change, that the community has responsibilities towards those of its members who have offended.

Probation, perhaps, is distinguished less by its instrumental objectives – after all, many other agencies are committed to public protection and reducing crime – than by the means by which this can and should be accomplished. Excesses of punishment, as advocated by punitive strategies, are corrosive for any society. There seems to be a strong association between punitiveness and scepticism about the possibility of change (Maruna and King 2004): the less people believe in the possibility of change, the more punitive they are likely to be – and the less likely to support non-custodial punishment for offenders. But in that case, perhaps a confident affirmation of probation's core belief in the possibility of change may be a powerful way of challenging punitiveness.

Again, contemporary preoccupations with effectiveness have risked suppressing the moral significance of criminal justice practice. Instrumental conceptions of criminal justice risk seeing an affirmation of human rights and other moral claims as an impediment to their objectives. As Garland (1990: 292) writes:

> the pursuit of values such as justice, tolerance, decency, humanity and civility should be part of any penal institution's self-consciousness – an intrinsic and constitutive aspect of its role – rather than a diversion from its 'real' goals or an inhibition on its capacity to be 'effective'.

Criminal justice and probation practice are not just ways of dealing with criminals, but ways of doing justice. They are therefore irreducibly moral activities.

Further reading

An excellent brief introduction to probation values is Nellis (2007b). Nellis and Gelsthorpe (2003) and Gelsthorpe (2007) are also insightful and important. Knight *et al.* (2008) is a wise and stimulating introduction to diversity and anti-discrimination. A good start to the enormous literature on discrimination in criminal justice is Phillips and Bowling (2007) (race) and Heidensohn and Gelsthorpe (2007) (gender). Her Majesty's Inspectorate of Probation publishes much valuable material about discrimination and diversity online. A case for human rights as the expression of probation values is argued in Canton (2009a). The European Probation Rules are discussed in Canton (2010b).

4   Punishment, sentencing and probation

This chapter considers the purposes and justifications of punishment. Although the main focus will be on the court's sentencing decision, many of the ideas and problems discussed here will recur throughout the book. Probation, after all, is essentially involved in giving effect to the court's decisions and the concepts explored here will be of relevance to probation staff in almost all aspects of their work.

Punishment: its purpose and justifications

Punishment involves a deliberate imposition, typically a hardship or loss of liberty or rights, on wrongdoers, by a recognised authority, as a censure for the wrong done. This calls for an account of its purposes and justifications.

The practices and institutions of punishment have many purposes and meanings. Philosophers have typically looked at justifications, while sociologists have explored the social, political, economic and cultural factors that shape punishing practices in different societies and indeed the way in which punishment may reciprocally influence the character of a society (Garland 1990).

Philosophers often begin with an initial distinction between *retributive* and *reductive* accounts (Cavadino and Dignan 2007). Retributivism holds that punishment is a fitting response to wrongdoing: offenders should be dealt with as they deserve and the proper punishment is one that matches the offence. Reductivism sets for punishment the objective of contributing to a reduction in future offending and considers some of the mechanisms by which this might be achieved.

In law, courts are required to have regard to several purposes of sentencing:

a   the punishment of offenders[1];
b   the reduction of crime (including its reduction by deterrence);
c   the reform and rehabilitation of offenders;
d   the protection of the public;
e   the making of reparation by offenders to persons affected by their offences
      (Criminal Justice Act 2003 s. 142).

(a) looks like a retributive principle; (b), (c) and (d) are reductive in intent; (e) goes beyond the initial philosophical distinction to suggest other ways of responding to wrongdoing.

The punishment of offenders

This is primarily a *retributive* principle. Retributivism (sometimes referred to as 'just deserts' or 'the justice model') insists that people should be punished as they deserve. This is just and proper in itself. It is not the consequences of the punishment that give it its justification: rather, the sentence should constitute due and proportionate punishment for the wrong that has been done. This principle and some of its corollaries – worse crimes should receive weightier punishments, like offences should be punished alike – have a strong intuitive appeal to many people. Even those who seek another purpose or justification for punishment can respect the objection that one punishment is too severe or another not severe enough for the offence. Indeed, whatever the primary justification for a particular sentence, its adequacy and appropriateness *as punishment* is one of the first and most prominent considerations.

But how is a fair and proportionate punishment to be determined? The court must look to the seriousness of the offence and will take account of 'any harm which the offence caused, was intended to cause or might foreseeably have caused' (Criminal Justice Act 2003, s. 143 [1]). The defendant's culpability – their responsibility for this harm – must also be considered. The punishment should then be made to 'fit the crime'.

Crimes, however, cannot be readily translated into punishments in this way. We all recognise (or think we can) when a punishment is obviously out of proportion – much too lenient or too severe – but when we try to identify a specific sentence it becomes very much harder. This is because crimes and punishments are *incommensurable*: there is no common metric that allows a straightforward calculation from crime to punishment.

It may, though, be possible to *rank* types of crime – in order of seriousness. There is broad consensus that (for example) crimes of violence are more serious than property crimes (Stylianou 2003). Punishments might next be ranked – perhaps on a scale of loss of liberty or limitation on rights. In principle, it might then be possible to 'read across' from one scale to the other. The *penal tariff* thus constructed would be a retributive device to ensure that like crimes are punished alike and that the more serious crimes are awarded the heavier penalties ('ordinal proportionality').

Yet crimes may differ in any number of ways, complicating the idea of 'like offences'. Theft, for example, is a very broad category and our perception of the seriousness of an offence of theft is influenced by many considerations – for example, the value of what was stolen, the impact on the victim, the motives and circumstances of the offender. There are always mitigating or aggravating factors – considerations that could be advanced to show that an offence is a less or more serious instance of its kind (Walker 1999). These typically relate to harm (the damage done was not so bad; the effect on the victim was particularly serious) and/or responsibility (the offender was provoked; the offence was carefully planned). These differences in harm and culpability should lead to more or less serious levels of punishment.

Even on a penal tariff, then, the 'read across' from crime to punishment is not at all straightforward. A further consideration (often overlooked) is the *impact* of the penalty: if punishment is to be in proportion to the wrong done, then the real impact of the penalty, different upon different people, cannot justly be ignored. This gives rise to another form of mitigation – mitigation not to show that the offence was a less serious instance of its kind, but to show that the standard penalty might have unexpected and perhaps disproportionate consequences. Examples include the vulnerability of the defendant, old age, disability, illness, family circumstances, effect on employment or accommodation (Easton and Piper 2005; Walker 1999).

Two other characteristics of a retributive approach must be noted. First, in any principled form, it sets *limits*: punishment may not be more severe than the offence merits. Nor, ordinarily, should it be less, although there may remain a place for special circumstances or for mercy (Walker 1999). Second, retributivism says nothing about the *form* that punishment should take. This needs to be emphasised because in many countries retributive punishment is too readily understood to entail imprisonment.

The Criminal Justice Act 1991 set this approach – punishment in proportion to the crime – as the main rationale of sentencing (although in certain circumstances courts were allowed to go beyond the deserved penalty to protect the public from sexual and violent offenders). While the Criminal Justice Act 2003, drawing upon the influential Halliday review of sentencing (Home Office 2001), (re)introduced a number of other sentencing objectives, seriousness still structures the sentencing framework. Seriousness sets thresholds: a custodial sentence (which here includes a suspended sentence of imprisonment) may not be passed unless the offence is *so serious* that a fine or community sentence cannot be justified (CJA 2003 s. 152 (2).); an offence must be *serious enough* to warrant a community sentence (CJA 2003 s. 148 (1).)

Reductive purposes

If retributivism *looks back* to the offence to determine the appropriate punishment, the next three statutory purposes of sentencing *look forwards* to influence the behaviour of the offender (or perhaps others) so as to reduce the incidence of offending in the future by one mechanism or another. This is why they are referred to as *reductive* approaches to punishment.

Since these approaches set out to achieve a reduction in offending, they are – at least in principle – amenable to empirical inquiry about their effectiveness (to what extent do they achieve their objectives to reduce crime? do they work?), even if the methodological difficulties are formidable (Bottoms 2004). Retributive punishment, by contrast, may not be investigated in this way since there is nothing, no future state of affairs, it sets out to achieve – just a fitting match between crime and punishment.

Reductive accounts often have their origin in the view that, since punishment involves the infliction of pain or deprivation of some kind, the impositions of punishment can only be justified to the extent that, by reducing offending, there is a net reduction in harm overall. In some accounts, punishment that goes beyond that required to reduce offending is by definition gratuitous and unjustified. The most persuasive reductive versions thus incorporate a principle of *parsimony*: to impose as light a punishment as is consistent with achieving reductive objectives. Parsimony – also known as *minimum intervention* – may not always be readily reconciled with the principle of proportionality on which retributivism depends (Tonry 1994). At the same time, the idea of minimum intervention, and indeed any principled approach to punishment, sets limits to what may be done in the name of punishment – an important ethical safeguard against cruelty and vengeance.

The reduction of crime (including its reduction by deterrence)

Since other ways of reducing crime are covered elsewhere in this section of the Act, Criminal Justice Act 2003 s. 142 (b) appears to refer mainly to deterrence. This is the idea that someone who is confronted with a vivid prospect of punishment might thereby be deterred (frightened off) from further offending. This encompasses both *individual deterrence* (for example, a suspended sentence of imprisonment is meant to make clear to that offender the consequences of any further offending) and *general deterrence*, which makes the ambitious claim that other people as well, contemplating a crime but knowing of the punishment that awaits offenders, might refrain through fear of this penalty.

Deterrence, which has an influential if sometimes implicit place in political debate about punishment, makes assumptions about how people reason. But do people reason in this way? Is fear of a relatively remote punishment enough to deter – especially if the prospect of detection or arrest seems unlikely?

A claim that deterrence does or does not 'work' must attend to at least three variables – the (potential) offender, the act in question, the anticipated punishment. It is possible (indeed entirely probable) that:

- some people are more readily deterrable than others;
- some types of crime in some types of circumstances are more susceptible to deterrence than others;
- some prospective punishments are more compelling than others.

And of course all these variables interact with one another. In a contested debate, the observation that deterrence is, in the nature of the case, *subjective* is compelling (Bottoms 2004): it is not the actual consequences but *the consequences that the person anticipates* that will (or perhaps will fail to) deter; and, if deterrence is to work, these consequences must *for this individual* outweigh the incentives to offend.

Plainly, then, assertions that deterrence 'works' (or doesn't) are over-general and misleading. Disagreements about the place of deterrence in sentencing really hinge on the extent to which increases in the levels of punishment offer a plausible means of reducing crime – or that lower levels of punishment lead to more offending. It is hard to find evidence to show that increases in the amount of punishment achieve deterrent gains or that reductions would lead to a higher incidence.

In truth, the criminal justice system is predicated on a very crude and limited understanding of motivation and incentives. The way in which some people make their decisions, their judgements about risks and pay-offs, about incentives and drawbacks are far removed from the rational calculation assumed by classical criminology (Newburn 2007: Chapter 5). Incentives may not always function in the way that 'common sense' leads us to think they do (Levitt and Dubner 2006) and discussions with offenders about what influences their behaviour reveal the limitations of any ambition to reduce offending mainly through reliance on threats of punishment. The idea of the 'reasoning criminal' may be a necessary rejoinder to any view that offenders are in some sense radically different: as Cornish and Clarke (1986) insisted, offenders mostly reason like everyone else. Yet the rationality that many people bring to their actions – especially in the type of circumstances in which crimes often occur, where reasoning may be distorted by rage, despair, excitement or intoxication – is bounded and incomplete.

With regard to the principle of parsimony (above), it must be noted that, if there is an optimum level of punishment – *just enough to deter* – no one knows what it is. An evidence base that would allow an optimal deterrent sentence to be calculated simply does not exist. In this way, deterrence, like most other aims of punishment, gives little or no guidance about the appropriate *amount* of punishment. It is worth remembering too that punishment is just one of the consequences of offending – and, given the relatively low rates of detection of at least some types of offence, one of the less certain consequences. Many people are 'deterred' by conscience, by habit, by self-respect, by anticipation of the reproach of others and there is no reason to suppose that the absence of such constraints can be remedied by increases in levels of punishment. Deterrence probably works best for those who need it least.

> It appears that the EU will require fortune-tellers to inform their customers that fortune-telling is . . . 'not experimentally proven'. This means that 'a fortune-teller who sets up a tent at a fun-fair will have to put up a disclaimer on a board outside.' . . . We may well ask, then, why it is so important for the fortune-tellers to inform the public that fortune-telling is 'not experimentally proven', when the same may also be said about the punishment prescribed by law. Perhaps there should be a placard posted in the front of Crown Courts saying 'not experimentally proven'.
>
> (Sherman 2009: 14)

There are also ethical objections that should be raised: is it justifiable to punish people beyond what they deserve in order to discourage other people? A court may, for example, reason that a particular offence should attract a heavier penalty because it is too prevalent and an example must be set. Is it defensible, though, to impose punishment beyond desert because of prevalence (hardly the responsibility of this defendant) or to use someone to set an example to others?

Discussion of the potential effects and limitations of deterrence will be considered further in Chapter 9, when issues of compliance and enforcement are discussed.

The reform and rehabilitation of offenders

Rehabilitation is both more and less ambitious than deterrence: less ambitious because it recognises that intervention will influence only this offender and therefore cannot significantly contribute to overall levels of offending; yet more ambitious because it tries to bring it about that people refrain from offending, not through fear, but because they no longer *choose to offend*. (Deterrence, after all, provides a reason not to get caught – not a reason not to offend.)

Little will be said about the principle here because it will occupy us in so many other places in this book (see especially Chapters 6–9). For now, it is enough to say that rehabilitation and reform can be taken to refer here to any individual intervention that is intended to contribute to reducing reoffending and which does not rely (or mostly rely) on threat or on incapacitation.

The protection of the public

Any effective reductive mechanism contributes to the protection of the public. The sentencing purpose envisaged here is incapacitation.

The Prevention of Crime Act 1908 (enacted the year after the Probation of Offenders Act and to some extent inspired by a similar understanding of what punishment should or might achieve) introduced *preventive detention*, providing in Part II for the prolonged detention of 'habitual criminals'. This was the first of a series of measures, introduced intermittently over many years, which tried to identify and detain people who are likely to offend and so prevent their crimes (Easton and Piper 2005). Extended sentences and the notorious US 'three strikes' sentences are other examples. The results of such measures are often disappointing. They are at least as likely to identify persistent and sometimes relatively minor offenders as to prevent grave crime. They also lead to disproportionately severe sentences in some cases.

Incapacitation does not depend on influencing the offender's mind, but imposes physical constraints to prevent offending. While there may be specific community measures to incapacitate, prison is the plainest example. Some argue that it is possible and defensible to identify and incapacitate those most likely to offend seriously or prolifically (who should not be assumed to be the same people). Others claim that our capacity to make such assessments is less reliable than is sometimes thought; that criminal careers are often shorter than appreciated by advocates of incapacitation; that high levels of incarceration would be needed to achieve even quite modest reductive gains (see Bottoms, 2004, for review of the evidence).

Certainly incapacitation must be of 'diminishing utility': even if a large number of crimes could be prevented by imprisoning the most prolific offenders, it does not follow that there could be comparable gains by imprisoning more and more people. Another limitation is that in many circumstances criminals 'replace' each other: for instance, 'when drug dealers are removed from a local neighbourhood it will often be a matter of days, if not hours, before they are replaced by new drug dealers' (Coyle 2005: 17). Hedderman (2006) points out that prison, by postponing and spoiling the opportunities to acquire the settled lifestyle with which desistance is typically associated, can prolong the risk-of-offending period. Almost all offenders will be released one day and even if the rationale for their detention has been incapacitation, public protection requires that imprisonment should at least have attempted to reduce the likelihood of their reoffending. Principled incapacitation is not mere warehousing.

Incapacitation, like deterrence, raises hard ethical problems as well as empirical questions about effectiveness. Is incapacitation (beyond what is deserved) punishing people for what they have not done – or at least not done *yet* and, if the term of incapacitation is well judged, indeed never will do?

Judgements about incapacitation rest on an assessment of *risk*. Arguments for incapacitation are most persuasive when there is reasonable confidence that the offender poses a risk of serious offending. But, since certainty is unachievable, how probable and how serious must a further offence be before an incapacitative sentence is justified? Although a distinction has been made between empirical and ethical questions, in practice they are entangled. Our views about the ethical acceptability of incapacitation are likely to be influenced by our confidence in the accuracy of these judgements: the higher the proportion of inaccurate assessments leading to unnecessary detention, the more uneasy we are likely to feel about the ethical propriety of this approach to sentencing. The assessment of risk will be taken up again in Chapter 10.

The making of reparation by offenders to persons affected by their offences

Reparation refers to the idea that offenders should make amends to a victim or perhaps to the community to repair the harm caused by their offence. In England and Wales, reparative approaches have been most fully developed in relation to working with young offenders (see for example Mahaffey 2009). Even here, though, reparation is seldom at the centre of the response to offending, while for adult offenders the idea has yet to achieve what many people see as its potential. Reparation is, after all, one way in which we might change the focus of criminal justice responses and involve victims and communities as well as offenders in the response to crimes – part of the vision of community justice.

But this idea is weakly represented in responses to crime or in the sentencing powers of the court. Criminal courts have power to award compensation in appropriate cases, although financial compensation is not always the best way to make amends and offenders are often not in a position to pay. Community service (unpaid work) has always included a reparative element (Chapter 11). That apart, the adult court has no sentencing power that supports reparation. And the principle finds no obvious place within the Offender Management Model (Chapter 7).

Note that while reparation may have reductive effects – it is hoped that the process will bring about more considerate behaviour in future – this is not its sole nor even its primary purpose. Indeed if reparative approaches, especially those that involve direct work with victims, are assessed only in terms of the offender's future behaviour, there is a significant risk of the victim being used as a component of a rehabilitative programme, with their interests subordinate to those of the offender. These matters will be taken up again in Chapter 13.

The several and conflicting purposes of sentencing

These specific sentencing purposes reflect the contested general purposes for criminal justice (Chapter 1):

*   due process – justice requires retributive, proportionate punishment, 'just deserts';
*   crime control – crime reduction is to be achieved by individual deterrence, general deterrence, incapacitation;
*   treatment – rehabilitation is to be brought about through individual assessment and the subsequent provision of appropriate interventions;
*   reparative – making of amends by offenders to those affected by their offences.

In any particular case these considerations may point to quite different sentences. A sentencer may, for example, have to decide among possible sentences – one which is fitting and proportionate for the crime committed, another which seems more likely to deter this defendant and others, and a third which constitutes the best prospect of rehabilitation. There can be no assumption that the most effective deterrent penalty is that which is justly deserved; or that either of these is congruent with the penalty suggested by rehabilitation or reparation. Where these purposes do point to different outcomes, it is for the court to decide case by case, within the parameters set out in law or sentencing guidelines. It is hard to see, then, how consistency in sentencing can be enhanced when the legal framework reflects such a range of different – and legitimate – considerations.

Two other general remarks should be made in this discussion. First, no particular sentencing philosophy deals very well with the question of the extent to which *previous convictions* should influence the penalty. The Criminal Justice Act 1991 (s. 29) stated that previous convictions and/or responses to previous sentences should not (other than in special cases) lead the court to regard the (current) offence as more serious. But the Criminal Justice Act 1993 (s. 66 [6]) soon changed this and said that a court 'may' take this into account while the 2003 Act now says that the court '*must* treat each previous conviction as an aggravating factor' – although regard shall be had to the nature of the previous offence(s) and the time that has elapsed (s. 143 [2] emphasis added). As we shall see (Chapter 10), previous convictions and responses to previous sentences may well influence risk judgements and assessments of suitability for some kinds of penalty. In retributive terms, however, the pointed question arises: how does this differ from punishing someone again for an offence for which punishment has already been served?

Second, while discussions of the philosophy of punishment often stop at the point of sentence, plainly the way in which the sentence is put into effect can support – or perhaps undermine – the sentencer's intention. The communications of punishment, notably, are not just the announcements in court, but are constituted by the form of the punishment and the manner of implementation (Duff 2001; Rex 2005). This is why the matters raised so far in this chapter have a special importance for almost all aspects of the work of probation. Similarly, the tensions that complicate the sentencing decision sometimes persist during the management of the sentence. For example, should retributive, deterrent or rehabilitative considerations be decisive in responding to non-compliance (see Chapter 9)? Should community service (Chapter 11) give priority to (retributive) punishment or to rehabilitation or to reparation? We are likely to find that these questions are no easier to answer then than in the context of the sentencing decision.

Task

Chris appears in court to be sentenced. A charge of assault occasioning actual bodily harm has been admitted. Chris had been drinking in the pub and had got into an argument. There are witnesses to say that the victim of the assault had been drunk and abusive, taunting Chris and making offensive remarks. Chris punched him in the face and kicked him on the knee. The knee became swollen and he was unable to work for a few days. Chris has one previous conviction, two years ago, for criminal damage, which also took place in a pub, and for which a fine was imposed. This has been fully paid. Chris admits to having drunk too much and expresses deep regret about the loss of temper and the violence. Chris is also said to have been suffering from depression at the time, following redundancy, but is now receiving medication, has got a new job and is generally doing well. Imprisonment would lead to a loss of employment. It is said on Chris's behalf that this is quite untypical and good character references are presented at court.

- What should be taken into account in deciding what Chris *deserves*?
- To what extent do you think this offence is mitigated by (a) the provocation? (b) the consideration that Chris had been drinking? (c) the suggestion that Chris was depressed at the time?
- Is the likely loss of the job a reason to avoid imposing a custodial sentence? (If you think this is a reason not to send Chris to prison,

would it be fair to send someone to prison whose position was exactly same except that they had no job?)

- How much weight do you think ought to be given to the previous conviction?
- Using your imagination to build on this scenario, try to think of other possible aggravating or mitigating circumstances. What sort of consideration do you think ought to tend to aggravate or to mitigate an offence of this type?
- How should the matter of *deterrence* be approached? What kind of penalty do you think would have deterred Chris in these circumstances? To what extent might others be deterred by any example made of Chris?
- What sort of intervention would be most likely to effect Chris's *reform and rehabilitation*?
- What sentence would best meet the purpose of *public protection*?
- Is there a way in which Chris might *make amends* for the wrong done? How? For example, would compensation be appropriate? Why or why not?
- If the answer to any of these questions is 'it depends', what does it depend on and why?
- You may have been reading this with an assumption that Chris is a man. If you were now to be told that Chris is a woman, what difference would it make, if any, to your answer to these earlier questions?
- If the different purposes of sentencing are in tension here, which one do you think should be given priority? And what sentence would you impose if you were the magistrate?

Summary

It has been argued here that punishment is essentially contested: it has many purposes set for it and a number of supposed justifications. Some of its purposes do not readily harmonise with some others and, case by case, courts have to decide which objective should be given the most weight. The empirical evidence underpinning sentencing decisions is very meagre. While sentencing is guided by law and by precedent, then, decisions are difficult because they depend on considerations that are often in conflict with one another and which are irreducibly moral. Since punishment aims for so much – and has objectives set for it that are mostly beyond it – the practices of punishment typically occasion dispute, frustration and disappointment. This constitutes what has been called the tragedy of punishment (Garland 1990; Canton 2007).

Further reading

Nigel Walker's *Why Punish?* (1991) is an excellent account of the main arguments in the philosophy of punishment. David Garland's *Punishment and Modern Society* (1990) is indispensable. Among the briefer introductions to these matters, Cavadino and Dignan's account (2007: Chapters 2 and 3) is particularly good.

5 Prison, community sentences and probation's contribution to sentencing

Punishment has been said to be over-determined, with an abundance of justifications and purposes (Nietzsche 1887/1998), many of which were considered in the last chapter. Yet both the *amount* and the *type* of punishment are *under-*determined, with none of several rationales pointing to a clear way in which the 'weight' of punishment is to be decided or how it is to be carried out. In the first part of this chapter, we consider trends in sentencing practice and in penal policy, which often reflect different views about what punishment might and should be, and what these developments have meant for probation. Discussion then turns to probation's contribution to sentencing through the pre-sentence reports which probation officers prepare for court.

Punishment, prison and community sentences

Although fewer than one-third of convictions for indictable offences (roughly, the more serious offences) lead to a sentence of imprisonment, prison still stands as the symbol and archetype of punishment in our society. People who are not sent to prison 'walk away' from court and non-custodial sanctions often appear as a poor substitute for the 'proper punishment' of imprisonment. Imprisonment is believed to be retributively apt, a potent deterrent and uniquely able to protect the public. For these reasons, prison comes to be seen as the standard that other sanctions must somehow try to match and with which they will be compared. Expressions like *non-custodial sentences* and *alternatives to custody* seem to concede that status to prison.

Between the mid-1960s and the early 1990s, there was a cross-party consensus that there were too many people in prison – perhaps far too many. Yet as crime and punishment became more 'politicised', politicians were anxious to avoid any imputation that they might be 'soft on crime'. The Conservative administration tried to resolve this conundrum by insisting that while punishment was fitting and proper, it did not have to take place in prison: the term *punishment in the community* began to be used (Brownlee 1998).

Table 5.1 sets out some of the legislative initiatives to reduce the prison population (discussed in Mair and Canton 2007). These initiatives have had a profound impact on the work of probation, which has had to provide almost all of these sanctions and to present them to an (often sceptical) public as realistic and

Table 5.1 Providing 'alternatives to custody'

Criminal Justice Act 1967	Suspended sentence
Criminal Justice Act 1972	Community Service Day Training Centre Hostel provision Suspended sentence supervision order Deferment of sentence Compensation
Criminal Justice Act 1982	Partial suspended sentence Tougher conditions in Probation Orders Day Centres (Schedule 11)
1988 Green Paper	Affirms punishment as the main purpose of community sanctions
Criminal Justice Act 1991	Combination Orders Curfew Orders Probation Order *as* (rather than instead of) a sentence Probation Order conditions clarified and strengthened
Crime Sentences Act 1997	s. 38 abolishes the need for the offender's consent to most community sentences
Crime and Disorder Act 1998	Drug Treatment and Testing Orders
Powers of Criminal Courts (Sentencing) Act 2000	Tougher powers on breach of community orders
Criminal Justice and Courts Services Act 2000	Orders renamed: Probation – Community Rehabilitation Order Community Service – Community Punishment Order Combination Order – Community Punishment and Rehabilitation Order Exclusion Order Drug Abstinence Order Tougher powers for courts on breach
Criminal Justice Act 2003	Generic single community order Tougher powers on breach, including a possibility of a term of imprisonment *even when the original offence was not imprisonable* (Sch. 8)

demanding punishment. Meanwhile, however, the prison population has followed its own trajectory – mostly upwards – without any apparent relationship to the increasing number of 'alternatives'.

Indeed analysis of the proportions of offenders sentenced to prison and to other penalties (Bottoms 1983) suggests that, rather than cutting into the prison population, 'alternatives' commonly take the place of other alternatives – or are imposed on offenders who might at other times been given a lesser penalty (see also Carter 2003). Between 1998 and 2008 the number of people receiving a custodial sentence increased by 2 per cent, but during the same period the number of community sentences *also increased* and was nearly one-third higher in 2009 (when the prison population was about 83,000) than in 1999 (when the prison population was 64,770) (Ministry of Justice 2010b).

Cohen (1985) argued that the relationship between prison and its supposed alternatives is more symbiotic than competitive: they work together to extend and disperse social control. While this thesis has had its critics (Bottoms 1983), it is still very difficult to point to contemporary examples of 'alternatives' leading directly to a reduction in the prison population. Even when replacing terms of imprisonment, community sentences typically displace (at best) those who would have served short terms of imprisonment and therefore tend to have no more than a modest effect on the prison population, which is influenced not only by the number of people sent there but by the length of time for which they stay (Fitzmaurice and Pease 1986).

One well-known hazard of non-custodial sanctions is their *net-widening* potential (Cohen 1985). They may deflect some offenders from custody, but draw in many more who might otherwise have been dealt with in less intrusive and cheaper ways. Over time, while probation may have worked with more serious offenders during and after periods of imprisonment, it has had to deal, on community sentences, with *less* serious offenders:

- less serious offences – an increasing proportion of those receiving community sentences are convicted of summary/less serious offences;
- less serious previous records – more first offenders, fewer have previously been in prison;
- lower assessed risk of reconviction on average (Morgan and Smith 2003; Mair and Canton 2007).

As well as involving more people in the nexus of social control, alternatives can perversely serve to increase the prison population. There is a 'recoil' effect (Bottoms 1987) whereby people sentenced to an 'alternative' come back to court and may be regarded as having failed on their last chance and deserving prison. The attempt to make community sanctions more demanding while simultaneously ensuring that they are more rigorously enforced is also likely to lead to more breach. As part of this same quest for credibility, moreover, courts are expected to impose weightier penalties for breach (Canton and Eadie 2005). A combination of these inter-related trends could tend to inflate the prison population (Tonry 2004; see also Chapter 9).

This very brief overview of community sanctions suggests a few fairly clear conclusions:

- the idea that the prison population can be reduced by providing 'alternatives' is an aspiration that has brought substantial disappointment;
- sanctions introduced as direct alternatives sometimes achieve some initial success in diverting people from terms of imprisonment, but over time go 'down tariff', widening the net to include people who had before been sentenced to other community sanctions or to financial penalties;

- the recoil effects of tough community sentences rigorously enforced could lead to increasing numbers going to prison for non-compliance.

Prison stands as a conspicuous failure, with approaching two-thirds of former prisoners reconvicted within two years of release (Hedderman 2007). Moreover, the more the number of people sent to prison, the higher this rate of reconviction is likely to rise (Hedderman 2008). Even so, in political debate it continues to hold a place as the standard which other sentences have to match. This may be because it is believed to meet three of the objectives of sentencing – punishment, deterrence, incapacitation – better than anything else, even though much of Chapter 4 attempted to show that confidence in prison's claims, even in these respects, is misplaced.

Probation has therefore had to describe its work and present its worth in the terms of a debate set by punitive priorities, to show itself as tough and prison-like. And its success in this respect, unsurprisingly, has been limited. Meanwhile, the progressive net-widening has brought onto probation caseloads offenders who not only do not need such levels of intervention, but for whom there is no evidence that probation interventions will be effective. This increase in workload dilutes probation's potential to work effectively with those who most need and might benefit from its interventions (Morgan and Smith 2003).

In the Introduction three penal policy strategies were identified. We now see these contradictory influences at work. The punitive strategy urges punishment; the management strategy recognises the costs and inefficiencies of prison; the ethical strategy is mindful too of the human cost of penal excess. This is strikingly articulated in these quotations from Secretaries of State in successive Conservative administrations.

> Prison can be an expensive way of making bad people worse.
>
> (Home Office 1990a)

> Prison works. It ensures that we are protected from murderers, muggers and rapists – and it makes many who are tempted to commit crime think twice . . . This may mean that more people will go to prison. I do not flinch from that. We shall no longer judge the success of our system of justice by a fall in our prison population.
>
> (Michael Howard, speech to Conservative party conference 6 October 1993)

> Too often prison has proved a costly and ineffectual approach that fails to turn criminals into law-abiding citizens. Indeed, in all of our experience, in our worst prisons it produces tougher criminals.
>
> (Kenneth Clarke, speech to Centre for Crime and Justice Studies, London 30 June 2010)

The Halliday report and the Criminal Justice Act 2003

A major review of sentencing was undertaken for the government by John Halliday (Home Office 2001) and many of the principles of the Criminal Justice Act 2003 are to be found in his report. Halliday was especially concerned to address perceived shortcomings in the Criminal Justice Act 1991, which was felt to be especially inadequate to deal with dangerous and with persistent offenders. Halliday also proposed a Sentencing Guidelines Council (duly established by Criminal Justice Act 2003 s. 167, though now superseded by the Sentencing Council, created in 2010). This was part of the strategy to enhance consistency in sentencing and improve its quality, using imprisonment only when necessary and rationalising the use of community sentences.

Halliday also recommended a single 'generic' community sentence, enabling the court to decide, case by case, on the requirements which would make up the sentence. This was duly enacted in Criminal Justice Act 2003 (s. 177), implemented in April 2005. The court could now impose one or more of these requirements:

1   unpaid work requirement;
2   activity requirement;
3   programme requirement;
4   prohibited activity requirement;
5   curfew requirement;
6   exclusion requirement;
7   residence requirement;
8   mental health treatment requirement;
9   drug rehabilitation requirement;
10 alcohol treatment requirement;
11 supervision requirement;
12 attendance centre requirement (under 25s).

The same set of options is available when the court imposes a Suspended Sentence Order (SSO).

There were two particular concerns about these developments, both impacting significantly upon probation. One was that courts might 'overload' sentences, including several conditions which may turn out to be too demanding (and therefore perhaps lead to breach and re-sentence) or that a court may feel that it had exhausted all its options and resort to custody when there was a further offence. A second concern was that the SSO would begin to displace the community order, with courts keen to combine rehabilitative interventions with the direct deterrent of custody, potentially accelerating reoffenders into prison.

Mair and Mills (2009), however, found that courts have not been overloading orders with large numbers of requirements: by and large, community orders are used like the separate orders that preceded them. As many as half of the requirements are rarely used. Breach rates remain high (around 40 per cent) – higher than the rate before the new orders were introduced. Mair and Mills found little evidence that either order was being used instead of short custodial sentences and half of orders made in magistrates' courts are for summary offences.

There has, however, been an increased use of the SSO, widening the net by drawing in numbers of people who might have been dealt with by a community order (or less). One reason why this was a particular worry was that breach of the SSO ought in law to lead to an immediate custodial sentence. Yet Mair and Mills (2009) found probation officers who complained that magistrates were often not responding as anticipated: warned by their supervisors that breach would lead to custody, offenders have found that often it doesn't and officers felt this detracted from the order's and their own credibility.

Probation reports for the court

Having discussed the relationship between prison and its 'alternatives' and reviewed recent developments in community sentencing, we turn next to probation's contribution to sentencing decisions through pre-sentence reports.

Preparing reports for the court is one of probation's main tasks. In 2008, probation staff prepared 216,353 reports – about three-quarters of them for the magistrates' courts (Ministry of Justice 2009d).[1] Once known as social enquiry reports, these are prepared 'with a view to assisting the court in determining the most suitable method of dealing with an offender' (Criminal Justice Act 2003 s. 158 (1) (a)).

The practice of social enquiry can be traced back to the very beginnings of probation. The earliest reports sometimes read less like an impartial exposition of information and more like a plea – typically a plea for mercy (McWilliams 1983). Later reports reflected a treatment ideology (McWilliams 1985, 1986): reports might become 'diagnostic tools' (Worrall and Hoy 2005: 100), identifying factors in the past that might illuminate the offender's present behaviour and proposing interventions accordingly. The reality fell some way short of this, with a great deal of material included without any very clear purpose, but with a vague idea that the more known about the offender the better.

> For myself I find that I welcome social enquiry reports because they make me feel cosy, inasmuch as they transform a 'case' into a human being; but, sadly, I am driven to the conclusion . . . that except in limited contexts . . . they do little to make me (or anybody else) in any sense a better sentencer.
>
> (Barbara Wootton 1978: 45)

But by the late 1980s even the aspiration had changed. With a loss of faith in the treatment model, any attempt to identify the 'causes of offending' or interventions to address them was looking forlorn. Too many reports were criticised for including 'historical' information that was merely irrelevant (Bottoms and Stelman 1988; Worrall and Hoy 2005). The Criminal Justice Act 1991 changed the name to *pre-sentence reports* (PSR), implying a more task-focused approach to the decision to be taken, rather than a general, discursive social inquiry, at a time when the Probation Service was in any case was being asked to disavow social work.

Contemporary pre-sentence reports

If reports used to be variable in structure and content, this is now tightly prescribed. A standard PSR will include:

1   sources of information;
2   an offence analysis;
3   offender assessment;
4   assessment of risk of harm to the public and likelihood of reoffending
5   conclusion (Probation Circular 18/2005).

Sources of information

In almost all cases, report writers interview the offender at least once, although they are expected to draw on other sources besides. The Crown Prosecution Service should enable access to depositions which give an account of the offence (from victims and witnesses) which are used to check and, as necessary, challenge the offender's own version. Victim personal statements may also be drawn upon. Where possible, factual information should be verified from other sources. In any event, the court is entitled to know the sources of information on which the report is based.

An offence analysis

Offence analysis involves a searching investigation into the circumstances of the offence, going beyond a description and looking in particular at the offender's intentions and motives – *what the offender took herself/himself to be doing and why*. In constructing this section, officers may ask:

*   *How* did you come to be here/to meet this person/to do what you did? How could you avoid this in future?
*   *When* did this take place? (looking not only for dates and times, but also events in the offender's life – for example, *just after I was made redundant* or *when I was in a really bad mood*).
*   *Where* did this happen? (looking not only for specific places, but also answers like *on the way to my mate's house* or *just outside the pub*).
*   *Who* were you with? Who suggested this? Who has been affected by this offence?
*   *What* did you actually do? What did you think afterwards? What do you think you might have done differently?

- *Why* (a common and obvious question, but to be used sparingly, because it can sound prosecutorial and often elicits defensiveness or withdrawal).

An analysis of this type not only illuminates the offence itself, but in the process normally reveals a great deal about the offender's risks and needs more generally. (For this '5WH' approach: see McGuire and Priestley 1985: 24.)

The offender's account will often be challenged, because the report author doubts (or anticipates that the court will doubt) its credibility; or because it is incompatible with information from other sources; or because it is does not fit with other things that the offender has said. There is considerable professional skill in such a challenge if it is not simply going to elicit more denial. It is hoped that through a process of exploration and negotiation author and offender progressively move towards *an agreed account of what was done* (Hudson and Bramhall 2005) – though in practice it is not always possible to agree and differences should then be recounted in the report.

This analysis has a direct bearing on judgements about culpability and therefore about seriousness. (The report is not concerned solely with the offender's welfare or even with ways of reducing their offending in future – Raynor 1980.) Whereas (arguably) the offender's legal representative's obligation is to present an account of the offence to their client's best advantage, the PSR analysis may disclose aggravating as well as mitigating factors. The best reports offer an understanding of the offence which enables the court to see an offence as an intelligible human action, however deplorable, in the context of the individual's circumstances.

Offender assessment

The offender assessment section sets out personal information relevant to an understanding of the offence and/or to the means most likely to reduce offending in the future. Previous convictions should also be considered here. Again, the report should go beyond mere description – the court has a list of criminal convictions from other sources; the PSR should *interpret* the record, relating it to the offender's personal history and explore its implications for the present decision.

This is particularly important now that the court must consider each previous conviction as an aggravating factor. An interpretation of the record contributes to a wise judgement about its relevance and the weight it should be given in sentencing. This kind of analysis is unlikely to be available to the court from any other source.

Assessment of risk of harm to the public and likelihood of reoffending

The section assessing risk of harm to the public and likelihood of reoffending draws upon the information and analysis in the preceding sections. It will cover the (properly assessed) risks of reoffending and look in particular at the risk of harm that the offender may pose to others. Since these judgements may have a decisive influence on the court's sentence, officers must be clear and explicit about how their assessments are arrived at.

This part of the report in particular alters, at least potentially, the relationship between probation and the defence. Reports have often been drawn on by the offender's legal representatives for mitigation, but there is here a possibility that the report's analysis will disclose risk factors that point to more intensive intervention or perhaps to a longer prison sentence. The assessment must therefore be rigorous, sound and well evidenced.

Conclusion

The standing of the conclusion used to be especially vexed. The report often culminated in a specific proposal, often referred to as a *recommendation*. But some sentencers objected that they did not want a 'recommendation' from a probation officer – this began to trespass upon their role – and the probation officer's opinion of what was best was just one of many considerations. Some sentencers, by contrast, welcomed a recommendation (Bottoms and Stelman 1988).

Sometimes recommendations were ignored (and sometimes openly deplored) for being 'unrealistic' – although our account of punishment (Chapter 4) reveals that the purposes of sentencing are contested, complicating the idea of what 'realistic' could mean here. Tata and colleagues (2008) also point to disparities among sentencers: a proposal that might be found unrealistic by one might be acceptable to another. Gelsthorpe and Raynor (1995) found that what courts minded most was *being told what to do* – a well-argued proposal, appropriately framed, would not be dismissed out of hand.

While the status of the conclusion might seem a rather arcane topic, it raises important questions. Report writers have sometimes been encouraged to champion the use of community penalties and to 'manage' resources. Examples include: the proposal of an 'alternative' where custody is likely; trying to persuade a court to use one community sanction rather than another; or an argument to show that probation involvement is unnecessary and that a financial penalty might suffice. Report writers have therefore constructed an argument to support a persuasive conclusion.

Sentencers, however, may see the sentencing decision as theirs and do not want to be 'persuaded'. To this extent, the dispute is one manifestation of the tensions and boundaries between the government and the judiciary over sentencing (Ashworth 2007) – a increasingly politicised debate as government tries to demonstrate its willingness and ability to reduce crime through sentencing, while the judiciary zealously defends its independence.

While research can inquire whether sentencers 'followed the recommendation', correspondence between recommendation and sentence does not necessarily mean that the court has been persuaded by the report (Hine *et al.* 1978). Perhaps report writers sometimes correctly anticipate or 'second guess' the court's decision – all the more likely now that the court normally gives an indication of the anticipated level of sentence when requesting a report.

In 2008, an immediate sentence was imposed in 88 per cent of the cases where custody was proposed; a community order was imposed in 71 per cent of the cases where it was proposed (Ministry of Justice 2009d: 12, Table 2.2). In 22 per cent of cases where a fine was proposed, the outcome was a community order – an indication, perhaps, that courts impose community sentences in many cases where probation officers feel this is unnecessary. The marked reduction in the use of the fine has been seen to lead to pressures on prison and probation caseloads (Carter 2003).

Contemporary debates about PSRs

Information or persuasion

Should reports be 'strategic documents involved in persuasive communication' or, on the other hand, just provide 'reliable, comprehensive information relevant to what the court is seeking to do' (Bottoms and McWilliams 1986: 260; Haines and Morgan 2007)? As we have seen, courts often do not want to be 'persuaded' and may well not accept probation guidance on sentencing as authoritative. Yet there have been times – especially perhaps when probation saw its principal contribution as the provision of alternatives to custody – when as a matter of policy authors tried to persuade sentencers not to send people to prison.

Authors were asked by courts to distinguish clearly between 'the facts' and their own opinions – a common-sense distinction which may be less straightforward that it appears. Bean (1976) drew on research to suggest that in some cases report writers first decide whether to present a case positively or negatively – to 'pitch' or 'denounce' – and then deploy the facts around that initial judgement. Cases are *constructed* (McConville *et al.* 1991): events and states of affairs can be characterised in many different ways and facts are looked for, interpreted and presented for particular purposes. It is not that probation officers mislead the court: just that, like others in this process, they are involved in case construction.

Much of the material in the report calls for *interpretation* – a concept that elides a tidy fact–opinion distinction. For instance, whether something is a *criminogenic need* and amenable to intervention – often the very nub of the report – is a matter for interpretation and judgement. Another example is *remorse*, often an influential consideration in mitigation (Sentencing Guidelines Council 2009) (certainly a lack of remorse is often seen as aggravating). Yet *how* the offender's attitude to the offence is to be elicited and understood is plainly a complex matter. Nor is this attitude static: the offender may have several, ambivalent and changing attitudes. For that matter, the probation officer may (often should) seek to influence the offender's feelings about their offending.

Discrimination in PSRs

Worrall and Hoy (2005: 104) draw attention to 'the image of the offender that is represented by the report' – an image which is often powerfully conveyed through nuance and tone. Things may be 'read between the lines', whether or not they were deliberately placed there. As in any other medium of communication, the message may not be received as intended (Tata *et al.* 2008). This seems particularly relevant to stereotypical racist or sexist characterisations.

Since the sentencing decision is a critical point in a criminal justice process that leads to the over-representation of black and minority ethnic groups in prison, there has been considerable attention to the way in which PSRs are written for these offenders. An inspection found that that the standard of reports for African-Caribbean offenders was not as good as for Asian and white offenders (HM Inspectorate of Probation 2000) – a finding still apparent in the follow-up inspection, although the position was improving (HM Inspectorate of Probation 2004).

Certain racial groups seem often to be represented in reports in a stereotypical manner. Hudson and Bramhall (2005) found that in discussions of *attitude towards the offence* – especially with regard to remorse – there were marked differences between reports written on Asians and white offenders. They suggest there is no 'discursive space' in which perceptions of seriousness and remorse can be explored, inhibiting the process of movement towards an agreed account (Hudson and Bramhall 2005: 730). This leads to more distancing, sceptical turns of phrase ('He tells me that . . .'; '. . . according to him') as well as sometimes suppressing aspects that are indispensable to an understanding of the offence – for example, that an offence was a response to racist harassment. While the same formal areas are covered, the lens of interpretation is quite different. Conspicuously, for the Asian offenders in their sample, there are imputations of family pressure linked to offending, which characterise the offender as over-susceptible and at the same time implicate the family and community in the offending. In this way, there is collusion with – and thereby endorsement of – stereotypes. Unsurprisingly, the presentation of weak character, strong and detrimental family influences and lack of remorse leads to assessment of higher risk and a less enthusiastic (or no) proposal for community supervision.

Hedderman and Gelsthorpe (1997) found that legal representatives sometimes deliberately conjured stereotypical accounts of women's personal circumstances to evoke the court's sympathy. They argue:

> The difficulty to be addressed is one of finding ways to challenge stereotypical pictures of men and women, without ignoring the fact that they often (but not always) do have different needs and responsibilities and these are often precisely the needs and responsibilities which fuel the stereotypes.
>
> (Gelsthorpe and Hedderman 1997: 58)

Similarly, experiences of racism are an important part of some individuals' circumstances which cannot be omitted from a report without losing key insights. Yet how such matters are dealt with calls for considerable professional skill – and for courage, both from authors and offenders. Again, discussions of sexuality and disability may be centrally relevant, but not easy to address. Probation officers must be self-aware and vigilant not only about *what* they are saying, but *how* they say it.

Fast reports

Perceived imperatives of efficiency and economy have encouraged the use of faster delivery options. Sometimes 'sentencers select the order for the offender and ask the court officer to report that he/she is a suitable candidate' (Worrall and Hoy 2005: 87). These are specific sentence reports. Fast delivery reports pose a set of specific (tick box) questions, are written quickly and may be presented orally (Bearne 2007).

While such reports are intended to be used only in the less risky and more straightforward cases, there is a marked increase in their use and a corresponding decline in the numbers of standard reports (Ministry of Justice 2009d: Chapter 2). There are at least two reasons to be troubled by these trends. First, for probation officers, the PSR has normally been a process of dialogue and negotiation, in anticipation of future work. A just sentence is the outcome of a just procedure, not merely a proportionate and fitting determination, and this requires offenders' active participation. Fast delivery options suppress this possibility. Mechanistic questioning can lead to mechanistic responses, in which offenders give the most superficial account of the offence and offer unrealistic commitments for the future – about, for example, their willingness and ability to cooperate with community penalties. Considering the earlier discussion about particular shortcomings in engaging with Asian offenders and achieving an understanding of their offence, the possible consequences of fast delivery should certainly be a matter of concern.

Second, as Whitehead (2008) shows, fast reports exclude any idea of *relational responsibility*

> which allows for different apportionment of blame between offenders and the circumstances in which they live and act . . . Lack of attention to contextual and relational aspects of culpability . . . results in injustices in that the poor and marginalised are punished more severely than others: circumstances of disadvantage which reduce legitimate choices are not constructed as reducing culpability, but as enhancing risk of reoffending.
>
> (Hudson 2005: 4–5)

To understand an offence requires an appreciation not only of motivation and immediate circumstance, but of the wider social context in which these motivations came to influence the offender, set the circumstances for the offence and circumscribed the offender's choices. Fast delivery minimises the opportunity for the probation officer to convey this to the court. This abstraction of the offender from the broad social context conceals information that is relevant to a just and wise decision. Since the offending of women in particular is often so bound up with experiences of disadvantage and oppression, such abstraction is especially likely to disadvantage them. It may be that 'justice delayed is justice denied', but justice compressed can be justice compromised, speedy justice justice spoiled.

Summary

In the first part of the chapter, we considered prison and its 'alternatives' and reviewed recent developments in community sentencing. In the second part, pre-sentence reports have been discussed. We noted that Barbara Wootton was sceptical that reports made for better sentencing, although she welcomed them as 'transforming a case into a human being'. Behind this observation, perhaps, is the aspiration that sentencing might become evidence-led and that a scientific understanding of the origins of offending might one day allow the selection of that penalty which would best fit the case. But this is forlorn if sentencing essentially involves moral decisions. Levels of retributive punishment could not, even in principle, be determined 'scientifically'; the evidence base to determine the optimal deterrent sentence does not exist (Chapter 4); and even the findings of 'what works' in rehabilitation can at best generate averages and probabilities and cannot tell us what would 'work' for this individual. But if, as we have argued, sentencing decisions rest on irreducibly moral (rather than legal or technical) considerations, transforming a case into a human being looks like an indispensable precondition for better sentencing.

Questions

- Why have 'alternatives to custody' failed to make much impact upon the size of the prison population?
- Should reports attempt to persuade the court to take a particular decision or simply convey 'the facts'?
- To what extent can (or even should) a court consider the wider social context of an offence if its duty is to assign a just punishment for the wrong that has been done?

Further reading

The evolution of community penalties is well discussed by Brownlee (1998). More recent developments are considered by Mair and Canton (2007). Solomon and Silvestri (2008) is an invaluable resource. For court reports, Bearne (2007) sets out a concise account of the legal and practice framework for PSRs. With due allowance for the many changes that have taken place since it was written, Bottoms and Stelman (1998) is still useful and interesting.

6 The supervision of offenders

What works, motivation

This chapter introduces what might be seen as the main work of probation, the supervision of offenders in the community. The emergence of cognitive behavioural approaches will first be considered. This way of understanding and influencing behaviour provided an evidence-based, theoretical coherence for probation practice and underpinned the claims that *what works* with offenders was now beginning to be understood: the characteristics of effective interventions could be identified and used to guide future policy and practice. The chapter concludes with some discussion of motivation, which is evidently crucial in any attempt to bring about change.

The emergence of 'what works'

What exactly do probation officers do? Early research saw probation as a method in itself (Raynor and Vanstone 2002: 57) – probation was what probation officers did. But the term concealed a wide diversity of practices. *Casework* – with underlying assumptions that treatment was needed to respond to offenders' individual difficulties and personal shortcomings – was the way in which probation officers used to describe their work, but that term too encompassed a variety of practices and theories. Counselling, psychotherapy, transactional analysis, family therapy, group work of many different styles, behaviourism and common sense advice were all said to be deployed – depending sometimes on an assessment of the individual's needs, but quite as likely on the practitioner's preferences.

Probation's inability to demonstrate its effectiveness in reducing reoffending led some officers to repudiate treatment and to focus on very practical forms of assistance, including advice about accommodation, employment and welfare rights. Others again recognised the common predicaments of many people on their caseload and felt that responses had to involve active work in the community or forms of political engagement (Walker and Beaumont 1981). If policy makers and managers were troubled by this theoretical jumble, they were not able to propose with confidence anything to take its place.

This theoretical confusion and pessimism began to change with the emergence of evidence that some interventions could be shown to reduce reconvictions (see especially McGuire 2007a; Raynor and Robinson 2009: Chapter 6). The statistical method of meta-analysis, analysing the findings of a number of individual evaluations – studies which by themselves would not necessarily be persuasive, but which in the aggregate were thought to amount to a compelling case – demonstrated these effects (McGuire and Priestley 1995). Meta-analyses were deployed to show that if programmes were implemented as designed and targeted at the right offenders, a measurable reduction in reconvictions could be shown to be achieved (Raynor and Vanstone 2002; for the limitations of meta-analysis and challenge to the inferences drawn, see Mair 2004). Structured interventions based on the principles of *cognitive behaviourism* were found to have the strongest evidence of reducing recidivism.

Cognitive behavioural approaches

Although work informed by the principles of cognitive behaviourism (CB) had been taking place in probation at least as far back as the late 1970s – for example Priestley *et al.* (1978) (and see Vanstone 2000) – its rise to prominence in England and Wales may be attributed to the support it received from Her Majesty's Inspectorate of Probation in the late 1990s and their determination to promulgate evidence-based best practice throughout the Service (Underdown 1998; Chapman and Hough 1998).

As the name implies, cognitive-behavioural approaches represent a convergence of behaviourism and cognitive psychology. Rejecting unobservable and therefore mysterious mental constructs (Skinner 1973), behaviourism insists that psychology should (can) only study overt and observable behaviour. Behaviour is learned by the conditioning of rewards and punishments. Albert Bandura (1989) emphasised a shortcoming in the behaviourist account of learning: learning takes place not only through direct experiences of reinforcement, but also through observation and contact with others. Humans do not simply react to stimuli: they interpret them, mental processes mediating between stimulus and response. Cognitive psychology, which studies mental processes – for example, attention, perception, memory and reasoning – makes good these limitations in behaviourism.

Both approaches – and their synthesis in CB – emphasise the importance of *learning*. If behaviour and thinking are learned, then perhaps change can be achieved through a different process of learning – including 'unlearning' of undesirable thought patterns and behaviours. In contrast to (at least some versions of) a treatment model, probation intervention could be seen as an educational endeavour, enabling people to acquire new ways of thinking and behaving and expanding their capacity to make choices. McGuire explains CB's understanding of learning as the outcome of

> the cumulative experiences to which an individual has been exposed, and the environment in which that has taken place. Socialisation and other inter-personal processes within families play the most powerful role in individual development, but similar processes also help explain the profound influence of neighbourhoods and peers (differential association). Alongside behavioural

development, cognitive learning occurs in parallel and influences the formation of attitudes, beliefs, and habitual patterns of thought. Variability in learning opportunities will affect the pattern of acquisition of skills for effective living, engaging in relationships, and solving personal problems. Different permutations of these variables interact with environmental factors (including crime opportunities), and influence the pathways along which individuals travel through successive maturational stages.

(McGuire 2007b: 46)

CB appreciates the importance of understanding the meanings and interpretations that people bring to their circumstances, to the things that happen to them and indeed to the way in which they understand themselves. The processes to which McGuire refers give rise to personal *schemata* – ways in which people organise knowledge, implicit theories about the way the world is and one's own place in it – which may be then imposed, like templates, on subsequent events (McGuire 2001). These patterns and habits of thinking become established (perhaps entrenched) and influence behaviour. For example, violent people often interpret interactions with other people in ways that precipitate violence (Toch 1972), as Figure 6.1 illustrates.

CB approaches can investigate these thought patterns and schemata and, where these are dysfunctional – for instance in their association with persistent offending – endeavour to change them.

Figure 6.1 A schema that may lead to violence

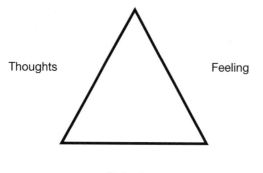

Thoughts   Feeling

Behaviour

Figure 6.2 The cognitive–behavioural triangle

CB recognises the interdependence of cognition (thoughts), emotion (feelings) and behaviour. None of these is prior and relationships of cause and effect operate in all directions, as the diagram in Figure 6.2 implies.

CB insists that people react differently to their social circumstances and that the ways in which they react are susceptible to change (McGuire 2007a). It can defend itself against accusations (for example, Gorman 2001) that it denies the significance of social factors in the origins of offending (McGuire 2001). Even so, there is a risk that the CB focus on the thoughts, behaviour and feelings of individuals could tend to marginalise other ways of understanding the origins of offending in social disadvantage and injustice (Kendall 2004). As Smith (1998, quoted in Barry 2000: 589) says 'an exclusive stress on offending behaviour entails the expectation that offenders, and not their social circumstances, must change, and encourages the abstraction of the offending act itself from the personal and relational context which could make it intelligible'. This criticism is all the sharper when considering the position of groups, perhaps especially women and offenders from black and minority ethic groups, whose offending behaviour and experiences of criminal justice can only be fully understood within that broader socio-political context.

CB had proved notably effective in the treatment of mental ill health. Many of the methods developed there – for example social skills training, problem solving, anger management, pro-social modelling and enhancing motivation – were now introduced into working with offenders. Assembling these methods into 'structured sequences that can be specified in prepared manuals, and so made reproducible' (McGuire 2007b: 46) provided the basis for offending behaviour programmes.

The central principles of 'what works' – the RNR model

When the Inspectorate published its influential reviews of the findings of research (Underdown 1998; Chapman and Hough 1998), CB approaches were seen to be the basis of most of the programmes that could be shown to 'work' – effectiveness typically being determined by reconvictions within a two-year period.

McGuire and Priestley (1995) drew particular attention to six characteristics of effective programmes. The first three of these characteristics – often referred to as the Risk, Need and Responsivity principles – have given the name *RNR* to the model (Bonta and Andrews 2007; Andrews and Bonta 2010).

Risk

The risk principle states that the higher the risk of reoffending, the more intensive and extended the supervision programme should be. The principle can accordingly be used to determine who should be worked with and to what level. As well as a principle of effective practice, it is a rational device for targeting resources on those most likely to offend again. There is some evidence that intensive work with low risk offenders may be counter-productive and lead to further offending (Andrews *et al.* 1990).

Much more will be said about the assessment and management of risk (especially Chapter 10). Here we note that, in accordance with the risk principle, assessed risk, more than any other single consideration, has come to determine the nature and intensity of probation supervision. Whatever risk assessment describes, predicts or weighs, therefore, it *assigns individuals to categories* – an act of ascription as much as description (Peay 1982). Most obviously, the offender management model (Chapter 7) assigns offenders to 'tiers' that mainly represent a gradation of risk. Eligibility for most accredited programmes is also determined by a risk of reconviction score within a specified range.

Needs

If the risk principle identifies those with whom work must be done, the need principle insists that the focus of intervention must be on those needs or factors associated with their offending. These are known as criminogenic needs. (The word *criminogenic* means *crime-causing* although it would be more accurate to say that these factors are known to be associated with offending: the causal relationships are often complex.) These differ from person to person, but there are some well-established factors that are known to be associated with offending, notably:

- procriminal attitudes ('thoughts, values and sentiments supportive of criminal behaviour').
- antisocial personality.
- procriminal associates.
- social achievement (education, employment).
- family/marital ('marital instability, poor parenting skills').
- substance abuse.
- recreation (lack of prosocial pursuits) (Andrews and Bonta 2010: 46).

As so often in matters of assessment (Chapter 7), these needs cannot always be easily determined. They call for the practitioner's judgement, patience and skill to gain the offender's confidence to talk about them.

While it may make sense to attend to criminogenic needs, it should be recognised that many needs are related to one another – a 'non-criminogenic' need could turn out to be an obstacle to a law-abiding life or to lie behind a more obviously criminogenic need. For example, low levels of confidence and assertiveness – even if not directly criminogenic – may interfere with social achievements like employment. Again, there may be some (criminogenic) needs that cannot be addressed until some other (less immediately criminogenic) needs have been attended to. It may not be realistic, for instance, to attempt to focus attention on anger management if someone does not know where they are going to sleep that night. Needs, after all, may interact viciously and people experience them in this way, even when it may be necessary as a problem-solving tactic to separate them out.

It is moreover a guiding principle of working with people that their own understanding and definition of their problems must be taken seriously. This is central to the *legitimacy* on which effective working relationships depend – practice being, and being seen to be, fair. This does not mean that an offender's perception of their difficulties may not be challenged or that skills of motivational enhancement may not be used to encourage other perceptions. But a hasty identification of criminogenic factors made without adequate regard for the individual's own view of their situation is unlikely to lead to a successful working plan. Even the best treatment will be ineffectual unless there is sufficient regard to its accessibility to the offender and to their motivation (see below).

Since criminogenic needs are associated with further offending – perhaps as 'causes' – and since they are, at least in principle, amenable to change, they can also be seen as dynamic risk factors (Bonta and Andrews 2007). While this insight could be said to contribute to effective risk management, the political and ethical significance of translating needs into risks is considerable (Hannah-Moffat 2005). Bennett (2008: 10) makes the point powerfully:

> the measure of risk includes consideration of issues such as accommodation, education, employment and financial management . . . These are factors that draw a link between social exclusion and offending (Social Exclusion Unit 2002). By embedding these within a structured assessment that may have consequences for an individual's continued detention, there is an argument that this is entrenching social exclusion within the criminal justice system . . . issues such as unemployment, poor housing and poverty are structural features of society, and if used to justify detention, they should, if anything, be extenuating circumstances.

The implications for women, whose offending often cannot be understood apart from the context of need and oppressive life circumstances, are especially disquieting (Hannah-Moffat 1999; Shaw and Hannah-Moffat 2000; Gelsthorpe 2001), but so too for offenders from minority ethnic groups (Bhui 1999) and mentally disordered offenders (Canton 2005). As Peay (1997: 697) puts it, 'At the worst, identification of people with distinctive needs becomes the occasion for special control'. In general, the transformation of need into risk has the consequence of redefining the most needy as the most risky and subjecting them to weightier and more intrusive punishments, exacerbating their social exclusion (Silver and Miller 2002). Some would take this as evidence of the influence of the power model (Chapter 1).

Need and disadvantage

Offenders on community supervision are disadvantaged on almost every index of need (Davies 1969; Mair and May 1997; Social Exclusion Unit 2002; Solomon and Silvestri 2008). The Social Exclusion Unit studied the characteristics of the prison population, very many of whom have been and/or will be subject to supervision in the community. They found their needs to be extensive and their ability to access services significantly worse than average – one aspect of their social exclusion.

> Compared with the general population, prisoners are *thirteen* times as likely to have been in care as a child, *thirteen* times as likely to be unemployed, ten times as likely to have been a regular truant, *two and a half times* as likely to have had a family member convicted of a criminal offence, *six* times as likely to have been a young father, and *fifteen* times as likely to be HIV positive.
>
> Many prisoners' basic skills are very poor. *80%* have writing skills, *65%* numeracy skills and *50%* reading skills at or below the level of an 11-year-old. *60 to 70%* of prisoners were using drugs before imprisonment. Over *70%* suffer from at least two mental disorders. And *20%* of male and *37%* of female sentenced prisoners have attempted suicide in the past. The position is often even worse for 18–20-year-olds, whose basic skills, unemployment rate and school exclusion background are all over *a third* worse than those of older prisoners.
>
> (Social Exclusion Unit 2002: 6, emphasis in original)

Among those on community sentences, around 14% are homeless or in temporary accommodation and nearly one-third have an 'accommodation problem'. More than half (55%) of offenders on community sentences are unemployed at the start of their sentence and/or have an 'education, training and employability' problem (*ibid*. 34). Nearly a quarter misuse drugs. Offenders are also often significantly at risk of criminal victimisation (see Chapter 13).

Offenders' health needs are increasingly recognised: by many criteria, their physical health is much worse than in the average population (Brooker *et al.* 2009). At least 40% per cent have mental health problems (Canton 2008a). Offenders under community supervision have a death rate four times as high as the general population and twice as high as people in prison. Rates of suicide have been found to be nine times higher among male offenders under community supervision than in the local population and higher than among prison populations (figures from Solomon and Silvestri 2008). Almost all these indices of deprivation and disadvantage are even more marked for women offenders (Fawcett Society 2009).

Offenders, then, in prisons and in the community, have greater than average needs and lower than average opportunity to access appropriate services. Once again, the ethical aspect of probation's work in the wider criminal justice system must be recognised. As an agency of crime control, probation may choose to focus on dynamic risks; but as an agency which affirms justice it must attend to needs *as needs*. Access to adequate health care, for instance, should not depend on its influence (if any) in reducing offending, but is necessary for its own sake. One aspect of the legitimacy of probation rests on the way in which it should oppose social exclusion as unjust – not only because of its contingent effects of offending.

Responsivity

The third component of RNR is the principle of responsivity. Responsivity is defined by Dominey (2007: 270) as 'Ensuring that all interventions, programmes and activities with offenders are run in a way which is engaging, encourages full participation and takes account of issues of identity and diversity.'

In general, cognitive behavioural approaches are most likely to make a difference (Andrews and Bonta 2010), although the often decisive importance of *relationship* (Chapter 9) is also increasingly recognised. Specific responsivity relates to individual differences. Consideration of this key principle has often looked first to the idea of 'learning styles' (see for example, Chapman and Hough 1998). Annison (2006), however, while respecting the importance of an understanding of the ways in which people learn, cautions against a deployment of the concept of learning styles that assigns people to over-generalised categories. Dominey's reference to aspects of identity and diversity, moreover, implies a much wider conception of responsivity – calling for consideration of culture, gender, ability and other considerations that may affect the way in which services should be delivered accessibly and effectively.

Other principles

In addition to these three defining precepts of the RNR model, McGuire and Priestley (1995) also emphasised other characteristics of effective programmes:

- Community base: programmes in the community are said to be more effective than those undertaken in prisons. This has an intuitive plausibility – after all, living in the community affords opportunities to put learning to the test in the real world. Programme completion, however, is associated with effectiveness (Harper and Chitty 2005) and, in principle, institutions should be able to ensure good completion rates.

- Multi-modal: offenders' problems are diverse, calling for a correspondingly diverse repertoire of interventions. It is implausible that one single method will be appropriate for all problems or (as the principle of responsivity reminds) for all people.
- Programme integrity: If the programme is to have its effect, it must be delivered in the manner intended. Andrews and Bonta (2010) found that RNR principles were often not implemented with the required rigour and this can detract from a programme's effectiveness. This may be especially important if we do not know the 'active ingredient'. It may be possible to evaluate the effectiveness of the programme, but the influential components and the precise mechanisms that bring about change may be much less clear.

RNR has sometimes struggled with this idea. Chapman and Hough (1998) warn against an over-rigid adherence to a manual script, but the degree to which it is permissible to depart from the (carefully worked-out) schedule is uncertain. Recognition of responsivity raises similar difficulties: if people learn in different ways can a programme – especially a group programme – accommodate this? Again, those who have worked on programmes recognise the need to respond flexibly to happenings in the group, which may lead to some departure from the schedule. If these changes are consistent with the aims and principles of the programme, then this probably enhances programme integrity, but again the parameters are unclear. Opportunities to learn in the moment – to respond to what is actually taking place – is a feature of a great deal of good teaching, but could compromise integrity unless managed in a way that is congruent with the programme's rationale.

These well-established principles should be supplemented by others that have emerged from the experience of actual implementation (Raynor 2004a), including:

- a renewed emphasis on personal skills of engagement and relationship (Chapter 9);
- the use of professional discretion – although as we have just seen there is an inherent tension here between allowing staff discretion and the requirements of programme integrity;
- recognition of and response to diversity;
- attention to 'the broader service context in supporting effective intervention' (Raynor 2004a: 200), including leadership, resourcing, training for and enthusiasm of those delivering programmes and the role of the responsible offender manager in supporting the interventions (Chapter 8).

Motivation

We have been considering the theoretical understanding of the processes of learning and change envisaged by cognitive behaviourism. This underpinned the approaches of most of the programmes that were found to be effective in achieving measurable reductions in reconviction. These programmes were characterised by some specific principles, centred around risk, need and responsivity (RNR). We turn next to consider motivation. All and any work with people to bring about change must strive to understand motivation and to work with its complexities.

An influential model used to understand motivation is *the cycle of change* (Prochaska and DiClemente 1992), illustrated in Fig. 6.3. Developed in the field of substance use, the *cycle* describes how people typically go through a number of stages when attempting to change established patterns of behaviour.

Each of these stages requires a different style of intervention and indeed adopting the wrong approach can be counter-productive. Table 6.1 adapts Ashcroft's (2007) summary to show how interventions must be appropriate to the stages of change.

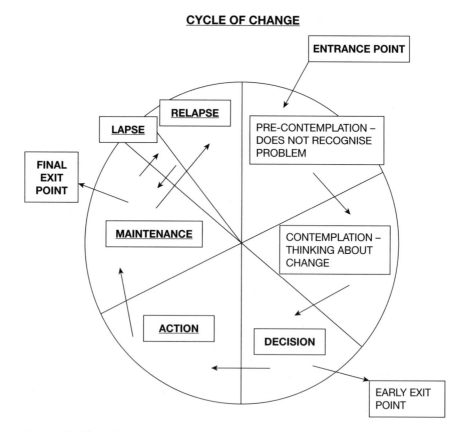

Figure 6.3 The cycle of change

Table 6.1 Matching interventions to stages

Stage of change		Matched Intervention
Precontemplative	At this stage, the person does not see the behaviour as a problem and has no wish to change	Rapport building Problem free-talk
Contemplative	Developing awareness of unease and a need to change	Identifying the positives and not-so-positives of *not* changing Building upon concerns
Preparation	Getting ready to make the change	Building optimism that change is possible Enhancing commitment to change
Action	Making the change (e.g. stopping drinking)	Identifying practical strategies to begin change
Maintenance	Sustaining the change	Relapse prevention training
Relapse	Recognising that lapses may occur	Identifying the learning experience of lapse Rebuilding commitment to change

The model has proved popular with practitioners and clients, no doubt because it accords with people's own experiences of the to-ing and fro-ing of trying to change. (Honest introspection – *what have I found to be motivating/demotivating?* – is a valuable resource here.) At the same time, the idea of phases and the metaphor of a 'cycle' is at risk of over-simplifying the dynamics of motivation: one phase does not always simply follow another, phases may be 'skipped' and, for that matter, perhaps people may be in more than one 'phase' at the same time. The phenomenon of *ambivalence* (Miller and Rollnick 1991) is characteristic of many offenders: wanting to change aspects of their behaviour and, at the same time, *not* wanting to change – perhaps because the perceived rewards of current behaviour are too great, or the costs of change too high or because they do not feel that change is achievable.

> The two basic and necessary forces of motivation are the push of discomfort and the pull of hope.
>
> (Compton and Galaway 1984: 136)

Miller and Rollnick (1991) explain the techniques of motivational interviewing. It is (emphatically) not a means of persuading people to do things that they do not want to do, but rather of working with their ambivalence and developing the positives. At the centre of this approach is the recognition that success in facilitating change 'occurs not by attacking the negative, but by fostering the positive'

(David Hawkins, quoted by Sandham and Octigan 2007). Motivational interviewing is a skilled technique, but many of its features can readily be incorporated into much of probation's work with offenders. These include:

- Seeking to understand the person's frame of reference, particularly via reflective listening.
- Expressing acceptance and affirmation.
- Eliciting and selectively reinforcing the client's own self-motivational statements, expressions of problem recognition, concern, desire and intention to change, and ability to change.
- Monitoring the client's degree of readiness to change, and ensuring that resistance is not generated by jumping ahead of the client.
- Affirming the client's freedom of choice and self-direction (Sandham and Octigan 2007: 168).

Motivational enhancement, however, cannot sensibly be confined to the techniques of motivational interviewing (Kemshall and Canton 2002; McGuire 2001: 71f.). Every aspect of engagement with offenders can be more or less motivational. Waiting times, the condition of reception areas, attitudes of staff, reliability of service – all these can support or undermine the offender's willingness to work with probation and indeed can influence their general motivation to change.

Sometimes obstacles to change can be very ordinary and practical. For this reason, Hudson (2007: 166) suggests that probation staff should routinely consider with the offender 'literacy, drug or alcohol problems as well as logistical considerations such as transport arrangements, work patterns and dependent care commitments' that may affect their chances of compliance.

In our later discussion of compliance (Chapter 9), it will be seen that legitimacy – the perception that one is being fairly and respectfully dealt with – and aspects of the relationship between the probation officer and the offender are critical in enhancing motivation.

Can people be 'coerced' into change? Don't people have to *want to change*? Robinson and Crow (2009: 101) consider arguments that the relatively scarce resources of probation supervision should be reserved for those who are motivated to change. On the other hand, they point to research to show that some interventions may be effective, even when participants are 'coerced'. Hough's (1996) review concluded that drug treatment, for example, was just as effective for those who had been coerced into treatment (on pain of being taken back to court for non-compliance) as for those whose participation was voluntary (Hough and Mitchell 2003).

To make sense of all this it is useful to remember the earlier discussion about fluctuations in motivation. Many substance users are ambivalent about their usage. Again, one person may at first attend under compulsion, but quickly become convinced of the value of the programme and then attend enthusiastically; another, attending voluntarily, may be put off by their first impressions of the programme or lose hope in their ability to change. Rumgay (2004) suggests that, while external constraints may contribute to initial participation, continuing involvement calls for internal commitment. An officer who instructs an offender to participate in a programme may be seen to be acting 'coercively', but is at the same time expressing a real concern that the offender should change and a belief that this is possible – providing the 'pull of hope'. *How* the instruction is communicated can in itself affect motivation.

There is no simple distinction between those who are motivated to change and those who are not. Levels of motivation change, sometimes rapidly; ambivalence is very common; signs of low motivation may arise from fear or despair as well as from any set determination to persist in the behaviour that needs to change; and if this is the case threat is very likely to be counter-productive. Motivational techniques do better by building on positives and blunt attempts to overcome an individual's uncertainties rarely succeed. Since the fulfilment of the court's sentence is not optional but is required of the offender, instruction must be given, but the manner in which this is done can make all the difference to motivation and to compliance. In Chapter 9, we take up this question in the context of understanding compliance.

Summary

In this chapter we have considered the emergence of a new confidence that there are effective ways of working with offenders. Programmes that were successful in reducing reconviction attended to risks, needs and responsivity (the RNR model), informed by cognitive behavioural approaches that recognise the mutual influences between thinking, feeling and behaviour. It was argued that the distinction between criminogenic and non-criminogenic needs is in practice not always easy to draw. The increasing tendency to regard needs as dynamic risks is not politically neutral: it can involve emphasising the risks posed by excluded and disadvantaged groups and make their right to have these needs addressed unfairly contingent upon some assessment of the relevance of these factors to their offending behaviour. Since probation is part of a system of justice and not just social control, its legitimacy depends partly upon its recognition of the needs of many of its service users and probation's responsibility to contribute to having those needs met.

The chapter moved on to discuss motivation, noting that this is complex and changeable and rejecting any simple distinction between those who are and those who are not 'motivated to change'. It seems likely that service has not infrequently been withheld on the basis of that distinction – for example, offenders being sent to prison because they were believed not to be able or ready to change. No doubt punitive approaches to working with offenders are impatient with the complexities of change processes. Bureaucratic strategies too are more comfortable with tidy categories and clear-cut distinctions. But managing and enabling change is often not like that and working with offenders' ambivalence, volatility, uncertainties and confusion is one of the most important skills needed by probation practitioners.

Questions

- What are the political implications of focusing on criminogenic needs (to the exclusion of other needs) and the regarding these as risk factors?
- What do you understand by the term *responsivity*? How would you go about assessing it?
- Consider something that you have wanted to change about yourself: what encouraged you and what made it harder? What implications do these insights have for probation practice?

Further reading

McGuire (2001) is an authoritative introduction to CB. McGuire and Priestley (1985) was profoundly influential and remains extremely useful. Cherry (2005) and Farrow *et al.* (2007) instructively discuss many of these topics.

7 Probation practice

The ASPIRE model, assessment, planning and the Offender Management Model

In the last chapter we considered an influential psychological paradigm – cognitive behaviourism (CB) – that offers a powerful explanatory account of learning and change. Strong claims were found to have been made for the effectiveness of programmes, based on CB principles, which helped offenders to 'unlearn' entrenched anti-social patterns of thought and behaviour and, by imparting new skills and teaching different possibilities, broadened their range of choice. We met the claim that programmes based on the principles of risk, need and responsivity (RNR) were most effective in reducing reoffending. The chapter ended with some initial thoughts about motivation.

In this chapter and the next, the details of practice will be looked at more closely. How are risks, needs and responsivity to be identified, assessed and used to guide intervention as RNR requires? We begin with the influential ASPIRE model, moving on to discuss assessment and planning. The Offender Management Model will be introduced. The next chapter will consider implementation, review and evaluation.

The ASPIRE model

ASPIRE is an acronym for Assessment, Planning, Implementation, Review and Evaluation, the phases that together make up a coherent and purposeful engagement with offenders. Figure 7.1 sets out the model graphically.

Roughly, *assessment* works out what the problems are; *planning* specifies what needs to be done and how this will take place; *implementation* involves putting the plan into effect; *review* and *evaluation* consider what has taken place – and may set the scene for a further assessment (what needs to be done next).

Assessment

Assessing what?

The RNR model suggests that the focus of assessment should be the offender's risks, needs and responsivity. Risks here include not only the likelihood of reoffending, but often, more specifically, the risk of serious harm that the offender is believed to present (Chapter 10). Criminogenic needs must then be identified, although, as we

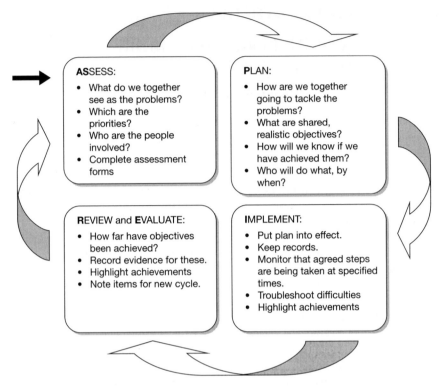

ASSESS:
- What do we together see as the problems?
- Which are the priorities?
- Who are the people involved?
- Complete assessment forms

PLAN:
- How are we together going to tackle the problems?
- What are shared, realistic objectives?
- How will we know if we have achieved them?
- Who will do what, by when?

REVIEW and EVALUATE:
- How far have objectives been achieved?
- Record evidence for these.
- Highlight achievements
- Note items for new cycle.

IMPLEMENT:
- Put plan into effect.
- Keep records.
- Monitor that agreed steps are being taken at specified times.
- Troubleshoot difficulties
- Highlight achievements

Figure 7.1 The ASPIRE process

Sutton (2001)

have seen, distinguishing between criminogenic and non-criminogenic needs is not always straightforward. Attention to responsivity requires some assessment to make sure that work with this individual is relevant and accessible – is *right for her/him*.

In addition, though, the practitioner will be forming initial views about the resources and interventions that probation might deploy to respond to assessed RNR – first of all, the individual's own abilities and resources, since principles of motivational enhancement encourage a focus on strengths rather than weaknesses. As O'Connell (2005: 25) warns: 'Some forms of assessment ... emphasise deficits, pathology, crises, failure and trauma. There is insufficient recognition of the coping strategies, the strength of character, the courage and the stamina that the client has needed to cope to date.' There may be support available from others as well: probation's services are just part of the potential response.

Assessing how?

How do probation staff undertake their assessments? Largely this used to be left to the judgement of individual practitioners, so that practice was variable. Their approach to assessment is usually referred to as *clinical*, though a better term might be person-by-person assessment. This relies on the practitioner's skills, experience and 'diagnostic' judgement and is therefore affected by the preferences or even the idiosyncrasies of the practitioner. Some matters of importance might not be raised at all in assessment and indeed may thus be made undiscussable, with the client feeling that they are somehow off limits. Such assessment allows scope for unfair discrimination, not least through stereotypical assumptions and attendant possibilities of bias and error.

This approach is conventionally contrasted with *actuarial* assessment (Kemshall 2007 and references there cited; Bonta and Wormith 2007; Robinson and Crow 2009).[1] This approach makes use of assessment instruments (C. Roberts 2007), forms that guide the practitioner to identify certain variables or risk markers that are known to be correlated with offending. The principle (and the arithmetic) are much like the actuarial tables that insurance companies use to assess risk and to decide on the level of premiums.

Probably the best established of these instruments is OGRS (Offender Group Reconviction Scale), now in its third version (Howard *et al.* 2009). Information is collected about a small number of (in principle) easily determined variables:

- age;
- gender;
- offence;
- number of custodial sentences when under 21 years old;
- number of previous convictions;
- age at first conviction.

Once these data have been put into the form on the computer they generate a *risk of reoffending* score, expressed as a percentage. (Other instruments may assign the individual to a category of high, significant or low risk of reoffending – Brown 2000; Kemshall, 2001, 2003). The calculation is based on the known reconviction rates of offenders who match this individual in the relevant respects. (Reconviction is not the same thing as reoffending, but it is the best proxy there is.) Over time, these instruments have been refined, as the actual reconviction outcomes are progressively 'fed back' into the databases. It is now confidently asserted that they have achieved impressive levels of accuracy and there seems near consensus that actuarial methods are significantly more accurate than clinical ones (Monahan 2004; Andrews and Bonta 2010).

> Suppose the use of an assessment instrument like OGRS generates a score of 70% per cent for an individual. This means that, of 100 people matched on the relevant variables, 70 will be reconvicted within two years and 30 will not.

Stephens and Brown (2001), however, discovered serious practical difficulties in probation's use of OGRS, including both unreliable data and appreciable differences between officers in 'scoring' the same case. Yet even if these problems could be overcome, OGRS cannot be used to make individual predictions. The factors that determine an OGRS score, moreover, are *static*: apart from age (getting older) and number of convictions, they do not change. OGRS, then, can take no account of improvements (or deteriorations) in attitudes or behaviour or assess the response to interventions. *Actuarial assessments thus detach assessment from case management.*

> OGRS cannot say whether *this* person is one of the 70 or one of the 30, how soon or how seriously they may reoffend or, crucially, what might be done to make a difference.

We need a mode of assessment that is rigorous and consistent (as person-by-person assessment usually is not), but also capable of informing subsequent planning and intervention (which purely actuarial methods cannot). 'Third generation'[2] instruments have been designed (C. Roberts 2007), which ensure that the relevant risks and needs are discussed and judgements are made systematically. These judgements should then point to the appropriate criminogenic needs as the focus and target for intervention.

OASys – what is OASys?

The best known of these instruments in work with adult offenders is the Offender Assessment System (OASys), routinely used in England and Wales and adopted (and adapted) by many other countries (Holden 2007 – from which the account below borrows heavily; Debidin 2009). It has five components:

1 risk of reconviction and criminogenic factor;
2 risk of serious harm to others (the general public, children, people known to the offender, staff, prisoners), risks to the individual (self-harm and suicide, personal vulnerabilities) and other risks;
3 summary sheet;
4 sentence plan;
5 self-assessment.

Risk of reconviction and criminogenic factors

OASys incorporates OGRS, but further requires practitioners to attend to a number of dynamic factors – ones that are changing and so in principle amenable to influence – and to assign a 'score' to these. The scores awarded represent judgements about the seriousness of the problem for this individual and its relationship with offending. Thus, 0 = no problems; 1 = some problems; and 2 = significant problems. The social, economic and personal factors OASys covers are:

- accommodation;
- education, training and employment;
- finance and income;
- relationships;
- life-style and associates;
- drug misuse;
- alcohol misuse;
- emotional well-being (including mental health);
- thinking and behaviour (including considering the consequences of their behaviour, seeing things from someone else's point of view);
- attitudes (towards offending, towards supervision).

(Health is addressed but not 'scored'.) These factors were chosen for their established association with offending. Each will be explored carefully and this will not depend on the practitioner's preferences or assumptions.

Risk of serious harm to others (the general public, children, people known to the offender, staff, prisoners), risks to the individual (self-harm and suicide, personal vulnerabilities) and other risks.

This section includes:

- a screening (to indicate whether a full risk analysis should be completed);
- an analysis, leading to a risk management plan;
- summary of risks of harm.

The risk management plan is one of the most important sections and often a focus of particular attention in audits and inspections. Plans are expected to include contact details of other agencies involved (information which may then be repeated in the sentence plan), their respective roles in the management of risk and often a clear contingency plan, setting out anticipated responses to possible events and developments.

Summary sheet

This section summarises identified risks and needs, showing the working priorities for the sentence and risk management plans.

Sentence plan

A (reviewable) plan setting out how the sentence will be put into effect.

Self assessment

A questionnaire which gives the offender an opportunity to record his or her views. In a large sample (n>100,000), Moore found that, while many offenders acknowledged that they had problems, 47 per cent thought they had *no* problems that were linked to offending. By and large offenders seemed less likely to identify offending-related problems than practitioners. Moore proposes that 'that attention should be paid to whether offenders have realistic perceptions of their own likelihood of reoffending and the link between particular criminogenic problems and offending' (2007: 6). Yet perhaps offenders may not always find it easy to think or talk in such terms or to disclose difficulties to practitioners (whether or not they identify them for themselves): this is a necessary reminder that assessment is an irreducibly human process and more than a routine matter of completing a form.

OASys can 'trigger' more specialised assessments. The form can also generate a template to be used in the preparation of a PSR (Chapter 5). Since OASys was developed jointly with the Prison Service, it potentially constitutes a common assessment framework and a shared vocabulary for discussing risk – an essential component of a 'seamless' sentence (Chapter 12).

Assessment and the models of criminal justice (Chapter 1)

Which models illuminate the contemporary use of assessment instruments? They seem to serve the *treatment model* by identifying those who may best benefit from various forms of intervention. But they also support a *bureaucratic model* assigning offenders to categories or levels of intervention to enable the routine allocation of resources. The *power model* would suggest that assessment instruments compound social disadvantage by reconstructing it – presenting it as either irrelevant (because non-criminogenic) or as dynamic risk factors warranting more intrusion and control (Silver and Miller 2002).

OASys – strengths and limitations

OASys is now central to probation's work. There had been anxieties about its size and complexity, but any assessment instrument must strive for a 'balance between comprehensiveness and use-friendliness' (Robinson 2003a: 120). Mair, *et al.* (2006) found that it was generally welcomed by practitioners for being specific and systematic and for ensuring a consistency of approach. Even so it is hard not to connect its size and demands with stories about the amount of time that staff spend in front of a computer (The Times 2009; BBC 2009).

The respondents in Mair and colleagues' study were also doubtful that OASys was sufficiently responsive to diversity – a criticism that can potentially be levelled against any standardised instrument (see Chapter 3). The Corston Report (2007) suggests that the origins and context of offending by women is different from male offending in important ways and that their respective criminogenic needs may not be assumed to be the same. Similar questions have been raised around other 'dimensions of difference' (Kemshall *et al.* 2004). Can OASys accommodate this diversity?

OASys is said to work well in assigning offenders to broad categories in terms of their prospects of reconviction (Moore *et al.* 2006); it does less well in anticipating the seriousness of any further offence (Bennett 2008).

Inter-rater reliability – practitioners rating the same cases in the same way – is critical and the rigour of OASys was intended to reduce the chances of discrepancies. Morton (2009) concluded that overall (inter-rater) reliability is 'moderate': some factors are rated in the same way by practitioners *quite reliably*– accommodation, lifestyle and associates, drug misuse – but others just *moderately reliably,* while *low reliability* was found for financial management, alcohol misuse, thinking and behaviour, risk of serious harm. It seems improbable that this type of discrepancy could be eliminated entirely and quite different assessments could continue to be made on the basis of the same information – which has serious implications for targeting for programmes and levels of supervision.

One challenge here is *instantiation*: an inescapably 'clinical' element in any actuarial scheme is the need to make an individual judgement to determine whether the risk factor is in fact present and to what degree. For example, 'attitude' may be an established risk factor, but there is still the question of determining what the individual's attitude actually is. And on this particular judgement there is just moderate agreement among practitioners. Moreover, the kinds of problems that offenders identify for themselves bear an uncertain relationship to what practitioners take to be their problems. Nor can many problems be readily captured by a tick, a yes/no or a score.

An implicit assumption is that there is a 'right answer', which practitioners and offenders are variably successful in getting. Notably the dominance of risk has encouraged the view that the principal virtue of assessment is 'accuracy' – a match with some independent fact. Yet even the most objective factors turn out to be less than straightforward. Being homeless or unemployed seem like relatively 'hard' facts, but there are varying degrees of *having somewhere to live* (from home ownership to being able to sleep at a friend's house) and different levels of employment (from full-time permanent employment to occasional casual work). Other factors – relationships, emotional well-being, thinking – are still less simple matters of fact.

The extent to which something is or is seen as a problem is still less a 'fact', varying with the individual's willingness to talk, being unaware or 'well-defended' or ambivalent, their (fluctuating) confidence and motivation, their concern about how to present themselves. Much too depends on the practitioner's skill in eliciting and exploring these matters and the trust they are able to gain.

Dealing with dynamic factors, OASys ought to be able to appraise progress or deterioration. But sometimes 'repeat assessments yield higher risk or needs scores because the offender has chosen to disclose more problems or the officer has learned more about the offender, rather than because risk or need factors have actually changed' (Raynor *et al.* 2000: 38). These 'disclosure effects' should again alert us to the shifting and elusive character of specifying and measuring personal problems.

While OASys is an RNR assessment, its primary focus is *risk*. Responsivity is not assessed with anything like the same rigour, even though it is plainly essential that the resulting work plan should be relevant and accessible to the individual. Here offender and practitioner are thrown back on a mode of person-by-person judgement that is considered inadequate to assess risk. Other risks – specifically the individual offender's own vulnerabilities – are by no means neglected, but again receive less detailed attention. Yet the disadvantages and vulnerability of so many offenders should lead us to expect that offenders are themselves significantly at risk. These risks often include ill-health and, for example, a considerably higher than average risk of suicide and self-harm (Akhurst *et al*. n.d.; Cowe 2007a, 2007b). Political rhetoric should not be allowed to obscure the obvious point that people may present a risk of reoffending *and also* be vulnerable.

Assessment as a human process

While most contemporary accounts of assessment begin with some discussion of assessment instruments, there are influential aspects to any encounter between two people that shape the way in which the process develops. For example:

- Both bring certain assumptions and beliefs, including schemata (Chapter 5) based on their previous experience of these or similar exchanges, what they have heard from others, and so on. (Probation staff have their own schemata, both personal and professional – Lurigio and Carroll 1985.)
- Both have a personal identity, shaped by structure, culture and biography (Critcher 1975) which could affect the encounter in a number of ways.
- Perceptions of the power held by the practitioner can influence the exchange too, perhaps overlaid and complicated by aspects of power associated with personal identity.
- Complex interactions among behaviour, thoughts and feelings mean that assessment cannot be reduced to a bureaucratic process: it is never a reading off of 'facts' about a person.
- Many topics can elicit –in both practitioner and client – anxieties, doubts and fears.

Appreciation of the human aspects of assessment is quite as important as a consideration of its technicalities.

Assessment instruments – summary

Instruments contribute to rigour and consistency in assessment. OASys goes beyond static, immutable risk markers and tries to engage with the real 'dynamic' circumstances in people's lives. Yet this calls for skills – interviewing, the gathering, interpreting, and recording of information, instantiation and judgement, emotional literacy (the ability to be aware of and work with one's own feelings and the feelings of others – see Chapter 9). These are irreducibly personal skills and the process and outcomes of assessment cannot be understood as a purely objective account of the 'facts of the case' from which levels of risk and need can be straightforwardly inferred: a failure to appreciate this can lead to a misunderstanding of the significance and value of assessment instruments.

OASys is not – and was never intended to be – a tick-box questionnaire. Robinson (2003a) found considerable apprehension among staff that it would remove professional judgement and discretion, but these skills are more than ever relevant in administering, interpreting and using OASys properly. While much research centres on the question of its 'accuracy', assessment is also – and quite as importantly – an exploration and a negotiation. The process should endeavour to arrive at a sufficiently shared understanding of the offender's situation to form a basis for future work. As in the discussion of fast delivery PSRs (Chapter 5), here too we might ask whether the managerial requirements of National Standards to complete these processes expeditiously could interfere with a task whose value lies at least as much in the process as its product.

Setting objectives and planning

Giving priority to its 'predictive accuracy' is at risk of isolating assessment – separating it off from the other phases of the ASPIRE cycle. The purpose of assessment, after all, is to inform planning and subsequent intervention: if an assessment cannot guide work in this way, then, no matter how accurate, it is not much use. RNR should expect, therefore, that assessment will attempt to identify the factors or problems to be worked on, informing the planning phase of the ASPIRE cycle where objectives are set and decisions taken about how to achieve them.

These objectives should emerge directly from assessment and are shaped by that process. Focusing on risk and need, RNR tends to generate objectives that are framed in terms of the reduction of risks and criminogenic needs. But this may be already an unpromising beginning (Farrall and Calverley 2006; Ward and Maruna 2007): RNR assessment is preoccupied with problems and shortcomings and thus generates *aversive* goals – things to avoid or to refrain from. Even when the objective appears to be a positive one – for example, the obtaining of employment – it is valued for aversive reasons, because getting work helps people to reduce re-offending, rather than because it is often a component of a fulfilling life (Chapter 9).

A rounded assessment should attend as well to people's strengths and potential. Even within the constricted framework of RNR, assessment ought to be exploring '"resilience perspectives", which, in contrast with approaches that dwell on risks and/or needs, consider the "protective factors and processes" involved in positive adaptation in spite of adversity' (McNeill 2006: 49). RNR is insufficiently sensitive to the specific goods or goals that individuals might want to achieve, their legitimate ambitions. An emphasis on *approach* goals – positive aspirations for achievement – stimulate motivation and the processes of change. It is not that assessment instruments are repudiated; on the contrary, they can be valuable: 'Potential issues of risk and need are presented to the client as areas for collaborative investigation' (Ward and Maruna 2007: 131). But they tend to shape planning and intervention towards mainly aversive goals, rarely dealing well with resilience, strength and aspiration. The mode and focus of assessment shapes the objectives that are set, as well, perhaps, as the 'tone' of subsequent supervision.

To plan seems to be a precondition of any professional, purposeful engagement. Yet circumstances change, especially for those with unsettled and problematic lives. (Re-)assessment must therefore be undertaken in response to significant events and developments, as well as periodically in any case, and these reappraisals may lead to changes of plan. Some objectives may emerge as more immediately compelling than had been appreciated; others may become apparent as the offender becomes more aware of or more prepared to disclose them; other objectives again may turn out to be much less relevant than had first appeared. Yet, not least because of the volatility of motivation (see Chapter 5), practitioner and client must work determinedly in an agreed direction.

A well-known (and perhaps weary) stipulation is that objectives should be SMART. Chapman and Hough (1998: 7.7) offer one account of this, saying that outputs and outcomes should be specified in ways that are:

*S*pecific
*M*easurable
*A*chievable
*R*ealistic
*T*ime scale attached

Chapman and Hough were discussing *organisational* objectives, but this acronym has become the preferred way of approaching plans for individual supervision too. The virtue of this approach is often taken as self-evident: how can progress or achievement be measured without a precisely specified and time-bounded objective? Evidence-led practice must have some way of securing reliable evidence of its effects.

Yet Trotter (1999) has emphasised the importance of working with clients' own perceptions of their problems. Not all problems lend themselves to responses that can be formulated as SMART objectives and the attempt to frame a problem to make it amenable to a SMART analysis can distort its character. John Raine (personal communication) proposes the idea of DIM objectives:

*D*emanding
*I*nnovative
*M*oveable

While this is not perhaps intended to be taken too seriously, it does present a sharp challenge to the pretensions of SMARTness. Not everything to which people reasonably aspire can in any significant sense be measured or even well specified: people may well have ambitions that are vague and distant, but nevertheless real and inspirational. Nor are the steps towards them always immediately apparent.

Planning, then, involves the identification of interventions and resources that may be deployed in response to the explorations of the assessment – what is to be done, how and by whom. Taking full account of responsivity, plans should be used to ensure direction and so that practitioner and client may call one another to account, but should also be sufficiently flexible to accommodate change. To work purposefully is to be guided by an objective; to pursue an objective that now shows itself to have been superseded or irrelevant is a mark of rigidity.

The emergence of offender management

OASys offers a rigorous and consistent approach to assessment; objectives are then to be set and plans agreed. Yet the ASPIRE process is incomplete without an operational structure and a systematic framework to deliver what is found to be required. We move next, then, to consider *offender management* and the Offender Management Model (OMM) which is intended to constitute just such a framework.

As we saw in Chapter 5, the range of problems that offenders experience calls not only for different modes or types of intervention (one principle of effective practice is that it should be *multi-modal*), but for different providers of service. If someone's criminogenic needs are identified as (say) substance misuse, short-comings in inter-personal skills and homelessness, they are likely to need access to several services. It makes no sense, as had long been recognised (Home Office 1990b), for probation to try to provide all such services itself: rather it should engage with specialist service providers on behalf of people under supervision. Probation accordingly developed partnership arrangements with a diverse range of agencies in the public and independent sectors which grew apace in the 1980s and 1990s (Rumgay 2007). The Social Exclusion Unit Report (2002) (Chapter 6) was a further stimulus: offenders should have fair and reasonable access to services enjoyed by everyone else. These developments also represent a much wider trend in criminal justice to involve other agencies and organisations in crime control (Garland 2001).

A proliferation of interventions and providers, if uncoordinated, could lead to confusion, inefficiency and ineffectiveness. Case management (Holt 2000), origi-nating in social work and community health care, emerged as the guiding strategy to provide coherent services. In 2001, the Home Office commissioned research into models of case management (Partridge 2004). The Social Exclusion Unit report (2002: 11), noting the fragmented way in which prisoners received services, proposed a 'form of case management . . . which should involve joint working between the Prison Service and Probation Service and other statutory and non-statutory organisations'.

These initiatives were given a different focus and imperative by the review into correctional services, led by Patrick Carter (2003), which 'found an urgent need for the different parts of the criminal justice system to work closer together' and proposed a restructuring of the prison and probation services to create a National Offender Management Service (Chapter 14). The aspiration to deliver a 'seamless service' raised operational as well as organisational challenges. This was to be achieved through *offender management*, a new term which in probation superseded *case management*.

The Offender Management Model (OMM)

The offender management model (OMM) prescribes the processes for managing individual offenders. (The sections that follow rely heavily on Grapes 2007.)

OMM does not imply any particular methodology or approach and is expressed in 'agency-neutral language and terminology' (Grapes 2007: 188). Treating 'every case as a project' (NOMS 2006: 44), an offender manager coordinates an 'end-to-end' process, including an individualised combination of interventions and experiences in which different service providers make their distinctive contributions. This calls for a teamwork approach, requiring mutual understanding, a clear sense of role in a collective endeavour and effective communication. The offender management team is made up of an offender manager, offender supervisor, key workers (providers of interventions) and a case administrator. Grapes emphasises that this conception of team affirms the contribution of *all* staff, including those whose work has sometimes tended to be taken for granted.

The offender manager must ensure that the processes of ASPIRE take place, but does not necessarily (and usually does not) personally undertake all the associated tasks. The offender manager, however, does undertake assessment, sentence planning, coordination, monitoring and evaluation, and takes strategic decisions about the case. The offender supervisor – a different *role* from the offender manager, although both roles can be (preferably are) held by the same person – provides the 'continuous human link' through regular contact with the offender, motivates and coaches the offender, 'oils the wheels' and reports developments to the offender manager. The supervisor role with serving prisoners (to whom the OMM also applies) is of particular importance since the prison-based supervisor will have much more direct contact than can the offender manager in the community. (For formal roles see Appendix 3 of NOMS 2006.)

Described by Grapes (2007) as 'model within a model', *tiering* assigns each individual to one of four tiers to determine the level and nature of subsequent involvement. Table 7.1 sets out the purposes and tasks associated with each tier.

The tiering attempts to realise two related principles – that resources should match risk and that involvement should be no more than necessary to achieve purpose. The single most important criterion that determines assignment to a tier is risk, as assessed by OASys, revealing the influence of risk management on the origins and character of the model (Robinson and Crow 2009).

The term *punishment* here, incidentally, should be understood as *giving effect to the order of the court* – there should be no suggestion that there is anything additionally punitive implied by the model. Nevertheless the term has occasioned some misgivings (for discussion see Burnett *et al.* 2007), especially among those who set a sharp opposition between punishment and rehabilitation (see Chapter 4). There is a political risk that, at the fourth tier, public protection imperatives might suppress the objectives of helping and changing as well as controlling – as

Table 7.1 The tiers of the Offender Management Model

Tier One	Punish	Arrangements made for the implementation of the sentence requirements, with due regard for decency, health and safety and the preservation of citizenship; monitor risk factors; 'signpost' to helping resources
Tier Two	Punish and Help	Motivation; referral to resources providing practical help addressing circumstances or situation - typically employment, accommodation, basic and life skills; support and encouragement of participation
Tier Three	Punish, Help and Change	Implementation of carefully planned programmes designed to achieve personal change, typically including offending behaviour programmes, drug and alcohol treatment; some social skills
Tier Four	Punish, Help, Change and Control	Intensive, inter-agency, multi-faceted programme to control and monitor behaviour, including surveillance and intelligence work. Typically, Prolific Offender Schemes and dangerous offender MAPPA 'packages'

(NOMS 2006: 48)

the OMM insists. Chapter 10 will argue that the skills of engagement that are needed to help and support change are quite as relevant in working with offenders believed to pose the highest risks.

Implementation of the model began in April 2005 and it was introduced in phases through to December 2008, being progressively extended to different groups of offenders. It was first applied to offenders subject to community orders and then extended to include many prisoners, including prolific offenders and those sentenced to Imprisonment for Public Protection (IPP). Most prisoners however are not yet managed in this way.

In probation, and to a lesser extent in prisons, familiar team structures were replaced by working arrangements designed to implement the model, with staff working in small clusters or units often known as Offender Management Units (OMUs).

Opportunities and hazards of OMM

The model's strengths are conspicuous. The idea that an offender manager leads assessment and planning and then ensures that relevant interventions are made available through appropriate referral to specialised providers seems both sound and sensible. Pathfinder projects (November 2005–March 2007) established 'that practitioners, partners and offenders at all levels and in all agencies, viewed it as "the right way to do things"' (Grapes 2007: 191).

Encouragingly, too, the OMM was soon supplemented by a Ministry of Justice paper (2008b) considering the implications of offender management for women offenders, avoiding the (usually tacit) assumption of much earlier policy that it was indiscriminately applicable to everyone. In particular, this policy paper emphasises the responsibilities of offender managers to have regard to the vulnerability of women offenders as well as to any risks they pose.

The most frequently expressed concern about the model, perhaps, is the possibility of *fragmentation*. Relationships are at the heart of probation work and some felt this would be jeopardised in a model that seemed likely to reduce the amount of personal contact between offender and probation officer (see Chapter 9). Robinson (2005) warned that good practice might be compromised and the morale and sense of purpose of staff undermined.

Defenders of the model have always recognised this risk. In an early influential monograph on case management, Holt (2000) emphasised:

- Continuity
- Consistency
- Commitment
- Consolidation.

Partridge's (2004) review of case management models echoes this, while Grapes (2007) notes that effective practice and desistance research suggest that these features are indispensable to the coherence and integrity of the OMM. Yet such insistence in itself acknowledges the *possibility* of fragmentation inherent in the model and the need to guard against this. Can the relational influences of probation be maintained when the offender encounters a succession of individuals who, for all their distinctive areas of expertise, are likely to have only a partial rather than an holistic understanding of the individual? What scope is there for an effective working relationship with someone who sees the offender no more than occasionally?

As we shall see in the next chapter, the best intervention work calls for the active participation of the offender manager – or perhaps the offender supervisor – helping the individual to apply the general learning from offending behaviour programmes and making critical connections between interventions delivered by different providers. The OMM encourages this, but there is a possibility that pressures on workload and resources will make insufficient allowance for the demands of the full and active role of offender manager. In that event, there is a real possibility of the fragmentation that Robinson feared.

Skidmore (2007c) writes about the relationship between offender management and models adopted by other agencies. Case management is an influential paradigm in many practice settings, but its procedures and priorities cannot be assumed to be the same for other agencies. In particular, there are critically important procedures in working to protect children within which the OMM must function and which it cannot presume to lead. Skidmore's other examples include work with drug misusers and with people who are mentally ill: again, it may not be assumed that the OMM will take precedence over the established practices of other agencies. As ever, inter-agency work, on which OMM depends, will call for mutual respect and patient negotiation.

Summary

In this chapter we have considered the first two phases of the influential ASPIRE model – assessment and planning. Methods of assessment have been discussed and an attempt made to identify the strengths and shortcomings of assessment instruments, with particular attention to OASys. After discussion of setting objectives and planning, the chapter went on to discuss the emergence of the idea of *offender management* and the development of the OMM.

The OMM makes a clear distinction between management and interventions and envisages that offenders should be referred to providers, within but also beyond the Probation Service, with the expertise to work with their identified needs. The next chapter goes on to look at these interventions and subsequent processes of review and evaluation.

Questions

- What are the strengths and limitations of assessment instruments? To what extent can they accommodate diversity?
- Assessment is here described as a 'human process'. What is meant by this and to what extent can assessment instruments allow for this?
- How can the OMM avoid the fragmentation that some of its critics fear and sustain effective working relationships in a succession of services and providers?

Further reading

Burnett *et al.* (2007) is a concise introduction to many of the topics covered in this chapter. Farrow *et al.* (2007) consider many of the implications for practice.

8   Probation practice – ASPIRE

Intervention, evaluation and the challenge of compliance

The last chapter discussed assessment and planning, the first two phases of the ASPIRE cycle, and ended by introducing the Offender Management Model (OMM), the operational architecture of contemporary probation work. In this chapter we consider the implementation of plans that emerge from assessment and the processes of review and evaluation which enable practitioners and offenders to see whether their objectives have been achieved.

Interventions

Assessment and planning are processes to determine what needs to be done and how this will be achieved. Subsequent implementation is diverse in character and intensity: for some intervention will involve a tightly structured programme; for others it will amount to referral to and engagement with services to address identified needs; for others again their involvement with probation may be not much more than a matter of reporting to their probation officer as required.

Accredited programmes

The *what works* initiative claimed to have identified the guiding characteristics of effective practice. But these principles were framed in very general terms. The logic of *what works* requires the design, implementation and evaluation of *programmes*. A programme – 'a planned sequence of learning opportunities' (McGuire 2007a: 158) – must be specified in sufficient detail to make it reproducible so that it may be delivered as intended.

'Pathfinder' projects were set up to run promising programmes and evaluate their effects. There were inevitable tensions between the political imperative to implement effective programmes expeditiously and, on the other hand, the requirement to evaluate them rigorously and to meet challenges of implementation (Raynor 2004a).

A panel, now known as the Correctional Services Accreditation Panel, was also established (Wham 2007; Raynor and Rex 2007; Maguire *et al.* 2010).

Accreditation criteria

A programme proposal is submitted to the panel who apply ten criteria to decide if it merits accreditation:

- a clear model of change
- selection of offenders
- targeting a range of dynamic risk factors
- effective methods
- skills orientated
- sequencing, intensity and duration
- engagement and motivation
- continuity of programmes and services
- process evaluation and maintaining integrity
- ongoing evaluation.

Ministry of Justice 2009c: Appendix C

Where these criteria are satisfied, the programme will be formally accredited. Accredited programmes came to be seen as the main type of intervention and the way in which the Probation Service would demonstrate its effectiveness. Almost all programmes originally accredited were designed to cognitive behavioural principles and were intended to influence people's attitudes and thinking (Chapter 5).

The following discussion offers some examples. (See Appendix B Ministry of Justice (2009c) for a full list of programmes accredited or recognised by the Panel. See also Hancock (2007a); McGuire (2007a); National Probation Service n.d.)

Some are *generic* programmes, designed to be relevant to offending of all kinds, including Think First and One to One. *Think First* (now replaced by a newer 'Thinking Skills Programme' in some areas, but among the best-established accredited programmes) involves four pre-programme sessions followed by 22 group sessions of between two and two-and-a-half hours. These focus on skills needed to change behaviour such as problem-solving, anti-social attitudes, tackling pressures to offend, victim awareness, moral reasoning, self-management and social interaction. The course is followed by a number of individual sessions.

One to One is a programme designed to be delivered individually. It covers much the same curriculum as Think First and comprises one pre-programme session of motivational interviewing, followed by 21 one-to-one sessions of between an hour and an hour and a half.

Other programmes are designed for specific types of offending or offending associated with specific criminogenic factors. For example: *Sex Offender Treatment Programmes* (SOTP) are designed to increase personal responsibility, make clear the consequences of offending, enhance empathy for victims, challenge the thinking patterns that lead to such behaviour and help offenders develop strategies to avoid reoffending (Snowden 2007).

Controlling Anger and Learning to Manage it (CALM) aims to reduce aggressive behaviour related to poor emotional control and conflict resolution skills. It comprises 24 groupwork sessions of between two and two-and-a-half hours. Through learning social skills, emotional management and cognitive techniques, offenders learn to understand and control their emotional arousal, skills to resolve conflict and how to deal with relapse.

The *Integrated Domestic Abuse Programme* (IDAP) aims to reduce the risk of domestic violence, violent crime and abusive behaviour towards women in relationships by helping perpetrators change their attitudes and behaviour. The programme involves contact with the victim or current partner and risk management through continual assessment and information sharing with other agencies including the police. The programme consists of 27 weekly two-hour group sessions and 13 individual sessions. Completion is usually over a period of not less than 27 weeks. The programme is followed by at least four relapse prevention sessions with the offender manager.

A criticism that came to be levelled against the *what works* initiative was that the programmes, and the evidence-base for their effectiveness, came from experiences of working with mainly young, white men and could not be assumed to be relevant to women or to offenders from Black and minority ethnic groups (for example Shaw and Hannah-Moffat 2004). McGuire (2005) persuasively rebuts some of these criticisms, even as he urges the need for further research and refined programme specification to meet different needs.

Specific programmes designed to meet such concerns include the *Women's Acquisitive Crime Programme,* designed for women whose crime is for financial gain, who have poor problem-solving skills, and who do not think through the consequences of their actions. There are 31 two-hour sessions, with additional work needed for those with a high risk of reoffending or with a high level of need. The programme is based on motivational techniques with an emphasis on emotional management and building healthy relationships.

Chapter 3 argued that unfair discrimination can arise both from the denial of difference (which here would be an assumption that programmes designed for white men must be suitable for everyone) or from the exaggeration of difference (which would here be an assumption that provision must be different).

It may well be unreasonable to ask a woman, perhaps with personal experience of male abuse, to be alone in a male group, or someone to be the only black person in an otherwise white group. This could be addressed through separate provision, although there are sometimes logistical and resource challenges for such provision. Calverley and colleagues (2004) found little support among male offenders from black and minority ethnic groups for 'BME only' groups. But a deeper criticism is that the programme design itself is gendered or race specific. Nor should culture be overlooked. For example, programmes for sex offenders and for domestic violence will explore and seek to change attitudes towards children and women, but these attitudes may well vary in different cultures and programmes need to be able to allow for and accommodate this. These questions are easier to raise than to answer, but an awareness of diversity is essential in any consideration of programmes and its neglect can lead both to injustice and ineffectiveness (Shaw and Hannah-Moffat 2004, but also McGuire 2005).

Interventions and pathways

The initial focus of *what works* was on offending behaviour programmes. Without genuine and fair access to opportunities for social inclusion, however, personal change is unlikely to be sufficient to bring about desistance.

The Social Exclusion Unit report (2002) influenced a National Action Plan (2004) which spoke of 'pathways' out of offending and identified a number of 'key areas' where strategy and services, commonly undertaken in partnership with other agencies, needed to be enhanced:

- accommodation;
- education, training and employment;
- mental and physical health;
- drugs and alcohol;
- finance, benefit and debt;
- children and families of offenders;
- attitudes, thinking and behaviour.

The *Guide to Working with Women Offenders* (Ministry of Justice 2008b) demonstrates how problems in these areas may have a different manifestation and significance for women offenders and accordingly require different kinds of response. The *Guide* adds other areas for attention (for example, emotional well-being) because of their association with women's offending, which raises pointed questions about whether these should receive attention for male offenders too (an exaggeration of difference?).

A huge range of policies and services address these pathways and what follows are no more than a few broad generalisations and examples.

Accommodation

'Appropriate and accessible accommodation is the foundation of successful rehabilitation and management of risk of harm to others. It is crucial to sustaining employment, treatment, family support and finances' (Home Office 2004b: 9). There are connections between homelessness and (re)offending (*ibid.*) (and, incidentally, victimisation – Chapter 13). The Supporting People scheme offers support to vulnerable people (including, though of course not only, many offenders) to help them live independently in the community through the provision of a range of housing support services (for detail, see Mulrenan 2007). Probation's active participation in these multi-agency arrangements has ensured that services are developed in ways that are relevant and accessible to offenders.

Employment, training and education (ETE)

'More than half the offenders who receive community or custodial sentences are unemployed at the time of conviction' (Bridges 2007: 117). The relationship between offending and unemployment is complex: does unemployment make offending more likely or do offenders find it harder to find work? (There are no doubt causal influences in both directions – Farrall and Calverley 2006.) Being in work brings opportunities and legitimate sources of income, as well as encouraging life styles and influential, informal social controls that conduce to desistance. Work can lead to a standing and a self-perception that gives people something that they do not want to risk losing through offending.

ETE interventions attempt to help people develop skills to enhance their employment prospects. This may include general education, specific vocational training, job seeking skills and/or work placements. ETE therefore involves multi-agency partnerships at both local and national level. Bridges (2007) observes that partnership with NOMS and probation has required partner agencies to consider public protection in their work with offenders.

Other important work here is *Education: Skills For Life*. Basic Skills are '[t]he ability to read, write and speak in English or Welsh and use mathematics at a level necessary to function and progress at work and in society in general' (Apiafi 2007: 110). Offenders have well above average difficulties in these respects and well below average opportunities to access the relevant services. Fifty-two per cent of the prison population have learning difficulties which would appreciably limit their learning and work opportunities (Rack 2005) and offenders under community supervision probably have a similar profile. All offenders should be screened, using *First Move* (National Probation Service 2007) and then referred as appropriate for a fuller assessment. This may lead to educational opportunities often provided through partnerships with local colleges of Further Education.

Accessible services?

Hollin and colleagues (2002) found that a number of offending behaviour programmes called for literacy skills that many participants lacked. A further study developed this inquiry and investigated three widely used general offending behaviour programmes (Davies *et al.* 2004). It was found that, as well as (and no doubt often associated with) literacy difficulties, as many as 35 per cent of offenders had speaking and listening problems. The programmes required levels of communication skills that perhaps no more than 26 per cent of the participants had attained.

Napo (2009) found very substantial numbers of offenders with communication difficulties on probation caseloads – about one-third of more than 2,306 offenders in the survey. While 32 per cent had difficulty in 'expressing themselves or understanding what is said to them', only one had had input from a speech and language therapist. These problems overlap with learning disabilities, where probation also faces a challenge to make sure that services are accessible (Martin 2007). Not all such difficulties are related to learning disabilities and/or communication problems, although they may be. In any event, appropriate attention to this seems essential and indeed in many cases a precondition of undertaking effective work of any other kind.

Mental and physical health

The relationship between mental health and offending is notoriously complex (Prins 1995). Probation has tended to regard mental ill health as a criminogenic factor, although Bonta *et al.* (1998) show that risk factors for mentally disordered offenders are substantially the same as for other offenders and that criminal history and other factors 'predict' more reliably than mental health factors.

An 'aspiration with a long history of failure' (Grounds 1991: 38) is that offenders who are mentally unwell should be diverted from criminal justice proceedings into medical care. Yet despite this long avowed policy and the setting up of some good diversion schemes, the numbers of prisoners with diagnosed mental health needs are increasing. Since probation staff work often with offenders – and no doubt victims – with mental health problems, mental health and learning disability need to be considered as responsivity as much as risk factors (Canton 2008a).

Offenders are also known to have more than average problems of physical ill-health and worse than average opportunities to avail themselves of appropriate services (Brooker *et al.* 2009). Lifestyles characterised by high levels of offending are typically stressful and hazardous. Whatever the relationship between ill health and offending, social justice requires that offenders should have access to the health services that they need and probation, in partnership with health care services, have a crucial contribution here.

Drugs and alcohol

The Church of England Temperance Society was influential in probation's origins (Chapter 2) and probation officers have always been aware of the effects of alcohol and other drugs. Misuse brings a range of problems, many directly associated with offending and/or as impediments to achieving a way of living lawfully. Possession of drugs and trafficking are offences in themselves, of course, and many drug users commit acquisitive crimes to fund their habit. The Action Plan notes:

> A third of offenders are drunk when arrested and the majority of prisoners enter custody with drug and alcohol misuse problems. Despite very high levels of need, many offenders will not have received any help with their problem prior to arrest. Women prisoners are more likely than men to have histories of severe poly-drug use and a greater tendency to be on hard drugs such as heroin.
>
> (Home Office 2004b: 27)

Treatment aimed at reducing harm and assisting users in controlling, reducing or stopping their substance misuse may include:

- *biological* interventions – for example, the prescription of substitute drugs like methadone or Subutex, detoxification, treatment for physical problems associated with misuse, reduction of blood-borne viruses;
- *psychological* interventions – for example, motivational interviewing and counselling;
- *social* interventions – attempts to reduce social exclusion, improve access to housing, employment and constructive interests and pursuits.

The term *bio-psycho-social interventions* is sometimes used (Malik 2007). Substance misuse accordingly requires the complementary and coherent involvement of a range of different agencies. Drug intervention services typically include:

- testing of people arrested for certain offences and a subsequent 'required assessment';
- arrest–referral services in police custody suites and courts to assess and to engage arrestees voluntarily in drug treatment;
- CARAT (Counselling, Assessment, Referral, Advice and Throughcare) services to assess and deliver care plans within prisons;
- CJITs (Criminal Justice Interventions Teams) working in the community, including referral to specialised services and/or to removing obstacles to stability or drug free lifestyles;
- rapid prescribing facilities for those with opiate dependency (Skidmore 2007a).

Finance, benefit and debt

'Poverty, one of the most enduring characteristics of the population with whom the Probation Service has its dealings, has become one of those topics which is almost never mentioned in polite probation circles' (Drakeford 2007: 210). Yet levels of material inequality have increased in the past 20 years and 'Single men, and those at the very sharpest end of disadvantage, have benefited the least from anti-poverty measures, and are treated, in social policy terms, as the least deserving' (*ibid.*). Drakeford indicts probation for its failure to speak up for service users who experience the most marked disadvantage.

Interventions here are largely confined to worthwhile and pragmatic initiatives around debt counselling, access to benefits and, for released prisoners, the provision of discharge grants. There are also projects to help prisoners to set up and manage bank accounts. To go further risks appearing to favour offenders above others in poverty – which a punitive strategy is unwilling to countenance. It remains the case that lack of money and ready opportunities to make it are among the most prominent obstacles to desistance mentioned by offenders (Sheffield Pathways Out of Crime n.d.).

Children and families of offenders

'Maintaining family relationships can help to prevent ex-prisoners re-offending and assist them to resettle successfully into the community. However, 43 per cent of sentenced prisoners say that they have lost contact with their family as a result of going into prison' (Home Office 2004b: 37). The impact on women is often especially acute and traumatic – not only for them but also for their children (*ibid.* and Ministry of Justice 2008b). Wedge (2007: 39) refers to 'separation, stigma, loss of family income, reduced quality of care, poor explanation given to children, and children's modelling of their parents' behaviour' and to associations with children's subsequent misbehaviour and offending. Yet despite the recognition of the impact on children of the imprisonment of their parent(s), emphasised in the Action Plan and (powerfully) in the Corston Report 2007, it is by no means clear that sentencing courts take sufficient account of these consequences (Sue King – personal communication).

Interventions on this pathway are most commonly led by the voluntary sector, working with probation, health, education and other services. The achievements of Sure Start have benefited offenders. Some prisons run parenting programmes to support prisoners in their wish to be good parents to their children. Yet generally policy and practice in this area receive less attention than they merit. Personal relationships are central to most people's conception of a 'good life' and regularly feature in individuals' accounts of desistance – especially intimate relationships with partners and/or children (see Chapter 9; McNeill and Maruna 2007).

Attitudes, thinking and behaviour

These are principally addressed through the offending behaviour programmes already discussed at the beginning of this chapter.

Reporting as instructed

Perhaps the most common experience of all is too readily overlooked – the regular reporting required of offenders. Burnett *et al.* (2007: 221) suggest that: 'The concept of 'supervision' in this model [*sc.* OMM] is reserved for day-to-day contact intended to encourage the supervisee's compliance and motivation.' Yet what takes place on these occasions is not well researched.

The offender manager or supervisor should be actively involved in coordinating the more structured interventions we have been considering so far and supporting the offender in making sense of it all. A potential misunderstanding is that the offender manager will assess, make the referral and then may step back, as it were, with no active role in the intervention. But Mann (2007) identifies strong offender management as a factor critical to the success of interventions. Roberts (2004) emphasises the vital role of the case manager in supporting attendance at pro-grammes and in helping offenders to apply the inevitably generalised lessons from programmes to their own particular circumstances. Such work exploits an inherent advantage that community-based programmes have over those delivered in prison – that the community offers 'real life' opportunities to put learning into practice, to rehearse, to reflect and to consolidate the learning.

Contacts with probation should no doubt try to achieve this, as well as reviewing developments, looking for and eliciting indications of changes to risk factors, all being done in a motivational and pro-social manner. But these encounters can often be brief and perhaps cursory – often some 15 minutes (BBC 2009). At worst, it can be reduced to a routine 'signing in' that Bailey (1995) found was resented by offenders and taken as a sign of probation's indifference. This must detract from motivation and the offender's engagement as well as compromising the opportunities for personal relationships on which so much good work depends. At best, routine reporting may be experienced as a continuing involvement and interest in the offender, but this is an aspect of the work that is potentially compromised by workload pressure and greater interest and investment in more structured interventions.

Some reflections on interventions

Several questions arise from this brief review of interventions. Should there be a separate provision of services for offenders? The aspiration should be to enable offenders to access services as do other members of the community. The provision of separate 'services for offenders' already looks like a bad start to social inclusion. Probation's usual task should be to work with service providers to encourage and advise them about any distinctive obstacles that offenders experience in accessing their services. Specific provision is better considered as a fall back where ordinary services are inaccessible or otherwise inappropriate. Provision should be on the basis of need, not the status of being 'an offender'.

The Asha Women's Centre in Worcester is a 'one stop shop' for women 'who are isolated by disadvantage to gain access to the resources which they need to help them address their problems and achieve their social and economic potential' (http://www.ashawomen.org.uk/). Probation played a major role in helping to establish the centre and offending behaviour work is available, but services and resources are designed less around interventions for offending than to facilitate social opportunities and effective community linkage (Roberts 2002).

What are interventions trying to achieve? A conventional objective is reduced reoffending, but some kinds of provision – for example around physical health or emotional well-being – seem intrinsically valuable and a failure to demonstrate an association with reduced convictions should not detract from its worth. Probation has a valuable role in enabling service providers to identify and gain access to some of their most excluded and needy clients. In general, partners should not see their work with offenders as a contribution to 'the work of probation/NOMS', but as a way of fulfilling their responsibility – to provide accommodation, employment, health care, etc. – for vulnerable groups, as a matter of social justice and equity. It is hoped, of course, that reduced reoffending will result and the pathways were identified precisely because of their associations with offending. At the same time, since all providers are likely to be required to demonstrate the effects of their work, it will be necessary to be clear about the expected benefits of some types of intervention and these should not always depend on (usually uncertain and often contestable) effects on reconviction.

Interventions can enable people to acquire the skills they need to change. But as McNeill insists 'offenders need *motivation* to change, *capacity* to be and to act differently and *opportunities* to do so. All three features need to be present for change to occur' (2009: 38 emphasis in original). The availability of opportunities is something that probation can influence to no more than a limited extent: the socio-economic order will determine if a society enables its members to thrive. Similarly principles like social integration call not only for change in the offender, but a society willing to accept and accommodate those of its members who have committed offences – for example, employers who will not unfairly discriminate on the basis of a criminal record. The very idea of pathways potentially constitutes a restatement of probation's traditional mission of advocating on offenders' behalf, of encouraging society to meet its responsibilities to offenders, not just to affirm their rights against them. This is a view that punitive strategies find it uncomfortable to articulate.

Review and evaluation

ASPIRE's final phase is *review and evaluation*, although in a cyclical model the process may begin again with further work to be done.

Dispassionate, systematic and rigorous evaluation is a mark of sincerity of purpose. Any profession that aspires to be 'evidence-led' must ensure that it seeks out, interprets, collates and learns from the consequences of its practices. One type of evaluation tries to discover whether intended purposes have been achieved (see generally Merrington and Hine 2001). Rejecting the contemporary conceit that probation has only recently discovered the importance of reflecting on the significance and consequences of its work, Merrington and Stanley (2007) map instructively changing conceptions of probation's purpose over time against the types of evidence that have been sought to gauge its effects. Yet probation typically sets several purposes, not all of which may be assumed to fit together easily. Moreover what probation expresses, the values which it attempts to realise in its work, what it says as well as what it does are all important, though not easily captured through usual methods of evaluation.

Evaluating the individual case

The aggregates and averages of research into effective practice shed little light on evaluation of the individual case. How is such evaluation to be conducted? Merrington and Hine (2001: 6.5) suggest:

> The case record final assessment should allow the possibility of drawing together the following threads for an overall evaluation of the case:

- compliance (attendance and completion)
- overall assessment of needs and risk, and change since start of supervision
- specific interventions and evidence of change related to them
- offender feedback on the experience and impact of supervision
- any further offending and prospects for the future.

But while all these threads are significant, none is straightforward to evaluate.

Compliance will be explored more fully in the following chapter. There we shall encounter the difficulty of determining what counts as compliance. Does formal compliance (Robinson and McNeill 2008) – keeping (enough) appointments – constitute a sufficient fulfilment of the court's order? Or is more required, for example a sincere attempt to 'address offending behaviour'? Evaluation can more readily deal with auditable episodes – attendance – than with more elusive ideas like *working hard to stay straight*, although these must be quite as important.

Comparing *needs and risks* at the end of supervision with the initial assessment is also relevant. But Chapter 7 raised some of the complications in gauging the reliability of such assessments. If someone now ranks their drinking as a serious problem, when it was not so identified earlier on, does this count as a deterioration? Or as progress in the cycle of change and in their trust in the assessor? It is also possible that an individual's life circumstances may have deteriorated in ways that cannot reasonably be attributed to shortcomings in supervision – and indeed may have been even worse, but for the timely support of probation.

Rather than await an outcome that may or may not occur over a follow-up period, evidence of a programme's effects can be investigated through psychometric tests, which attempt to assess attitudes believed to be associated with the propensity to offend. The CRIME-PICS II Manual (Frude *et al.* 2009), for example, gauges attitudes and changes in offending-related problems.

Again, *specific interventions* may have taken place, but these are neither necessary (some people will change without their benefit) nor sufficient (some will not benefit whatever the quality of intervention) to bring about change. Interventions are typically just one component in the overall implementation of the sentence plan and just one element (often a modest one) within the changes in someone's life. It can be difficult to disentangle the several factors that have influenced the offender in the relevant period. Again, some changes are easier to identify than others.

Offender feedback has been extensively used, although the extent to which it is structured (for example, through an 'exit interview') varies, as does the way in which the findings from such interviews are collated and used to guide practice. Some officers may be more assiduous than others in eliciting such feedback. Should the feedback be taken by an independent person – a colleague who has not been involved in supervision, perhaps, or even someone outside the organisation? In any case, some of the most important aspects of probation work – the extent to which the individual has felt respected and dealt with fairly, quality of relationship, encouragement, provision of accessible opportunities – cannot be captured (or at least cannot be understood) by reconviction or other 'measures'. They can at best be elicited through careful attention to the individual's responses. Offenders view the opportunity to give feedback very positively (Will Hughes – personal communication) and often say that such opportunities have been all too rare.

No less importantly, some of the effects of probation may be delayed but enduring (Farrall and Calverley 2006). Work may have raised possibilities that will only be realised later on. Challenges to attitudes may have given rise to resistance or resentment at the time, but may nevertheless be valuable – and their value may in time come to be seen by the offender personally. Sometimes, 'over time, impacts become stronger' (Farrall and Calverley 2006: 66) – an insight which calls into question the type and timescale of much evaluative research.

The litmus test of effectiveness is usually taken to be *further offending*, during and perhaps in a follow-up period after supervision. But desistance – stopping offending and staying stopped – is better seen as a process than an event, often marked by lapse and relapse on 'a zig-zag path' (for example Bottoms *et al.* 2004). There is a need, then, for more nuanced methods of evaluation – too simple to see reconviction as a failure, its absence as success.

The effectiveness of an intervention is usually assessed by looking to see if there have been any convictions within a period at risk following that intervention. Note that reconviction is not the same as reoffending (and indeed some types of offence have a much lower 'clear-up' rate than others). It must also be relevant to consider:

- the seriousness of any further offence (perhaps there has been another conviction, but for a much less [or maybe much more] serious offence);
- the number of further offences (presumably several offences should be considered more of a failure than just one);
- the intervals between offences (for some people longer periods of time without offending represents real progress).

Not all evaluations capture these considerations, although some can. 'What works?' is not a matter of yes-or-no, but rather of more-or-less.

It will be at the point of evaluation that the virtue of SMART objectives (Chapter 7) will become apparent: the SMARTer, the easier it will be to see if they have been achieved. Sometimes it may be possible to see that objectives *have* been met, although the more usual experience, perhaps, is that there has been progress towards some objectives and less or none towards others. Where objectives have not been met – or incompletely met – what can be learnt? Perhaps the objectives were inappropriate or were superseded by other developments in the individual's life. The extent to which objectives have been met is certainly worth gauging, then, but the implications for the individual and for future work will still need to be interpreted, shared and negotiated. Again, concentration on the fulfilment of intended consequences can distract attention from other consequences – unintended and maybe unforeseeable, whether good or bad. The capacity of criminal justice interventions to generate unanticipated and perverse outcomes is notorious (Canton 2010a).

Farrow *et al.* (2007) offer many insightful thoughts about the importance of ending well. This should not only involve evaluation in the usual sense, but include working through some *what ifs* with the individual, including anticipation of relapse and 'contingency plans'. The final evaluation should also attend to the quality of the practitioner's work – a contribution to their continuing professional development which probation perhaps insufficiently exploits.

What works?

Offending behaviour programmes are typically evaluated in terms of their reconviction rates – comparing actual rates with those that an OGRS score would anticipate. What does the evidence tell us now? There are a number of authoritative recent reviews (see Further Reading) in which there is often a tone of disappointment, although it is not always clear whether the disappointment is with the outcomes of the programmes, the amount and adequacy of the research, or more particularly the extent to which the research strategies have been able to capture the programmes' effects. Moreover, the extent to which findings are viewed as a disappointment depends upon what might reasonably have been expected. That said, the demonstrable and marked reduction in anticipated rates of reoffending that policy makers hoped for have probably not been achieved – though maybe this was never a reasonable expectation in the first place.

Research has made some useful discoveries. Raynor (2004a) notes that programmes that had encouraging outcomes in a pilot stage, once 'rolled out', often fail to achieve such impressive results: the enthusiasm of the staff who were involved in the first programmes, their commitment to and understanding of a new programme may not be carried across when the programme is delivered elsewhere. Other contextual factors – staff training, committed leadership, targeting (making sure the right people attend), resourcing and the support of offender managers – can make a decisive difference. The success or failure of programmes is probably powerfully influenced by interaction among all these factors, as well as by the personal characteristics of those who participate in the programmes. The context of implementation is therefore receiving more considered attention than it did in the first heady days of *what works*. The volatile political environment and the radical organisational changes in probation that have coincided with the period of implementation also seem likely to have had unsettling effects (Raynor 2006; Stanley 2009).

One finding that seems quite robust is that people who complete programmes do better in terms of reconviction than those who begin and drop out. For that matter, these 'non-completers' do worse than matched control/comparison groups: arguably to begin and not complete is worse than nothing (Raynor 2004a). This finding exposes some of the complexity of interpreting results. Plausibly, those who complete programmes are those who are best motivated, have personal circumstances that are sufficiently settled to get them to sessions, probably have the benefit of involved and active offender managers and so on. But is it any surprise that it is these people who show lower rates of reconviction? There is always the problem of isolating one factor as influential among the many that obtain – not just interventions but everything else that is going on in someone's life – including (perhaps especially) their own resolve to desist.

Like any other evaluation of sentencing outcomes, interpretation is complicated by selection effects – the characteristics of offenders receiving different sentences differ greatly and these characteristics (for example, age, gender, previous convictions) appear to have much more influence on subsequent offending than do the sentences themselves. Further 'selections' take place when probation staff make decisions about who should participate in programmes, who should be 'breached' in response to non-compliance (and will probably then not complete) and so forth. Some researchers seem to regret that *random controlled trials* seem rarely achievable (Harper and Chitty 2005), although others (Stanley 2009) doubt that such trials would disclose what we most need to find out.

Even if we could establish confidently *that* some intervention 'works', the reasons for this may still be unclear. Meta-analysis cannot yield this type of understanding. Equally, there may be several reasons why an intervention fails to work (for example, poor implementation, wrong offenders) quite apart from any shortcomings in the conception of the programme itself. Qualitative inquiry into processes, self-report (from offenders and practitioners) and the observations of others are also necessary complements to meta-analysis. We need to know not only *that* an intervention works, but also *how*. This understanding is a precondition of development and enhancement.

Meanwhile, strong confidence in RNR is still expressed (Andrews and Bonta 2010) and Stanley (2009) insists that there are positive results associated with completion of programmes that should not be disregarded. This is surely right. Even so, it seems implausible that there is (or could be) a straightforward cause and effect relationship between intervention and reduced reoffending. Some who would regard the quest to discover 'the cause' (or even 'the causes') of crime as naïve and misconceived still seem to think that there may be causes of desistance. In the next chapter we will see that the process of desistance typically involves living a life in which offending has no place and this requires opportunities, as well as the motivation and skills to take advantage of them. These cannot be provided by offending behaviour programmes alone.

Summary

In this chapter, we have continued discussion of the ASPIRE model by reviewing implementation and the interventions that probation may facilitate. There has then been consideration of review and evaluation, ending with a short summary of what research into effectiveness may now be telling us. Behaviour and change can usefully be seen as a function of motivation (people do what they *want* to do), within the constraints of what they are *able* to do, but also of the *opportunities* open to them (Canton 2007; McNeill 2009). Interventions concentrate on skills and abilities – skills of thinking and reasoning, problem-solving, social skills, educational and employment-related skills. But without opportunities to thrive, the potential to desist will not be realised. None of this is to devalue the achievements of the last ten years and it is essential to continue and enhance interventions. People need skills and motivation to navigate the world however they find it, but a world of social inclusion and fair opportunities is needed to support the process of desistance.

Questions

- If many general offending behaviour programmes require linguistic skills that many participants simply lack, what are the implications for the probation service?
- Does the provision of discrete 'services for offenders' just aggravate their social exclusion?
- How should interventions with substance users be evaluated? Is their primary purpose to minimise the harm associated with substance use? Or to reduce usage? Or to bring about fewer reconvictions?

Further reading

For a sound and insightful review of contemporary interventions, see Robinson and Crow (2009). Recent appraisals of what evidence is now telling us about what works include Raynor (2004a); Harper and Chitty (2005); McGuire (2007); Merrington and Stanley (2007); Stanley (2009); Raynor and Robinson (2009).

9 Desistance, good lives, relationships, compliance

In the last three chapters, we have seen that contemporary probation has been dominated by the risks, needs and responsivity (RNR) model. In this chapter, other perspectives are considered – ones that propose different starting points and other ways of understanding the processes of personal change, with implications for the way in which probation can work with these processes. Sometimes these perspectives can complement the RNR model, but at other times they pose challenges to it.

The *good lives model*, with its origins in the study of desistance, is first discussed. This challenges RNR while accommodating many of its insights and achievements. This model reaffirms the value of the professional relationship between probation officer and client – something that RNR lost sight of, perhaps, but is now increasingly recognising as indispensable to offender engagement, supporting change and bringing about compliance (Burnett and McNeill 2005). Other insights into human behaviour, marginalised by the dominance of cognitive behaviourism, are next discussed. The importance of emotions is considered. The chapter concludes with a discussion of compliance, without attention to which the very viability of community supervision must be in question.

Desistance and good lives

The study of desistance has become increasingly prominent in Anglo-American criminology. Criminology has often centred on questions like: what is different about offenders? What are the reasons why people offend? But maybe there is nothing so very different about offenders. There are many explanations of why and how people come to start offending, all arguable and inconclusive. Bluntly, the reasons are not known and the chances are that even if they were known, nothing much could be done about them anyway – not at least through the mechanisms of criminal justice.

Desistance studies begin by recognising that quite a lot is known about the circumstances in which people come to *stop* offending and how this desistance is sustained. Accounts (see Further Reading) typically begin with the *age crime curve* – the graph that shows clearly that convictions tend to become much less numerous as people get older. Ward and Maruna (2007: 154) suggest that perhaps

85 per cent of repeat offenders will have desisted by age 28.) But as Weaver and McNeill (2007: 90) put it:

> Age indexes a range of different variables, including biological changes, social and normative transitions (and the associated social meanings ascribed to them), life experiences, the impact of social or institutional processes, and internal factors such as motivation or attitudinal change. Age in itself is not, therefore, the explanation.

Getting older is for many people associated with acquiring social ties and commitments – family (including parenthood) and other personal relationships, employment and other social bonds – that offer legitimate opportunities, leading to lifestyles in which opportunities and motivation to offend have no place and bringing compelling reasons to 'go straight'. The informal social controls exercised by partners, friends, employers, colleagues and which arise spontaneously from living full lives are a much more compelling inducement to good behaviour than the external controls of criminal justice. (An influential criminological theory – control theory – explains connections between offending and such 'social bonds'. See Newburn 2007: Chapter 11.)

Yet desistance research suggests that propitious life circumstances are not sufficient: it is how these circumstances and events are understood, interpreted and incorporated into ideas of self (Maruna 2000; McNeill 2003). A distinction has been made between 'primary' desistance – stopping offending – and 'secondary' desistance, where the individual comes to see her/himself no longer as an offender but as a different kind of person, ceasing to regard crime an option for excitement or as a likely response to difficulties (Weaver and McNeill 2007 and references there cited).

Why do 'we' not offend? Perhaps we do – probably the great majority of people commit a crime at some point in their lives (Karstedt and Farrall 2007). Still 'most of us' do not go through life battling our criminogenic needs and risk factors. For example, it seldom occurs to us to take things that don't belong to us and, if it does, we are immediately checked by the thought that this would be stealing. We are not offenders: this is not what we do. It is this way of understanding ourselves that is incorporated in the idea of secondary desistance.

Such changes in self-identity feature prominently in individuals' accounts of their desistance (Maruna 2000; Farrall and Calverley 2006). Desistance depends on how people react to external opportunities and circumstances – or, better, how they *interact* with them, making opportunities and recognising developments as opportunities. A sense of *agency*, acting and accomplishing, self-determination and a concern (and responsibility) for others are all typical components of a desisting self-identity. The self-identity is constructed and sustained by a narrative, an 'internal moral conversation' (Vaughan 2007), that comprehends past offending even as it disavows it in affirming a very different future.

Offenders are not 'moral strangers' (Ward and Maruna 2007: 125): their aspirations are the same human goods as others', though the means they choose are inappropriate and distorted. Working with offenders involves helping them to develop legitimate means of achievement. People typically desist by coming to live *good lives* (Ward and Brown 2004; Ward and Maruna 2007), their criminogenic needs and risks transcended by ways of living in which crime increasingly has no place.

Insights from desistance studies and some implications for probation

Among the insights these perspectives bring are:

1   The importance of social capital – cognitive behavioural interventions *by themselves* are not (could not be) enough (Farrall and Calverley 2006). People need opportunities to acquire and sustain lives that will transcend their offending behaviour. The relationships and social bonds involved depend not only upon individuals' abilities and motivation, but also on the availability of opportunities – a function of the socio-political order beyond the reach of criminal justice practices. Nor have the most eloquent proponents of RNR ever claimed otherwise. McGuire (2005) rightly rejects a false opposition between the personal and the social: cognitive behaviourism fully acknowledges the relevance of context; equally, desistance perspectives recognise the value of interventions to enhance abilities and skills to take advantage of opportunities and probation's role in encouraging and motivating.

2   Attention to offenders' own accounts – what they have found to be incentives and obstacles to desistance, what they experience as more and less valuable in their dealings with probation (Maruna 2000; Farrall and Calverley 2006). Much of the criminological tradition treats offenders as objects rather than subjects, inquiring into the 'causes' of their behaviour. But normally we approach an understanding of human behaviour not through causes but through reasons and by attending to the meanings with which individuals invest their behaviour (Canton and Yates 2008). Since self-identity and 'narrative' are central to the process of sustaining desistance, offenders' perceptions become the start and focus of working to support change.

3   The central place of relationships – offenders often speak of the value of a probation officer's practical help in identifying and resolving obstacles to desistance, but especially emphasise the sense of personal interest and concern, of partnership and cooperation (Farrall 2002). Probationers refer to a sense of loyalty and personal commitment that helped them to go straight (Rex 1999). Personal encouragement – the *pull of hope* (Chapter 5), together with fairness and openness – can be powerfully influential. Authority and challenge, disagreement and even conflict are part of this too, but the relationship is sustained by a recognition that there is a genuine concern for and interest in her/him as a person.

4   A challenge to research – *what works* has usually been evaluated in terms of reconviction within a specified time period, but this (in itself) fails to illuminate *how it works* – a significant constraint on the development of

innovative practice. Desistance studies attempt to redress this. Most empirical studies recognise desistance not as an event, but as sustained process – one that may involve 'drifts' in and out of offending (Matza 1964), with lapse and relapse (compare the cycle of change – Chapter 5). Again, as we saw in the last chapter, Farrall and Calverley (2006) insist on a longer timescale within which to assess the influence of work which may have an impact much later on – for instance the words of a probation officer becoming incorporated into a slowly but steadily developing desistance narrative. Desistance studies offer a different understanding of the process of change, an awareness of the possibility of reoffending along the path to desistance and the contribution of probation (Bottoms *et al.* 2004).

Desistance approaches, then, have considerable implications for probation, offering a new paradigm for practice (McNeill 2006). Table 9.1 sets out the difference between RNR and a desistance paradigm.

These approaches urge a reframing of some of the questions and assumptions of RNR, arguing that it:

- pays insufficient attention to individuals' strengths;
- is preoccupied with aversive goals, whereas approach goals constitute stronger motivation;
- concentrates on the techniques of what works (with the implications that change is a process led by intervention), rather than an offender-led process which probation should support;
- over-emphasises the past that the individual needs to disavow, by attending all the time to past patterns of offending;
- neglects *how* the process of change occurs;
- leads to risk management strategies that can tend to increase risk through a conception of risk that neglects social context and circumstances and through stigmatising and exclusionary approaches (Chapter 10).

Table 9.1 Differences between RNR and a desistance paradigm

'What works'/RNR model	*Desistance paradigm*
Intervention required to reduce re-offending and protect the public	Help in navigating towards desistance to reduce harm and make good to offenders and victims
'Professional' assessment of risk and need governed by structured assessment instruments	Explicit dialogue and negotiation, assessing risks, needs, strengths and resources and offering opportunities to make good
Compulsory engagement in structured programmes and case management processes as required elements of legal orders imposed irrespective of consent	Collaboratively defined tasks which tackle risks, needs and obstacles to desistance by using and developing the offender's human and social capital

Excerpt from McNeill (2006: 56)

Pathways to desistance may not be assumed to be the same for women as for men (Rumgay 2004). McIvor *et al.* (2004) found that in many respects processes of desistance are the same, although women and men speak of different incentives to desist and express them differently. This, perhaps, is what the good lives model might lead us to expect: there are likely to be many and different conceptions of a good life, varying with structure, culture and personal biography; yet, the consolidation of an identity in which offending has no place is likely to be common to all.

Relationship

Cognitive behaviourism in probation arguably lost sight of relationship. Reflecting on the value of trust and mutually respectful relationships, Robinson and Raynor (2006: 342) insist that, at its best:

> 'What Works' developments are full of similar ideas: for example, the use of 'Socratic questioning' to challenge people to think for themselves, and the development of skills and motivation to help people to overcome obstacles and take charge of their own lives. These are in reality far more human and collaborative processes than are conjured up by the technocratic language of 'interventions' and 'offender management'.

Yet, as implemented in the context of managerial imperatives and the political priorities of punishment and control, such processes often seem reduced to formal if not bureaucratic techniques.

From a range of perspectives, however, the critical importance of relationships has more recently been reasserted (Burnett and McNeill 2005). A milestone in research here was a meta-analysis undertaken by two of RNR's most influential proponents: Dowden and Andrews (2004) stressed the principles of 'core correctional practice' as:

- the firm, fair and clear use of authority;
- modelling pro social and anti-criminal attitudes, cognition and behaviours;
- teaching concrete problem-solving skills;
- using community resources (brokerage);
- (and, 'arguably the most important' component) forming and working through warm, open and enthusiastic relationships.

These principles are emphasised in the offender management model (Chapter 7) and have encouraged a strong contemporary interest in 'offender engagement'.

The value of relationships

Probationers I interviewed seemed aware of the efforts required to *sustain* a decision to stop offending, efforts on which they were more willing to embark where they felt committed to and positively engaged in the supervisory process.

(Rex 1999: 371)

The fifth and final component of CCP (Core Correctional Practice), relationship factors, is also arguably the most important.

(Dowden and Andrews 2004: 205)

The supervision process begins with the establishment of relationships and the effectiveness of every subsequent part of the process will depend in part on the quality of the relationship, though good relationships alone will not be enough to bring about change.

(McNeill *et al.* 2005: 39)

the main impact of the correctional services is considered to arise from the personal relationships developed with an offender.

(NOMS 2006: 12)

[principles that must inform practice include] the centrality of human relationships to the process of change

(Farrow, Kelly and Wilkinson 2007: 9)

the quality of the relationship between offender and worker is pivotal to effective intervention

(Ansbro 2008: 232)

the relationship in itself is a tool that can effect change . . . the quality of the rapport is in itself an instrument of intervention.

(*ibid.*: 241)

Staff should be selected partly on their ability and potential to build high quality relationships with a difficult clientele and then be given training that further enhances these skills.

(Andrews and Bonta 2010: 50)

Probation agencies shall aim to reduce reoffending by establishing positive relationships with offenders . . .
(Council of Europe 2010: European Probation Rules: Basic Principle 1)

Establishing a positive relationship between the helping professional and the client appears central to many theories of therapeutic change.

(Bonta *et al.* 2010: 15)

This calls for a much more attentive and assertive inquiry into offender perceptions. The 'user voice' is being heard more often (Aldridge Foundation 2008) and there is a major research initiative, the Offender Management Community Cohort Study, to investigate the experiences of offenders under supervision (National Centre for Social Research n.d.).

Some factors common to all well-delivered therapeutic interventions – warmth, empathy, engagement, congruence, therapeutic alliance, fairness, encouragement – seem more valued by clients and more efficacious than the specific characteristics of any particular method (McNeill *et al.* 2005). Ross *et al.* (2008: 477) conclude that 'The therapeutic alliance between a therapist and client is a vital part of therapy and treatment outcome' and explore some of the complexities of creating such an alliance.

Other ways of understanding people can complement – and sometimes challenge – the theoretical dominance of cognitive behaviourism. Fleet and Annison (2003), for example, set out some specific ways of working with offenders – including crisis intervention and solution-focused approaches (see also Cherry 2005, 2007b). These approaches can contribute to the effective engagement which is a precondition of any useful subsequent work and/or represent feasible and pragmatic responses to pressing problems of living – around income, accommodation, employment – that cannot wait for the benefits of a sustained and sequenced programme. Indeed it can be precisely through patient and respectful assistance in times of distress that a relationship is built.

Some of the concepts of psychoanalysis illuminate the ways in which relationships are formed and sustained Smith (2006). It is not that psychotherapy is being presented as a competing paradigm to CB, but it is a reminder that theories (other than CB) can offer ways of understanding and working with troubled people with complex needs, as well as making sense of the interaction between practitioner and client. What psychotherapeutic approaches emphasise, too, is the indispensable importance of understanding and working with *emotion*.

In summary, attention to relationship, stimulated by the good lives model, suggests that the client should (and probably will in any case) determine the direction and pace of therapeutic intervention and is, in these respects, uniquely placed to assess the value of their involvement with probation. When asked what is valued, clients often refer to the personal relationship as influential in engagement and in supporting change in their own lives.

Feelings: the missing side of the triangle?

In Chapter 6, the cognitive-behavioural triangle was introduced – a graphic representation of the mutual influence among thoughts, feelings and behaviour (see Fig. 6.2). But most of the interventions that have been considered so far attempt to modify behaviour by influencing cognition – the thoughts associated with patterns of behaviour. What happened to the third side of the triangle? While the role of feelings is theoretically acknowledged, their place in CB interventions has received much less attention.

Knight (forthcoming) emphasises the value of *emotional literacy* in probation practice. By emotional literacy is here meant the ability to be aware of one's own feelings, the feelings of others and the effects these have, not least their effects on the working relationship. It includes too the ability to work with emotions constructively and to deploy them for therapeutic benefit. Many of the emotions that offenders may feel are dysfunctional – for example, fear, anger, resentment, despair – and can interfere with processes of change. The worker's own feelings can also inhibit the therapeutic alliance and, especially when unacknowledged, find inappropriate expression with unhelpful consequences for an effective working relationship.

Motivational work is a conspicuous example of the need for emotional literacy: the practitioner must recognise the client's feelings and the effects upon her/him of the practitioner's words and behaviour. Another example is pro-social modelling, which Cherry (2007a: 243) defines as:

> The process by which the practitioner engages the offender in an empathetic relationship within which they actively reinforce pro-social behaviour and discourage anti-social behaviour and attitudes particularly by acting as a good, motivating role model.
>
> (Trotter 1999, 2007; Cherry 2005)

The influence here depends as much or more on the practitioner's behaviour as on their words and the level at which people's behaviour has its influence is the emotional level. Again, the active reinforcement of 'pro-social' behaviour calls for praise and encouragement, but knowing when and how to praise, when to be optimistic and when to allow someone to express their unhappiness and confusion, calls for emotional awareness. In giving praise, for example, it is emotional literacy that makes the difference between effective encouragement and being patronising: without emotional literacy pro-social modelling is at risk of becoming (and being seen as) no more than a manipulative technique.

Empathy is fellow-*feeling*; emotions are central to relationships. CB accommodates this theoretically, but the influence of this insight is much less apparent in probation policy and practice. Practitioners of course do develop and deploy their emotional skills, but this is insufficiently valued and discussed in the theories and policies of probation. The emotional can indeed be viewed with suspicion: to be emotional is the antithesis of professionalism. Assessment must be objective, untainted by emotion. But emotion is always operative and its disavowal is a denial, a failure to acknowledge – and thus to deal with – these feelings.

In Chapter 10 the technical and procedural issues of the assessment and management of *risk* will be considered. Reviews commonly attribute serious further offences to failure to follow guidelines, to staff bearing responsibilities beyond their role competence or experience, to heavy workloads. But when we ask questions like *how could they have been so careless/thoughtless/remiss?* do we give sufficient attention to the emotional dimensions of working in complex contexts? Dangerous offenders are disturbing, their behaviour can be demanding, unpleasant and threatening. The possibility of having to challenge and confront them, however professionally necessary, raises anxieties and fears in those who work with them, making it easier to deny some possibilities than to envisage and deal with them (Prins 1999; Tuddenham 2000). Emotional literacy is therefore central to the assessment and management of risk.

Compliance

Studies of relationships and offenders' perceptions have refreshed the debate about compliance with community penalties. Compliance is a long-standing problem in probation work. An unenforced community penalty is indistinguishable from 'getting away with it'. Probation has a duty to give effect to the orders of the court and can achieve none of its purposes without the offender's attendance and participation. Yet community penalties require people to do things – to keep appointments as instructed, to participate in (or refrain from) activities, to work – which they might otherwise choose not to do. This creates the possibility of default.

As probation strives to establish itself as a 'credible' punishment (Chapter 5), trying to demonstrate its punitive credentials to a sceptical public, enforcement is ever more politically salient (Hedderman and Hough 2004). The more that is asked, the greater the potential for default. The combination of greater demands and more rigorous enforcement is likely to entail more breach proceedings and, at least potentially, larger numbers of offenders sent to prison in response (Canton and Eadie 2005).

Enforcement has reassuringly 'tough' connotations that satisfy proponents of a punitive strategy. Policy has been ever more prescriptive about responses to default, with a reliance on the threat of breach and return to court. Yet our discussion of motivation (Chapter 6) demonstrates the likely limitations of threat and coercion in bringing about active cooperation. It may be more productive, therefore, to reframe the question and, instead of preoccupation with responses to default, consider carefully what makes offenders most likely to comply.

The debate was given an invaluable change of emphasis and direction by Anthony Bottoms (2001). He identified several dimensions to compliance, as Table 9.2 summarises. Most people in most circumstances certainly take account of the anticipated costs and benefits of their actions (instrumental compliance). Even this is far from straightforward, though: incentives do not always work in quite the expected way (Chapter 4). People do not always reason as the economics textbooks would anticipate: their 'rationality' is bounded and incomplete. Indeed what counts as a cost or a benefit is by no means the same for everyone in all circumstances. Bottoms further distinguishes *constraint-based* compliance – for example, the extent to which conduct is guided or circumscribed by physical restrictions, the 'compliance' brought about by external parameters – and compliance *based on habit and routine* (typically unreflective patterns of conduct, which, for offenders, cognitive behavioural interventions aspire to change).

Most important here is what Bottoms terms *normative* compliance, which itself has a number of aspects. Among these is the idea of attachment – for example,

Table 9.2 Dimensions of compliance

Instrumental/prudential compliance Often people calculate (what they perceive to be) the costs and benefits of different courses of action	a) Incentives b) disincentives	a) What are the incentives for the offender to comply? (and what are the incentives not to comply?) b) are there any disincentives to complying?
Normative compliance Often people are influenced by considerations of right and wrong, supported (or as it may be undermined) by their perception of what other people expect of them	a) Acceptance of/ belief in norm b) attachment leading to compliance c) legitimacy	a) It may be possible to build upon on the offender's normative beliefs to increase compliance. (Compliance as *the right thing to do*) b) Bottoms notes that *attachment* to individuals – families or 'significant others' – can be a factor in securing compliance. The relationship with the probation officer can be influential here c) Individuals must feel that the demands being made upon them are fair and reasonable
Constraint-based compliance Often people do what they do because there are external constraints that make other courses of action inaccessible or impossible	a) Physical restrictions or requirements (natural or imposed) b) restrictions on access to target c) structural constraints	a) For compliance with probation, this is mostly about the management of time and space – accessibility, transport, timing of appointments, attention to practical obstacles etc.
Compliance based on habit or routine Often people do what they do . . . because that's just what they do	Much compliance is routine and unreflective	CB links altered ways of thinking link with altered behaviour. Programmes attempt to influence this aspect of compliance

Adapted from Bottoms (2001: 90)

'attachment' to someone who demonstrates concern for and personal interest in the offender may promote compliance. This highlights the value of relationship: it can be a sense of obligation and loyalty to a probation officer that brings a reason to cooperate and indeed to go straight (Rex 1999). Smith (2006: 371) speaks of the potential of 'the quality of the relationship with the supervising officer, if he or she becomes someone whom the offender would rather not let down, and whose good opinion the offender values and wishes to keep'.

A further aspect of normative compliance is *legitimacy*. People are more likely to comply with expectations of them and to accept decisions – *even decisions that go against their own wishes* – when they are persuaded that these are fair (have been fairly arrived at) and reasonable (Tyler 2003). This implies explanation, dialogue and negotiation with the offender about how the court's Order is to be fulfilled. It also implies respect for diversity, the right 'to be treated not as a composite offender but as fully human, socially and culturally differentiated offender' (Gelsthorpe 2007: 301).

The challenge in practice is to make these different aspects of compliance work together. Enforcement policy has tended to limit itself by concentrating on the single, instrumental dimension of threat. Assuming that non-compliance must be a result of recalcitrance or back-sliding, insufficient attention has been paid to the complexity and ambivalence of motivation. Yet probation practice has acquired a sophisticated understanding of motivation (Chapter 6). The cycle of change, for instance, recognises that motivation is variable and shifting; the insights of motivational interviewing show that resistance cannot just be suppressed. None of this seems to have had much influence on enforcement policy, which, dominated by punitive and managerial approaches, retained its faith in the efficacy of threat of breach – even though many offenders on supervision have a substantial history of being unresponsive to threats of this kind (Hearnden and Millie 2004; see also Chapter 4 on *deterrence*). Preoccupation with threat may have led to a neglect – perhaps even an undermining – of the possibilities for enhancing compliance through the normative influences of relationship and legitimacy.

There are no doubt many reasons why offenders fail to comply or comply variably with the legal requirements of supervision and, unless supervisors consider the reasons behind non-compliance, their response may simply miss the point or make matters worse. For example, nothing is more demotivating than helplessness – a sense that change is impossible – and if this despondency leads to non-compliance the threat of breach is likely to make things worse. Bonta *et al.* (2010: 15) conclude 'a preoccupation with the conditions of probation, or the enforcement role of the probation officer, presents obstacles to the establishment of a positive relationship and may interfere with the offender's rehabilitation'.

Degrees of compliance

What counts as compliance? Minimally it requires a respect for the formal legal requirements of supervision, but practitioners aspire to more than this, compliance with the spirit as well as the letter. Bottoms (2001) distinguishes between short-term compliance (fulfilling the formal requirements) and the longer-term compliance of desisting from offending. A further distinction is between formal and substantial compliance (Robinson and McNeill 2008). Compare, for example, one offender who unfailingly keeps appointments and resolutely resists or avoids attempts to 'address offending behaviour' with another whose attendance is unreliable but seems genuinely if variably intent on changing their ways. Audits typically miss this distinction, overvaluing simply turning up for appointments (Canton 2008b).

Rigid, unfair or unreasonable responses to non-compliance can lead to further non-compliance and subvert the legitimacy on which longer-term, substantial compliance may depend. Robinson and McNeill (2008: 441) propose:

> to the extent that supervisors and the agencies within which they operate are concerned with longer-term compliance (or desistance from crime), their best hope arguably rests in encouraging compliance mechanisms that allow for the internalization of controls implied in commitment (via beliefs, attachments and eventually the development of new habits and routines) rather than the imposition of constraints or appeals to threats or rewards.

The compliance that probation ultimately seeks *is* desistance. Just as the dimensions of compliance must be made to work together to support the effective implementation of the order of the court, so must they sustain desistance. External incentives, including threats, are weak and contingent, giving reasons not to get caught; probation strives to bring it about that people refrain from offending because they come to see it to be wrong and to have no place in their self-identity.

Finally in this discussion, the 'integrity' and mutually reinforcing character of these conceptually separate dimensions of compliance should be noted. Employment, for example, makes a difference to habits and routines and lifestyles, but also brings informal social controls with both constraint and normative implications. More than this, it changes what people come to regard as a gain or loss – what counts as an instrumental incentive for them. While it can be instructive to separate out these dimensions in discussion, it is the relationship between them that can determine behaviour and promote compliance and desistance.

Good lives and criminal justice strategies

The good lives model is a natural ally of an ethical understanding of criminal justice. A punitive strategy is unlikely to concern itself with the welfare of an offender. The 'othering' of offenders may reject any suggestion that offenders' aspirations have a legitimacy or that they should be helped to achieve them. Emphasis on risk makes it harder to see offenders' 'value as human beings and easier to regard them in rather punitive terms' (Ward and Maruna 2007: 167).

Managerial perspectives tend to envisage technical solutions to non-technical problems. Interventions have an unquestionable value, but desistance studies point to the importance of social capital – opportunities to go straight as well as the motivation and ability to do so.

The ethical strategy embodies recognition of the essential humanity of people who have offended and an awareness that their primary goals and aspirations are usually much the same as those of everybody else.

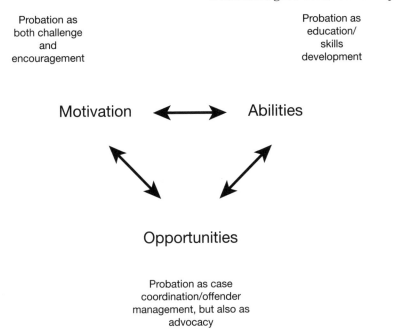

Probation as
both challenge
and
encouragement

Probation as
education/
skills
development

Motivation ⟷ Abilities

Opportunities

Probation as case
coordination/offender
management, but also as
advocacy

Figure 9.1 Behaviour as a function of motivation, abilities and opportunities

Summary

In Chapters 6–9 we have set out an understanding of probation that identifies its role in influencing key determinants of behaviour – motivation, abilities and opportunities. Figure 9.1 shows this as a diagram. The importance of motivation has been emphasised and it has been argued that staff should deploy both challenge and encouragement (both the push of discomfort and the pull of hope) and must develop the emotional literacy to do this wisely and well. The role of interventions, programmes and services can be invaluable in helping people to learn how to manage without offending the problems that beset them, to develop the skills they need to thrive. Yet desistance studies show that motivation and skills may not be sufficient: people need genuine opportunities to develop and to lead lives in which offending has no place. Reintegration implies not only a motivated individual, but also a community willing to believe in the possibility of change and to respect the legitimate interests of ex-offenders.

In this chapter we have discussed the findings from desistance research and considered their implications for probation practice. This perspective by no means involves a rejection of the insights and achievements of RNR, but it does pose challenges to that paradigm. Reflection on the elements of a *good life* reminds us that personal change calls not only for motivation, but also for social capital so that people have fair access to socially inclusive services and genuine opportunities to thrive. The origins of offending are bound up in the social order and responses to it cannot just rely on the mechanisms of criminal justice. Probation has a role here – in advocacy, in the negotiation of access to inclusive services – but the success of its work here will depend on wider socio-economic factors.

Good lives has stimulated the rediscovery of relationships, which offenders often refer to when reflecting on what they found most valuable in their dealings with probation. Discussion of relationships led us to a consideration of emotional literacy: practice cannot be reduced to the technical activity of managing or delivering interventions. The chapter concluded with a discussion of compliance, drawing parallels between some of the insights of desistance studies and discussions of compliance. An ambitious objective for probation practice to keep in view is to bring about long-term compliance with the law and that is what desistance is.

Questions

- Why do 'we' not offend? How big an influence is the threat of punishment?
- Emotional literacy has been argued to be fundamentally important to practice. Is it something that can be taught in training? How?
- What can probation staff do to enhance 'normative compliance'?

Further reading

A very brief introduction to desistance is Weaver and McNeill (2007). This could usefully be followed by McNeill (2003), Maruna (2000), McNeill (2006), Farrall and Calverley (2006). For tensions between desistance approaches and the priorities of contemporary probation, see Farrall (2007). Ward and Maruna (2007) offer a stimulating account of *good lives* and its relationship to RNR. On relationships, McNeill and Burnett (2005) is a good beginning. On emotional literacy, Knight (forthcoming). On compliance, see especially Bottoms (2001) and Robinson and McNeill (2008).

10 Probation, risk and public protection

This chapter considers the role of probation in *public protection*, especially through the assessment and management of risk. Discussions of risk used to be concerned mainly with the identification of a small number of 'dangerous offenders', but risk has now become central to all aspects of probation work. The risk posed by all offenders is now routinely assessed and the outcome of that assessment determines the type and intensity of intervention that will follow. After some discussion about the contemporary significance of risk and approaches to its assessment, we look at probation's work, in partnership with other agencies, with 'high risk offenders', going on to consider how some of the principles established here have been extended to work with other groups of offenders. The chapter will conclude with some reflections on risk in probation, in the wider criminal justice system and the extent to which society has been made safer by these developments.

Public protection and criminal justice

The priority that *the public must be protected* has been a dominant theme in penal policy in recent years (Garland 2001; Loader and Sparks 2002; see also Chapter 1). This has led to a revived interest in the concepts of *risk* and *dangerousness*.[1]

Among the many complex and inter-related reasons for this 'renaissance of dangerousness' (Bottoms 1977) are:

- The 'risk society' – our times are highly 'risk-aware', anxious about the many hazards of 'modernisation': the unforeseen impacts of technological advances and innovations (for example, pollution, the impact of human activity on climate, nuclear waste, the proliferation of weapons of mass destruction). There is a felt need to attempt to understand and control these uncertain threats which increase our sense of vulnerability and risk awareness. This includes heightened sensitivity to the risks posed by some offenders.
- The politics of criminal justice – political parties in many countries have promised to make the public safer, partly through the identification and management of dangerous people.
- The rise of 'alternatives' – the attempt to limit the size of the prison population through the provision of 'alternatives to custody' and systems of early

release sharpens the question about who '*should*' be in prison, to which the conventional answer is: the most persistent and the most serious offenders. *Bifurcation* (Bottoms 2007) refers to policy to reduce levels of punishment for less serious offenders, at the same time increasing them for more serious and dangerous offenders. The thought that dangerous people are in prison brings a sense of reassurance, even if this feeling is often misleading and confuses prevention with mere postponement.

- High profile cases – early release decisions and other aspects of the criminal justice process have been believed to have led to grave crimes. This has become embroiled in the politics of criminal justice.
- 'Targeting' – if resources are limited, it makes sense to concentrate them on people most likely to reoffend seriously. This idea is also supported by 'the risk principle' (see Chapter 6).

Dangerousness

Although largely superseded in operational practice by the discourse of *risk*, the term *dangerousness* still has a powerful resonance in political debate. But what should we understand by this word? To describe someone as dangerous is to attribute to them a disposition or propensity to behave in certain – usually violent – ways (Walker 1980). Even if someone has committed a very serious offence, it would be misleading to describe them as dangerous unless it was believed that they were likely to behave in this manner again. It is to say something about the likelihood of their *future* behaviour, even if such judgements are usually made mostly on the basis of their past.

Dangerousness is an elastic category that stretches as thresholds of tolerance change (Bennett 2008). The term *dangerous offenders* is usually applied selectively – for example, to people thought likely to commit murder, rape and serious assaults. It is less commonly applied to (for example) those who repeatedly drive under the influence of drink and, rarely, to manufacturers who pollute the environment toxically or employers whose neglect of health and safety regulations endangers or leads to the death of their employees or others (Dorling *et al.* 2008). It is becoming more common to recognise that some perpetrators of domestic violence should indeed be described as dangerous, although, again, it is not usually they who are in mind when popular debate agitates about dangerousness. This selective attribution of dangerousness cannot be explained by differences in the levels of harm involved and are best understood as a manifestation of the Power Model (Chapter 1) which allows some to impose their own priorities on the political debate.

To release or detain

Much early research on this topic was concerned with how to determine whether individuals were (no longer or still) dangerous and the associated question of release from prison. (Although the way in which this is discussed has markedly changed, there is still much to be learnt from a revisiting of this early work, notably Bottoms 1977; Walker 1980; Walker 1996). How sound were these assessments of risk? An influential review (Floud and Young 1981) showed that any known method of risk assessment at that time was *either* so restrictive that it failed to identify many people who were really dangerous *or* so 'inclusive' that it brought in many who were not: even the soundest methods would lead to the detention of two people who were *not* dangerous for every dangerous person detained.[2]

Since the factors that determine the soundest actuarial assessments (like OGRS – Chapter 7) are static and immutable, an ascription of dangerousness will become ever harder to cast off. It is scarcely surprising, then, that decision makers 'err on the safe side' (Hood and Shute 2000; Tuddenham 2000). A mistaken judgement that someone is not dangerous leads to (can indeed only be identified by) a crime, often a grave crime that captures the headlines and stands as an accusation against professionals who are held to have made a serious mistake. Detaining people who are not dangerous leads to no such alarming event. Our uncomfortable awareness that detention involves a profound limitation on human rights and impoverishment of life troubles us less than the shock of a grave crime.

But while this early research considered such questions as dangerous or not dangerous, to release or not to release, this is not usually the form in which the problem presents itself to criminal justice practitioners. For example, almost all prisoners are going to be released at some point. The question then becomes *when and in what circumstances will it be safest to release this prisoner?* There is an inevitable concern about releasing offenders who are still believed to pose a risk. But the better approach is to ask: is it safer to release this person now (perhaps under supervision and in reasonably propitious circumstances) than it will be to release them later (perhaps without any supervision and in less promising circumstances)? Equally, when an offender is under supervision in the community, developments may lead to increased concerns, but while a return to court or recall to prison may be considered, the question is commonly *what is to be done to reduce and manage the risks* – a question that does not yield a yes/no, true/false answer.

From dangerousness to risk

The language of *dangerousness* raises hard questions about the assessment and management of people who pose a high risk of harm. Yet the discourse has its limitations: the term *dangerousness* evokes alarm, but prompts no useful ideas about how to respond. Talking of risk, by contrast, as we shall see, challenges us to be more specific and begins to show how problems might be approached and risks reduced.

Yet the language of *risk* can bring its own confusions. Probation in recent years has tried to distinguish between 'risk of reoffending' and 'risk of serious harm', but confusion about the application of these terms persists (Mackenzie 2007). Behind much of this muddle lies a failure to distinguish between the *likelihood* of an offence and the *impact* (harm) of that offence – a distinction blurred in the expression *high risk offenders*. Figure 10.1 tries to clarify this.

The *y* (vertical) axis
is a scale of *impact*, i.e.
the higher on the scale,
the more harmful the
consequences of the
anticipated event

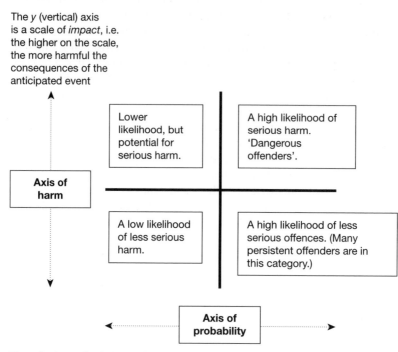

The *x* (horizontal) axis is a scale of *likelihood*: the further along the line, the more *likely*

Figure 10.1 Risk, harm and likelihood

Although the top right quadrant includes the most 'dangerous' people, in many ways it is the top left quadrant that poses the greatest difficulty for assessment and management. Many grave offences have been committed by people whose risk (likelihood) of offending was no greater than medium or low whose assignment to that level of risk had meant that the intensity of supervision was correspondingly medium or low (Craissati and Sindall 2009).

Approaches to assessment

How, then, do probation staff go about assessing the likelihood of further offending? In Chapter 7, we saw how assessment has developed in probation from an unstructured and perhaps idiosyncratic approach into the rigorous and systematic process exemplified by OASys. A powerful influence on these developments was the perception that clinical (person-by-person) assessment is inaccurate and that actuarial instruments are more reliable. It was indeed largely clinical methods that were favoured at the time when risk assessments were found to be so inaccurate.

Actuarial methods are now said to be significantly more accurate than clinical ones (Monahan 2004; Andrews and Bonta 2010). That said, such instruments tend to do less well in anticipating the *seriousness* of a further offence. This is partly because of the low base rate: grave crimes are rare and actuarial techniques struggle to comprehend rare events (see note 2).

But what does 'accuracy' mean in risk assessment? It implies a correspondence between an assessment and an outcome. But *there is no event that an actuarial risk assessment predicts*. While the product of an actuarial risk assessment is often referred to as a *prediction*, then, it is better understood as a probability judgement. A prediction is confirmed or falsified by future events, but the quality of a probability judgement depends rather on the soundness of the probability calculation.

This resolves the paradox that 'successful prediction should actually lead to prevention, and thus prove itself wrong' (Moore 1996: 28). When someone is assessed as high risk, this should lead to a risk management strategy and, where this is successful, the risk will not be realised. If this were *prediction*, it would be wrong – falsified by the outcome; as risk assessment, of course, it is perfectly sound. In short, probation officers do not want to 'predict' serious crimes: they want to do everything they can to reduce the chances of them happening. While the debate would often suggest that *accuracy* is the first virtue of risk instruments, it is in their potential to guide practice to reduce risk that their value truly lies. And here actuarial instruments are substantially limited.

A 'third generation' of assessment instruments tries to reconnect the assessment with the management of risk by combining the actuarial calculations of OGRS with a systematic assessment of dynamic risk factors to guide planning and intervention (Chapter 7). But dynamic risk factors should not be understood as facts to be read off in a straightforward way: they must be elicited and interpreted. This challenge is especially acute for risk assessment, since: 'Many calculations of risk are inevitably made at a crisis point in the management of the case and therefore in the life of the client' (Moore 1996: 5) when levels of anxiety and (sometimes mutual) suspicion are high. In these circumstances, the willingness and ability of people to explore sensitive, crime-related needs may affect the reliability of the information they give and their expressions of intent.

While risk instruments, then, appear to offer a secure anchor in a confusing and sometimes frightening context, their reassurance can be misleading. Best understood as systematic and rational mechanisms to assign people to a level of supervision commensurate with their risk of reconviction, they are sometimes presented as confident anticipations of the future. As Oldfield (2007: 279) writes:

> It is disturbing to find descriptions in pre-sentence reports of offenders, being, for example, of 'Medium Risk of reoffending with a Low-Medium Risk of Serious Harm'. Using such categories to convey information to sentencers seems fraught with interpretive difficulties and also serves to decontextualise the messy reality of life into what, superficially, appear to be 'scientific' categories.

Tuddenham (2000: 174) commends:

> Reflexive risk assessment . . . a dynamic, self-questioning process, which explicitly accepts that knowledge is subject to perpetual revision, and that the

wider social and political context has an influence on the practice of risk assessment and management.

Assessment is a continuing process, but (re)assessment should be more than the iterative administration of an instrument: it calls for perceptiveness, sensitivity and openness to the possibility of change.

This approach to risk assessment is very close to the reflective practice commended by Lord Laming in his review of child protection (2009). The role of supervisors and colleagues in supporting practitioners is especially emphasised. The practitioner's emotional responses – including denial and fear – influence their interpretation and assessment of risk: assessment is much more than a technical and dispassionate process (Moore 1996; Prins 1999; Tuddenham 2000).

Procedure and regulation are always mediated and interpreted by practitioners as they try to apply them to the realities of practice (Robinson and McNeill 2004; see Chapter 15). Tuddenham (2000: 173) reminds us of the need for 'an appreciation of the effect the assessor will have upon the assessment'. As Ballucci (2008: 175) puts it, 'contrary to the belief that risk tools remove the subjective nature of the . . . process, such practices not only still exist but are necessary for risk tools to operate'.

Actuarial instruments treat risk as a property of individuals. Yet even the most dangerous individuals refrain from offending for almost all of the time. Risk is a property of individuals *in* places and circumstances, *at* particular times, *with* other people – offenders and victims – and these entirely unpredictable situational contingencies and interpersonal dynamics are what give rise to serious crimes.

> violence is frequently circumstantial: the capacity to predict violence is likely to be limited by the fact that whether an individual is violent or not will depend on a range of circumstances and contingencies, on a particular constellation of events that are themselves hard to predict.
>
> (Busfield, 2002: 77)

Stealing a car can lead to a death; a burglary can turn into a grave assault. Actuarial approaches rightly insist that risk factors should be reliably correlated with offending, but it is often the combination and interaction of these factors that leads to further offending (see also Craissati and Sindall 2009). All assessment instruments struggle to capture this.

From assessment to management: systematic individual assessment[3]

Another approach to assessment involves a detailed and systematic analysis of the circumstances in which the individual is most likely to reoffend, including an examination of past patterns to try to anticipate and manage these circumstances in future (Scott 1977; Moore 1996; Prins 1999; Tuddenham 2000; Brown 2000). This kind of painstaking and thorough analysis is systematic, so avoiding the potential idiosyncrasies of clinical methods, but is also individualised and directly relevant to attempts to reduce risk. The analysis leads to neither a prediction nor a probability estimate, but conditional propositions – '*If* [these specified circumstances] obtain, violence is more likely . . .', '*Unless* this [safeguard] is in place . . .'. This type of judgement seems just the type of guidance that would be of most value to practitioners attempting to reduce risk in individual cases.

Such an approach exploits one of the advantages that the discourse of risk has over that of dangerousness: it challenges people to be *specific*. To say that someone is dangerous evokes alarm and fear, but does not prompt the necessary questions. Speaking in terms of risk prompts several specific questions, as set out in Table 10.1, which will need to be addressed in order to anticipate and prevent future harm.

Table 10.1 Trying to prevent serious harm: some questions

Who is likely to be harmed?	The offender may pose more of a risk to some person (or people) rather than others
How seriously and in what way?	What exactly is likely to happen in this case? Will the harm be life-threatening?
How soon might this happen?	Some risks are immediate, but some build up, as it were, over a longer period
In what circumstances will it be more, or rather less, likely to occur?	An analysis of the individual's behaviour in the past can illuminate this
What can be done to influence these circumstances?	A review of risk circumstances is a precondition of effective intervention
What is the worst that has previously occurred, and in what circumstances?	The degree and 'quality' of violence in the past (Scott 1977) is important evidence here, though the offender may escalate their violence to a new level
Is there a pattern that can be discovered in the past behaviour or the circumstances that led up to it? If so, is this pattern continuing or recurring?	Appropriately interpreted, patterns of behaviour associated with past offending can inform the risk management plan
What is the individual saying about likely actions? And does the individual want to be stopped?	To what extent can the offender be recruited into the risk management strategy (see below)? Some offenders are much more troubled than others about the likelihood of reoffending
What is the individual indicating?	The offender's behaviour is often valuable evidence as much as their words
What information is there from other sources?	There may be a number of people with knowledge of the offender – not only professionals, but friends and family who may have a strong commitment to preventing the offender from further crime. Good communication and interpretation of relevant information is of course crucial. Many inquiries into serious offences committed by offenders under supervision have pointed to failures of communication (Canton 2005)

This type of analysis is a precondition of effective risk management. Since such considerations have an immediate and obvious relevance to the day-to-day work of managing risk, it is not surprising that practitioners 'fall back' on person-by-person approaches, especially in the hardest cases (Kemshall and Maguire 2001; Robinson 2002).

Summary of key points

- Clinical/person-by-person risk assessment is often said to be inaccurate.
- Statistical/actuarial methods are said to be more accurate, but they yield group probabilities from which the level of an individual's risk may not be inferred.
- Even if such methods could produce an estimate of individual risk, they offer no guidance about how to reduce it.
- Such methods therefore break the required link between risk assessment and risk management.
- Actuarial methods are least reliable in the assessment of the likelihood of serious harm – partly because of the low base rate, i.e. grave crimes are rare.
- A thorough approach involves identifying circumstances in which people have offended in the past and endeavouring to recognise *and influence* these circumstances in the future.
- Risk assessment can never be a technical procedure, but necessarily calls for professional judgement.

Multi-Agency Public Protection Arrangements (MAPPA)

Risk reduction calls for sound inter-agency working (Prins 1999). As Moore (1996: 8) explains:

> One of the most common weaknesses identified in risk assessment is the tendency for it to be carried out by single disciplines, or even individuals. The range of information necessary is rarely to be found within the training and expertise of one profession.

Inter-agency work involves sharing information, collaborative risk assessment and management and the rational deployment of skills and resources to reduce risk. Agencies with their different responsibilities, authority, knowledge, skills and resources should achieve much more in a coordinated endeavour than when working separately (Rumgay 2007).

Multi-Agency Public Protection Arrangements (MAPPA) were set in place to assess and manage the risks posed by the most dangerous offenders. By the late 1990s, many areas had developed inter-agency arrangements and this was formalised by the Criminal Justice and Court Services Act 2000 (ss. 66–68) which placed an obligation on the probation and police services in each area to put arrangements in place to manage 'relevant sexual or violent offender[s]' (Kemshall and Wood 2007a).

The Criminal Justice Act 2003 (s. 325 [1]) brought the Prison Service into these arrangements and the three agencies 'acting jointly' became the designated 'responsible authority'. Other agencies have statutory duties to cooperate: social services, youth offending teams, Jobcentre Plus, local education authorities, local housing authorities, registered social landlords, strategic health authorities, Primary Care Trusts, NHS trusts and electronic monitoring providers.

A comprehensive description of the arrangements may be found in the compendious MAPPA Guidance 2009 Version 3.0 (NOMS 2009). Briefly and broadly (see Hodgett 2007 – on which the following paragraphs draw heavily), arrangements involve: identification of relevant offenders, sharing of information among agencies, assessment of a risk of serious harm and the subsequent management of that risk. Relevant offenders are in three categories:

1   registered sex offenders during their period of registration;
2   other sex offenders and violent offenders, following a term of 12 months imprisonment or longer, and usually for the duration of licence or statutory supervision;
3   other offenders whose offending behaviour suggests a capacity to cause serious harm to the public where the responsible authority reasonably considers that this is likely.

Once a relevant offender has been identified and initially assessed, MAPPA prescribes three levels. (It is to be noted, incidentally, that these levels may not be assumed to correspond with the 'tiers' in the Offender Management Model [Chapter 7]. While there may be some future alignment, these categorisations developed separately and arguably with insufficient reference to each other.)

- MAPPA 1: Ordinary risk management – the risk posed is judged to be manageable by one agency, without significantly involving other agencies.
- MAPPA 2: Local inter-agency risk management – the active involvement of more than one agency is necessary, but the level of risk or the challenges of managing it fall short of the threshold for MAPPA 3. Increases in assessed risk or key stages (for example anticipated release from prison) are among the reasons to call a MAPPA meeting here, convening all agencies with a contribution to make to a collective management of the case. A senior representative from the most appropriate agency will convene the meeting.
- MAPPA 3: MAPPP – Multi-Agency Public Protection Panel – the offender is assessed as posing a high or very high risk of causing serious harm, calling for close co-operation at a senior level, perhaps because of the complexity of the case and/or because of the unusual resource commitments it requires. Offenders will be the subject of (usually monthly) meetings with a core membership of senior managers. Arrangements for chairing these panels vary from area to area. Core panel members should receive full information in advance of the panel.
- MAPPA invariably seeks to identify risks, using approved assessment instruments. Perhaps it could be said that while instruments may be extremely

helpful in deciding who should be considered in a MAPPA meeting, their value lessens once specific responses have to be agreed and put into effect. Sometimes, no doubt, the panels will apply a set of questions (rather like those on page 135) to consider risk and response systematically.

Meetings are also required to take full account of the interests of past and/or potential victims. Investigation should take place and information gathered actively and shared as appropriate. Risk management plans should be agreed, with decisions recorded and implemented. The position should be reviewed regularly.

Representatives of different agencies and disciplines need to negotiate a common set of standards and construct a vocabulary in which to discuss their concerns. At what level, for example, does a risk become unacceptable? What is it to 'monitor' someone or some state of affairs? Police, probation staff and mental health professionals may understand something quite different by this term. These differences do not vitiate inter-agency work, but they need to be taken properly into account. Negotiations around such matters, familiarity with the approaches of other professions and respect for their contribution have helped to consolidate MAPPA. Kemshall and colleagues (2005) identified areas of good practice and made recommendations on organisation and practice. They generally found 'evidence of greater effectiveness and consistency' (2005: 1).

Yet inter-agency work notoriously presents challenges, as well as opportunities (Maguire *et al.* 2001; McGuire 2002; Rumgay 2003). Maguire and Kemshall explored how cultural tensions were sometimes acted out in meetings in MAPPA's early years (Maguire *et al.* 2001; Kemshall and Maguire 2001). Probation officers sometimes felt a strain in being expected to set aside traditional occupational priorities like rehabilitation: many were already uncertain about the pre-eminence of public protection within the discourse of their profession (Robinson 2002) and uncomfortable that needs were now reinscribed as risk factors (see also Chapter 6; Hannah-Moffat 1999). MAPPA could exacerbate these anxieties.

Risk practices are 'significantly mediated by the practices and values of staff and the culture of the organisation within which they are working' (Kemshall and Wood 2007a: 384). There are also formal and informal differences of power which may be mitigated by the mutual respect that good inter-agency work should generate, but may nevertheless remain influential and make it easier for some agencies to assert their priorities (Rumgay 2003).

Risk and compliance

What is it to manage risk? Finkelhor (1986) suggested that for an offence to take place the offender must have:

- motivation (in some sense must *want* to commit the crime) and then must overcome;
- internal inhibitors (conscience, guilt, fear – both self-interested/deterrent and ethical constraints that check misbehaviour);

- external inhibitors (for example surveillance [being watched], security devices);
- victims (perhaps by deceit, threat or force).

Arguably probation's distinctive contribution is in working to strengthen internal inhibitors (helping people to understand the consequences of their actions, enhancing victim empathy). Other agencies may think first of external inhibitors, especially surveillance, which seem not to depend on the (precarious) consent of the offender. But other mechanisms of compliance (Chapter 9) have their influence here too: the most reliable constraints are internal rather than externally imposed. A risk management strategy must therefore attend to aspects of self-control, to the individual's anticipation of hazards (and avoidance of risky situations) and to the internal dialogues that may motivate offending or neutralise inhibitors. Professional relationships are therefore a large part of effective risk management:

> Supervision is not primarily a surveillance and crime control process, but a framework of support. Monitoring depends centrally on the maintenance of a relationship . . . with every effort being made to achieve co-operation, openness and trust. Surveillance that is onerous and outside a framework of support may reduce the co-operation and disclosure on which effective continuing risk assessment depends.
>
> (Grounds, 1995: 56)

This insight raises sharp questions about the role of the offender in a risk strategy. The offender may sometimes be defiant, resistant, secretive and manipulative and at other times biddable and cooperative: this ambivalence and fluidity is exactly what understandings of motivation would lead us to expect.

A disregard for the offender's role in the strategy can jeopardise the legitimacy on which compliance may depend (see Chapter 9; Bottoms 2001; Robinson and McNeill 2008). Mere compulsion is a weak and temporary control: *legitimacy* is needed if active compliance is to be secured. Undue reliance on threat is most unlikely to be effective and mechanisms of compliance must be made to work together.

Effective continuous review, moreover, depends upon knowledge of changes and developments. Attempts to disregard the offender's reaction can close off two critical sources of information: invaluable information from the individual offender (Moore 1996) and from carers, families and friends who are sometimes closest to the individual. This information is much more likely to be forthcoming in the context of a relationship of confidence and trust.

So far as possible, then, offenders should be actively involved in the implementation of the risk plan (Canton 2005). It is naive to depend upon the co-operation of some individuals whose motivation to desist from offending is low or uncertain; but to suppose that a risk plan can be managed without regard to the offender's responses to it involves a naiveté of another kind. The usual professional relationship skills of probation staff are therefore relevant here, notably skills of *engagement* (Tuddenham 2000) so that risk management is not something separate from the processes of supervision.

Summary of key points

- Multi-agency arrangements recognise that agencies together can achieve much more than they can working separately.
- Effective inter-agency work can be difficult to achieve because of (legitimate) differences of agency responsibility, priority and professional culture.
- Risk assessment instruments have a value in constituting a common framework to discuss risk, but their role in guiding practice is limited.
- Undue emphasis on control can be self-defeating, especially if it fails to take into account the offender's compliance with risk management.

Serious further offences

Probation has tried hard to learn from experience when offenders under supervision have committed serious offences. (Mead 2007; see especially http://www.justice.gov.uk/inspectorates/hmi-probation/risk-of-harm-to-others.htm) No doubt there is more to be learned, however. The great majority of such offences are not committed by those subject to MAPPA arrangements, or by those ranked as high risk by OASys or assigned to the fourth tier in the OMM. Craissati and Sindall's (2009) sample had mostly been assigned to the medium level of risk (see also Ansbro 2006), demonstrating limitations of these classifications.

Inquiries sometimes discover that procedures were not followed and may attribute this to staff inexperience or shortcomings in training, or perhaps to weaknesses of implementation or under-resourcing. Few if any inquiries have taken the further step of claiming that *had the procedures been appropriately followed, the serious offence would not have taken place.* Tuddenham's remarks about reflexive judgment seem insightful here too. Undue confidence in an apparently objective assessment and the reassurances of superficial compliance collude with practitioners' anxieties and fears to make it harder for them to appreciate developments which in hindsight seem clear (Prins 1999). Many of these factors have a 'feelings' component, not just cognitive and procedural aspects.

A systematic study of 'near misses' could be also be instructive (Mary Anne McFarlane – personal communication). How to identify these is not straightforward: no offence has taken place. Even so, these could be considered as *case studies of what worked.* There is relatively limited dissemination of good practice in this respect – in contrast to the reports on serious further offences which often reaffirm what is already recognised to be good practice.

Probation and crime reduction

Prolific and other priority offenders (PPO) programmes

MAPPA's achievements encouraged an extension of its approach. PPO programmes were set up in response to a recognition that a relatively small number of offenders account for a disproportionately large number of crimes (Moore 2007).

The aspiration is that, if these offenders could be identified and checked, many crimes could be prevented. Yet the identification of this group is notoriously difficult (Hagell and Newburn 1994), whose members are in any case constantly changing, 'with 40 per cent of persistent offenders desisting from offending without official intervention and many being replaced each year by new persistent offenders' (Moore 2007: 204).

Crime control and punitive strategies sometimes fail to distinguish *persistent* from *serious* offenders. These are distinct groups, conceptually and empirically: the people who offend most are by no means necessarily those who commit the most serious offences (see Figure 10.1 on page 132). Losing this distinction can work to the especial disadvantage of those women who commit a number of relatively minor offences, but may find themselves subject to intensive interventions (Shaw and Hannah-Moffat 2004).

The PPO strategy has three complementary strands (Criminal Justice Joint Inspection 2009):

- prevent and deter – stopping people from becoming prolific offenders;
- catch and convict – apprehending, convicting and enforcing;
- rehabilitate and resettle – offering rehabilitative interventions.

Many offenders on the scheme have substantial records of burglary and robbery, quite commonly associated with drug use. They are offered support, but also subject to intensive supervision and surveillance so that any offending would be more than usually likely to be detected. Some interventions are found supportive and helpful, but constant 'checking up' can be experienced as intrusion or harassment.

How are such schemes best evaluated? Further convictions could show the scheme working as it should (through the strategy's *catch and convict* strand) or as failing in its *rehabilitate and resettle* component. A simple measure of reconviction is inadequate here: many on the programme will reoffend – their high OGRS scores make this likely – but their offending may well be greatly reduced in frequency or seriousness (Merrington 2006).

Typically many objectives are set for schemes and achievement of all of them cannot readily be shown. Ironically, the two principal objectives – reduced reoffending and diversion from custody – turn out to be those where evidence of success is least persuasive. Other objectives – intensive interventions as a punishment to match a serious offence, provision of rehabilitative opportunities, public protection – may constitute a more plausible focus. Merrington (2006) points out that the schemes have some features – close surveillance, quick response, fast-tracking into programmes, established inter-agency procedures – that make them especially suitable for public protection work.

While evaluative research is guardedly optimistic about the effect of PPO schemes (Homes *et al.* 2005), Farrall *et al.* (2007) suggest that concentration on reconviction could overlook developments in people's lives – perhaps in employment or in personal relationships – that may not have an immediately measurable effect, but may nevertheless be significant on the 'zig-zag path' to desistance (Burnett 2004: 196). Perhaps the schemes should best be understood as a contribution to 'buttressing primary desistance' (see Chapter 9) on the way to more enduring change. But this change is not something that the schemes alone can ensure.

Integrated offender management

People serving sentences of under 12 months who are not subject to formal supervision on release have attracted particular attention. Perceived shortcomings in working with this group, many of whom commit several offences in the year after release (Social Exclusion Unit 2002), has prompted a further initiative, *integrated offender management* (IOM).

This scheme tries to build on the achievements of MAPPA and PPO, recognising that 'that some high-priority/highly damaging offenders may fall between the gaps in current arrangements' (Home Office and Ministry of Justice 2009: 3). This initiative importantly includes *non-statutory* offenders, those not subject to formal supervision, and also those who have been 'down-graded' from PPO schemes. Like MAPPA, police and probation are lead community agencies, but many others are involved – for example accommodation, health and education services.

These schemes are still very new and their effectiveness is not yet clear. Approaches to their evaluation should, however, learn from PPO research (Farrall *et al.* 2007) and consider the difficulties of understanding short-term interventions in the context of complex and uneven processes of desistance. Access to rehabilitative services is a component of these schemes. But social inclusion ought to mean that people have access to services as of right as citizens or members of the community: it should not be contingent on their inclusion in a crime reduction project. Nor, while effective inter-agency work is to be welcomed, should all agencies be encouraged to see their role as in the service of crime reduction. Unintended consequences must also be considered: perhaps some interventions can make things worse, for instance by aggravating social exclusion through stigmatisation, disrupting spontaneous developments towards desistance or by undermining legitimacy with service users.

Schemes of this type should also have regard to proportionality and to the rights of offenders. The punitive strategy is dismissive of the idea of offender rights, while a management strategy is over-focused on the instrumental objectives of reducing risk. Yet some jurisdictions would look with dismay at the potential intrusion into the lives of ex-offenders and ponder compatibility of these initiatives with Article 7 of the European Convention on Human Rights (which includes the principle *no punishment without law*). IOM and similar schemes are among a range of preventive sanctions and measures that are less a response to what an individual has done than a pre-emptive intervention in anticipation of what it is believed that they might do – an increasingly common characteristic of contemporary penality (Garland 2001; Ashworth and Zedner 2008).

Other contributions to a safer society – crime reduction

Crime reduction is the contemporary – and doubtless more realistic – reframing of crime prevention initiatives which originated in the late 1970s and early 1980s. Since the reasons why people become offenders are largely unknown and in any case unlikely to be amenable to much influence, it may be better to look at the particular circumstances in which crimes take place and to see how the environment might be manipulated to prevent them or, if they do take place, increase the chances of the offender's apprehension. This is 'situational' crime prevention. 'Social' crime prevention recognises that educational and social provision, especially with those most likely to offend, can make a significant difference.

A well-known framework (Brantingham and Faust 1976) distinguishes:

- primary prevention: through various forms of environmental design or manipulation, notably ' target-hardening' (barriers, locks, immobilisation devices) and surveillance ('natural' – making the sites of offending more visible – or through devices like CCTV);
- secondary prevention – identifying and working with those considered most likely to offend ('at risk of offending');
- tertiary prevention – working with known offenders to reduce the incidence of their offending.

The probation service is, most obviously, engaged in tertiary crime prevention. Yet it may have important contributions to make at other levels besides. Probation staff come to know a great deal about the circumstances in which offences take place. But while these insights are undoubtedly put to good use in working with individual offenders (that is, at tertiary level), it is not at all clear that such information is collated and deployed to contribute to primary crime reduction. Again, OASys collects data that could be analysed and interpreted to identify community profiles and patterns of criminogenic need (Debidin 2007). Yet it is hard to say how consistently, systematically or reliably this type of analysis takes place or influences service provision.

Relatedly, one of the consequences of probation's increasing distance from its community (see Chapter 14) is a diminution of its capacity to contribute in these ways. When probation officers travelled 'the patch', they met other people and came to know a great deal about the community they served. Exchanges of information still take place, through crime and disorder reduction/community safety partnerships, at management levels, but it is not so clear that this takes place among practitioners (except, of course, in the management of individual cases). This 'softer' intelligence, once part of the repertoire of probation staff, is indispensable in understanding the social (and criminogenic) characteristics of a community. Seeing people only in the office risks abstracting them from the social context in which they have come to offend and in which their desistance is to be accomplished.

Again, secondary prevention could be enhanced through community work to enhance social capital (Boeck 2007), but contemporary probation's commitment to this seems uncertain. Smith and Vanstone (2002: 827) argue for a wider social engagement for probation, transcending its preoccupation with tertiary crime prevention, and challenge the service:

> to maintain its long tradition of recognizing the impacts on crime and victimization of inequalities and disadvantage, which means both developing its own services for the excluded and marginalized, and contributing to preventive social programmes aimed at improving the life chances of the most deprived.

Do the political priorities of public protection and its associated practices and procedures make for a safer community? Their contribution here is established and valuable. At the same time, there are other ways of comprehending risk, especially those that put a greater emphasis on public awareness and responsibility – the responsibilities of all adults to contribute to the protection of vulnerable people – and public education to enhance a more sophisticated understanding of the origins of serious offending and the possibility of reducing it (Kemshall and Wood 2007b).

Perhaps some approaches and procedures are counter-productive. It has been suggested that their carers' risk aversion is bad for children's development (BBC 2007). Again, a preoccupation with the idea that dangerousness is an identifiable and manageable property of individuals warrants intrusion, expansiveness of the category and distracts from other forms of social danger (Bennett 2008). Emphasis on the dangers that strangers might present could divert attention from the vivid risks that can confront people in their own homes – domestic violence against women, child abuse and the abuse of the elderly and vulnerable. Registers and schemes can only respond to those who have been recognised, but the population of 'dangerous offenders' is constantly being replenished. It is also possible that some interventions can corrode the trust and reciprocity which should bind a community and make it safer, so undermining systems of natural protection. The anger indulged by punitive approaches and the managerial response that supposes that the solution is to identify and check individuals both lead to social exclusion, whereas it is societies with the greatest social inclusion that have the best chance of reducing offending.

Summary

In this chapter, we have explored the emergence of risk as the guiding priority of probation policy and practice. The strengths and limitations of assessment instruments have been discussed. While actuarial instruments have a value in targeting, in performance management and in the accumulation of the evidence necessary to lead practice, in the individual case their worth is much more limited. To the working practitioner, trying to reduce the likelihood of reoffending, risk assessment matters just to the extent that it informs risk management. The importance of reflexive risk assessment has been emphasised, with an insistence that risk cannot be assessed or managed in a technical manner, but calls for the judgement and self-awareness of reflective practitioners.

The most effective risk management strategies should endeavour to command the understanding and, so far as possible, consent of the individual: risk and compliance must be considered together. Coercion is an uncertain, weak and temporary form of control. Respect for individuals and concern for their interests are not only ethical requirements, but are much more likely to enhance compliance and reduce risk: pre-occupation with risk may therefore turn out to be ironically self-defeating. While policy accounts are sometimes framed as if control and public protection call for quite different modes of practice, many of probation's skills – developing relationships of mutual respect and trust, eliciting and interpreting information, attending to the vagaries of motivation, awareness of the effect of one's own feelings and working constructively with those of the offender – are every bit as important here as in other aspects of probation work.

After discussing MAPPA and associated developments that try to 'target' persistent and serious offenders (groups that must be carefully distinguished), we turned to probation's uneven and (under-achieving) contribution to crime reduction at levels other than the tertiary. Finally we raised the possibility that some measures bring heightened mistrust, defensive practice and harassment of offenders. They therefore tend to increase rather than reduce these risks by corroding trust and reciprocity on which community safety may ultimately depend.

Questions

- Is detention to prevent serious offending justifiable? Is this morally different from punishing someone for what they have not done – and, it is to be hoped, never will do?
- Why is the author sceptical about the accuracy – and indeed the value of concentrating on the accuracy – of risk assessment instruments?
- Do you agree that some interventions and measures could make things worse?

Further reading

Moore (1996), Kemshall (2003) and Robinson (2003b) are excellent introductions to these matters. The account of crime reduction offered here is very cursory. For introductions to by what is now a vast literature, see Tilley (2009), Tilley (ed.) (2006), Crawford (2007) and Garland (2001).

11 Community service

What is community service?

Community Service[1] (CS) involves doing work for the benefit of the community as a punishment for an offence. It is a relatively inexpensive sanction for crimes of medium seriousness that commands wide levels of public support in most countries (Tonry 1998). It is extensively established across Europe: the probation service implements or organises CS, in one form or another, in all but one of the 33 European jurisdictions covered by van Kalmthout and Durnescu (2008).

In England and Wales, the statutory basis of CS is the requirement to undertake unpaid work as all or part of a community order or a suspended sentence order. The requirement is measured in hours – now between 40 and 300 hours (Criminal Justice Act 2003, s. 199 [2]), although for much of the history of CS it was between 40 and 240. In 2008, more than 96,000 offenders were ordered to perform unpaid work as all or part of their sentence (Ministry of Justice 2009a) and nearly one-third of all community orders made in 2007 had unpaid work as the sole requirement (Solomon and Silvestri 2008).

The nature of the work undertaken is determined in consultation with the offender and varies considerably, but can include:

- practical or manual work (often undertaken in groups) – for example, painting and decorating, gardening;
- personal working for people with particular needs – for example, the elderly or people with a disability;
- working in a workshop, typically on probation premises.

There are often opportunities too for offenders to use some of their hours in education or work-related training and to gain qualifications.

In the early days of CS, there was a marked gender difference with disproportionately fewer women receiving these orders (McIvor 2004; Worrall and Hoy 2005: 120), and while the numbers have found a balance, there are still differences between the genders in how the measure is used, the age profile of men and women undertaking CS and the likelihood of completion (McIvor 2007).

A 2008 *Snapshot of Unpaid Work* shows that environment/conservation, painting/decoration, cleaning and maintenance and 'charity shop' together account for some two-thirds of hours worked. Over two-thirds of this work comes from commissions from the voluntary sector, local authorities and community groups.

In support of a visible unpaid work initiative, Jack Straw, Minister of Justice, commented 'It's crucial that the public ... has a say in what community punishments offenders receive' (Ministry of Justice 2009a) and at the Community Payback website (http://www.direct.gov.uk/en/CrimeJusticeAndTheLaw/Prison AndProbation/DG_1820800), people are invited to nominate appropriate projects. The best CS schemes, however, have always been active and imaginative in inviting referrals from the community and in seeking out tasks that would be of genuine benefit.

Meanwhile, the government has been celebrating the amount of unpaid work undertaken and its benefits to the community. The website announces that in 2008/09:

> Over 62,000 offenders completed Community Payback.

> Over 8 million hours of work were undertaken.

> Work valued at over £45 million (if paid at the minimum wage) was carried out.

The term *payback*, however, has an (intentional?) ambiguity: paying back can evoke thoughts of retribution or revenge as well as making amends. The expression itself prompts thoughts about the different purposes of community service and it is to this that we next turn.

The contested purposes of community service

In 1994, Manchester United star Eric Cantona was sentenced to two weeks' imprisonment for attacking a spectator at Crystal Palace's ground. Hearing the appeal against sentence, Judge Ian Davies imposed a community service order for 120 hours and said: 'We express the hope that he will be able to be used in carrying out his public duty to the community by helping young people who aspire to be professional footballers . . . and others who merely aspire to play the game and enjoy it.' Greater Manchester Probation Service duly arranged for him to coach 720 children after the judge said the footballer should be given *work which made use of his skills and helped* young people.

(*The Times*, 1 April 1995 – emphasis added)

Do you agree with the comments of the Judge? Can you think of another point of view?

The history of community service could be recounted around changes of conception in and dispute over its purposes. In practice, community service has always had to try to reconcile tensions among competing objectives. The changes in name are just one manifestation of this: the original Community Service Order was renamed a Community Punishment Order (Criminal Justice and Courts Services Act 2000, s. 44) to emphasise its punitive character, then blandly retitled 'unpaid work' (when the single community order was introduced by the Criminal Justice Act 2003), while the intermittent emphasis on *community payback* is meant to draw attention to its reparative aspects (for example, Ministry of Justice 2009b).

The power to order offenders convicted of offences punishable by imprisonment to undertake work on behalf of the community was first enacted in the Criminal Justice Act 1972. The Advisory Council on the Penal System (ACPS) had proposed the introduction of this sanction (ACPS 1970 – the *Wootton Report*) and argued that the order would be welcomed by proponents of different penal philosophies. Some would see it as punishment – an apt, more constructive and cheaper alternative to prison; others would emphasise its reparative character – making amends for wrongs done; others again would point to 'the value of bringing offenders into close touch with those members of the community who are most in need of help and support' – presumably an experience that would support rehabilitation and enhance reintegration (ACPS 1970:13).

Although this broad appeal had been seen as a strength at the time, the Chair of the Committee, Baroness Wootton, later confessed herself to be 'slightly ashamed, [at] an undisguised attempt to curry favour with everybody' (Wootton 1978: 128). She went on to say, however, that this 'lack of clarity in the objectives of the scheme . . . has been both criticised as a weakness and applauded as a virtue' (*ibid.*). It made community service versatile even as it made it vulnerable to appropriation by those with a set or exclusive view of its purpose, while Willis (1977) argued that its 'chameleonic' character was constraining its potential as a genuine custodial alternative. But, for good or ill, different objectives for community service were embedded in the scheme for the start.

Community service as punishment

> Graham Smith, Chief Inspector of Probation, said that punishing the soccer star by allowing him to coach youngsters may have given the impression that such penalties 'let criminals off'. 'The *orders were meant to be a burden*', said Mr Smith . . . 'It is not an occasion for a defendant to receive additional approval or to further recreational and professional opportunities. It is certainly not for turning people into heroes.'
>
> (*The Times*, 1 April 1995 – emphasis added)

> Do you agree that the decision could have given the impression the Chief Inspector feared? Does the decision make a hero of Mr Cantona?

Community service *as punishment* was part of the scheme from the beginning. The arrival of community service anticipated the policy of *punishment in the community* by some 15 years and the idea that the probation service might be involved in the implementation of punishment was novel and, for some, disquieting. The Probation Order would not, at least at that time, have been understood or presented in that way – it was *instead of* punishment. Those uncomfortable with punishment as the primary rationale of a probation-administered sanction may have felt, though, that this was a price worth paying if CS were to realise its potential in displacing sentences of imprisonment. To be a credible alternative to prison, it was felt, CS had to be (and be seen to be) punitively demanding.

The scheme was introduced in pilot areas and subsequently made available nationally. In some of the pilot areas, the policy was that community service orders should only be imposed in cases where, but for this power, the court would otherwise have imposed a custodial sentence. Early research was therefore much preoccupied with the place of community service on the penal tariff – was CS really taking the place of prison? The question was all the more pertinent when there were no signs that the introduction of CS was leading to a reduction in the prison population (Willis 1977). Early research suggested that perhaps between 45 per cent and 50 per cent of those sentenced to CS would probably otherwise have gone to prison, but the rest would not (Pease *et al.* 1977; McIvor 1992). This looks like some gain, to be sure, though Bottoms (1987) warned that there was a risk of a backlash effect: when offenders breached their order or offended again, they might be sentenced to custody by a court that would regard the CS order as a last chance that had now been abused. And this was possible even when the order had *not* been intended to be a direct alternative to prison. Moreover, as we shall see, while CS may have held its place reasonably well in its early years, more recently it has gone 'down tariff' and been used for less serious offences and less serious or risky offenders.

When, from the mid-1980s onwards, *punishment in the community* came to be seen as the defining characteristic of non-custodial sanctions, the punitive aspects of community service were still more strongly emphasised. Arguably, CS was particularly suited to this policy: hard work is probably easier to characterise *as punishment* than the less obvious and less visible demands of probation supervision. It is not coincidental that the first set of National Standards, promulgated in 1988, were for CS (only). These sought to tighten enforcement practice, but also insisted that at least some part of every order should be 'demanding'. Although this was usually taken to mean that work should be hard and physically laborious, it was also recognised that some assignments could be *emotionally demanding*: for example, for some offenders the experience of working with people with a serious disability might make such emotional demands.

Commenting on the new standards soon after they had been issued, McWilliams (1989) defended a primarily retributive justification for CS, but argued that this by no means entailed that tasks should be manual rather than non-manual, impersonal rather than personal. Nevertheless, the idea has persisted that CS will be more readily acceptable and replace imprisonment in more cases if tasks are seen to be physically tough and taxing. It is this that lay behind Graham Smith's insistence (see below) that 'it is involuntary labour containing thoroughly unpleasant features' – a view, incidentally, that would have dismayed the Wootton Committee – and the contemporary argument that unpaid work must be seen to be 'tough' (Casey 2008).

The political need to present CS tasks as intrinsically unpleasant has undoubtedly constrained a great deal of valuable reparative and rehabilitative work. Whitfield (1998) tells the instructive story of a group of community service workers who went to Romania in 1991 and worked hard to construct an orphanage. The reaction of the Home Office to this manifestly worthwhile – and surely exacting and 'tough' undertaking – was to prohibit any such future projects in case 'going abroad' was taken as a some sort of reward for misbehaviour.

Alexander Paterson famously said that people 'are sent to prison as a punishment, not for punishment' (quoted Ruck 1951:13) and this seems like a useful precept for contemporary CS as well. The punishment is the demand on time and labour – a principle that has often been used to challenge demands that work must be arduous or laborious. Once the court has determined the length of the unpaid work requirement, it is the rehabilitative and reparative potential of the work that should determine the placement.

Meanwhile, there has been a long-term trend towards using community service for less serious offenders – displacing other community penalties and fines more than imprisonment. In the years leading up to Criminal Justice Act 2003 CS was moving down the tariff: proportions of defendants with convictions for summary offences, of first offenders and of offenders who had not served a previous custodial sentence – each an index of CS's place on the tariff – were all increasing. As for 'risky' offenders, two-thirds of those given a Community Punishment Order had OGRS scores (see Chapter 7) of less than 30; in comparison and contrast, of those receiving the ostensibly low-tariff penalty of a fine, 60 per cent had OGRS scores above 60 (Morgan and Smith 2003). Whether attempts to make community service 'tougher' is a plausible solution to this trend is another matter.

We should also note that the tariff position has often been different as between women and men. McIvor (1998) found that women in Scotland were being given CS where there was no significant risk of custody, with an associated failure to use the sanction to divert women from short custodial sentences. More recently, the general tariff decline could foreseeably widen the net even further for women offenders.

Community service as rehabilitation

Cedric Fullwood, chief probation officer of Greater Manchester, said: 'We take heart from the assessments . . . which speak of Mr Cantona's

> *rehabilitation and exemplary behaviour.* Mr Cantona was *greatly challenged by this order.*'
>
> (*The Times* 26 April 1996 – emphasis added)

> Are you persuaded by Mr Fullwood's assertion? In what way do you think that Mr Cantona might have been 'greatly challenged'? How might these challenges be explained to someone who protested that it was no challenge for a footballer to be asked to play football?

The probation service has often been uneasy about affirming the rehabilitative potential of community service, even though this was undeniably part of the original vision. Early on, courts sometimes expressed the hope that CS would be of benefit to offenders – not least in instilling working disciplines and improving prospects of employment. But the probation service, while not disavowing such benefits, preferred to encourage the use of the probation order where there were recognised needs to be addressed. After all, no recognisable 'treatment' interventions were attempted – not in the sense that treatment was understood within the social work paradigm that prevailed when CS was introduced. No less significantly, the service was anxious about the possibility that community service, if used as a rehabilitative measure, might divert people from probation orders rather than from prison.

It has always been the case, of course, that many of the offenders on CS are quite as beset with problems as offenders on probation, posing challenges for enforcement and completion (see Eadie and Willis 1989). It is also true that the offenders' experience of the two sanctions might show that CS was often found to be beneficial, even when demanding (McIvor 1992). Nevertheless, this difference in characterisation – probation for rehabilitation, CS for punishment – has continued to influence the way in which they are seen and implemented. Ellis and colleagues (1996) found, for example, that CS was enforced much more robustly than probation. More recently, Rex (2005) found that staff in CS and in 'field' probation units have significantly different ideas about what the respective measures are *for* and what messages they do and should convey – as indeed do offenders, victims and magistrates.

Caution about the rehabilitative aspirations of CS continued even when research (authoritatively summarised by McIvor (2002)) showed that offenders on CS achieved lower than expected rates of reconviction. McIvor herself had earlier shown connections between (reductively) effective outcomes and the type of work undertaken. Offenders' perception of the worth of their work influenced their commitment and their participation; tasks could be demanding, even tough, but they had to have worth and meaning; and where work was found to be meaningful, not only were there fewer enforcement problems, subsequent rates of reconviction were lower (McIvor 1992).

McIvor's findings were very influential in a number of probation services in England and Wales. The value of the work assigned became a prominent consideration with the aspiration that, through worthwhile accomplishment, offenders' sense of self-esteem would be enhanced and subsequent reoffending accordingly reduced. These ideas were to influence the later development of enhanced community punishment, as we shall see.

Even so, for the reasons set out, probation was wary of promoting the reductive potential of CS, especially during the period of punishment in the community, for fear of compromising its place as 'an alternative to custody'. But when probation shifted emphasis towards effectiveness and 'what works', and was relatively more reticent about punishment, CS had to be characterised in a different way. Effectiveness, measured through reduction in reconviction, was now to be the principal focus and justification of probation practice and the potential of CS to contribute to this had to be affirmed. Community service orders made up a significant proportion of ambitious government targets for the completion of accredited programmes. But CS could only be a credible part of this strategy if the scheme were to be allowed to accommodate rehabilitative purposes and were subject to systematic evaluation of its effects.

In 1999, therefore, projects were established to investigate 'what works' in community service. Different 'pathfinders' variously emphasised:

- pro-social modelling – supervisors acting as models and consciously implementing the principles of reward, encouragement and 'pro-social expressions and actions';
- skills accreditation – offenders were enabled to undertake some of the hours of their order in developing work-related skills and achieving qualifications;
- tackling offending-related needs – using the order to address problems associated with their offending – for example, enhancing people's abilities to solve their problems without offending (Rex *et al.* 2004).

Summarising early findings from the evaluation of the pathfinders, Rex and Gelsthorpe (2002) reported demonstrable gains, including reductions in 'procriminal attitudes and self-perceived problems' (321), although they wisely cautioned that much more needed to be learnt about *how* these positive influences actually operated. The pathfinders, then, were sufficiently encouraging to lead to the implementation of a scheme of *enhanced community punishment* (Rex *et al.* 2004).

Presenting itself in the language of effective practice (National Probation Directorate 2003), enhanced community punishment represented an assimilation of CS into the mainstream of evidence-led, crime-reductive probation practice. Its main features were:

- integrated case management–a systematic, planned and 'holistic' approach, based on an assessment of risk and need through OASys;
- pro-social modelling – with staff, especially supervisors, demonstrating appropriate attitudes and behaving in ways which offenders might emulate;

- problem solving/cognitive skills modelling – the workplace would be likely to pose practical problems which offenders might learn to solve and also develop skills to apply to other difficulties in their lives;
- guided skills learning – the work might enable people to obtain vocational qualifications and thus enhance employability;
- placement quality standards – all placements and projects had to meet a specified standard (National Probation Directorate 2003).

The value of the real experiences of work was especially emphasised. The learning on accredited programmes might be seen as artificial and remote, whereas

> Community Punishment is particularly valuable in providing opportunities for learning in real situations and in a very concrete and practical way, in contrast to the more conceptual learning methods of other forms of supervision. Enhanced CP enables this contact to be used to target a range of dynamic risk factors.
>
> (National Probation Directorate 2003: 5)

A comparable point could be made about pro-social modelling (see Chapter 9). The opportunities to 'model' appropriate behaviour and problem-solving skills in a work setting may well more extensive and more 'real' than in office encounters (Mair and Canton 2007). Again, praise, an important ingredient of pro-social modelling (Trotter 1999), offered in the context of community service, where effort and achievement are readily apparent to supervisors, beneficiaries and others, has a spontaneity and authenticity – in contrast to the rather contrived (and maybe even condescending?) praise bestowed in an office. Such opportunities were accepted enthusiastically by CS supervisors, who were found to have 'embraced the pro-social modelling agenda' (HM Inspectorate of Probation 2006: 7).

The principles of 'core correctional practice' (Dowden and Andrews 2004) include the firm and fair use of authority, pro-social modelling, teaching concrete problem-solving skills, forming and working through warm, open and enthusiastic relationships. It is clear that community service offers quite as much scope for working with offenders in these ways as many other probation encounters – and probably more.

Some areas were very enthusiastic about enhanced community punishment, but for others it was logistically complex and indeed expensive. This was a particular challenge in those areas that found it hard to resource small groups. The principles of enhanced community punishment set limits on the number of people in a working group. Such constraints also have implications for the type of work that can be undertaken. Here as elsewhere, costs and logistics as much as philosophy can determine policy and practice developments.

Unhappily, moreover, the introduction of enhanced community punishment coincided with an awareness that it was being used for less and less serious offenders. Drawing attention to this marked tariff decline, Morgan and Smith (2003: 11) wrote 'NPS is shortly to roll out an accredited system termed "enhanced community punishment", a system which the data suggest *almost two thirds of offenders currently on* [Community Punishment Orders] *do not need'* (emphasis added). And not only was there no need for this type of intervention, based on their OGRS scores, there was little evidence to show that they would benefit from it.

It remains the case that the rehabilitative potential of CS is considerable (McIvor 2002), although, as we shall see, there are political as well as practical challenges to the achievement of that potential.

Community service as reparation

> Mr Smith said in his annual report: 'It appeared an enormously popular sentence; *the youngsters themselves gained from it.*' But he added: 'The purpose of community service is quite clear: *it is involuntary labour containing thoroughly unpleasant features.*'
> (*The Times* 26 April 1996 – emphasis added)
>
> Do you agree with Mr Smith? If the Order had contained 'thoroughly unpleasant features' would the youngsters (or Mr Cantona) have gained from it? On balance, do you think this was managed in the right way?

While there are other sanctions that punish and/or try to rehabilitate, community service was the first – and is arguably still the only – adult sentence with a reparative purpose. There is no small irony in the consideration that at just the time when 'making reparation' was instated for the first time as one of the statutory purposes of sentencing (Criminal Justice Act 2003, s. 142), community service was seeking a different rationale as a reductive measure.

The idea of making amends for doing wrong has an immediate and compelling intuitive appeal (Wright 2008). Stern (1999) recounts how the point and value of CS as reparation was immediately appreciated in the African jurisdictions to which it was introduced. That CS is appropriate and fair is grasped readily by offenders, victims and members of the public, according the sanction a legitimacy that other punishments often lack – a factor both in successful completion and in subsequent reductions in reoffending (Killias *et al.* 2000). Indeed this is something that Bottoms's important work on legitimacy and compliance would lead us to expect (Chapter 9).

Reparation through community service almost never takes the form of work with direct benefit to victims. The term *community* payback recognises that redress might be offered to the wide community. Work that directly undoes harm done by crime is not the usual CS experience: the *Snapshot* shows that no more than 13 per cent of all hours worked could be understood in this way ('community safety' – 7 per cent; graffiti/litter removal – 6 per cent). The reparation of CS, then, is often indirect and *symbolic*. As we have seen, however, in the context of the

Cantona case, not every kind of task is understood by everyone as an appropriate 'symbol'. As Rex (2005) insists, punishments and the manner of their implementation send a message, but *what* message, *how* it is received and *by whom* are often less than straightforward considerations.

In Turkey CS as a requirement of probation is still novel. The newspaper *Today's Zaman* (2009) reported on a case where a defendant vehemently objected to being asked to plant trees as his community service:

'I prefer to be jailed, rather than planting trees. It is not because I am against nature. Just the opposite: I have planted many trees in my life, but to be forced to do so is against human dignity.' [The judge had been using this punishment to bring about reforestation.] But human rights activist and lawyer Yusuf Alataş is not sure about the fairness of reforesting through such sentences. 'The punishment should be relevant to the crime. The aim of punishment is deterrence, not environmentalist activities,' he said. 'If someone harms the environment, pollutes it . . . to punish this person by sentencing him to plant trees is a reasonable and useful probation, but planting trees as punishment is not relevant for every kind of crime,' explained Alataş.

Some of the less obvious considerations upon which a CS scheme may depend, then, include:

- a cultural view of what counts as making amends;
- a particular cultural attitude towards labour and the extent to which it can constitute either punishment or reparation;
- popular and judicial attitudes about what constitutes socially useful activity;
- some 'fit' between the crime and the CS tasks assigned;
- an employment context (the availability of and remuneration for work) (Canton 2006).

These are all important considerations, perhaps especially when CS is being established in a country for the first time. It should also be noted that these considerations are *gendered* and will make a difference to the way in which CS is used for women and men.

Community service for reintegration

Reintegration is closely associated with both rehabilitation and reparation, though conceptually distinct. John Braithwaite (1989) emphasised the value of *shaming* in effective punishment. But this shaming, he insisted, must be *reintegrative*: punishment should involve censure, but the shaming must take place in the context of a recognition that the offender is a member of the community, that punishment will come to an end and that the ex-offender is then entitled to their original standing.

Reintegration through community service is an idea to be found in the Wootton Report (ACPS 1970), where the suggestion that offenders might work alongside (non-offender) volunteers represents one way in which reintegration might be achieved through the mode of punishment. Again, offenders, having completed their assigned hours, were often given – and readily accepted – opportunities to continue to work in the same setting (Flegg 1976). This reintegrative potential has more recently been affirmed again by others (Gelsthorpe and Rex 2004; McIvor 2007), who have emphasised the value of enabling workers on CS to have direct contact with the beneficiaries of their efforts. Rex and Gelsthorpe quote McIvor to the effect that the most rewarding placements are 'reintegrative and entail some reciprocity and exchange in which the offender both offers service to others and is given the opportunity to acquire skills' (2004: 205).

The visible unpaid work/community payback initiative, emphasising the contribution of CS to the community, could therefore support reintegration. McIvor notes that if ECP set the offender as the principal beneficiary, community payback centres on benefit to the community. But, she warns, demanding tasks – or stigmatisation in the manner in which these are carried out – could spoil this and instead lead to an exclusionary, disintegrative mode of shaming (McIvor 2007). The National Probation Service (2005) emphasises the importance both of manifestly demanding punishment and the value of work to the community, but as we have seen these aspirations are not always so easily reconciled.

Not only reintegration but *any* plausible objective of CS depends upon its legitimacy – with courts and the public, with offenders and with direct beneficiaries – and this calls for careful attention to diversity and avoiding unfair discrimination. The manner in which CS is carried out can only support reintegration if it is administered fairly and inclusively. As Goode puts it,

> Schemes must be organised to maximise inclusion. Work sessions must be arranged so as not to prevent the offender being readily available to seek or take up employment if unemployed. Unpaid Work should not conflict with an offender's entitlement to benefit, or disrupt education or training activities. They must take account of religious and cultural requirements. The views of lone women or black or minority ethnic group offenders must be sought and taken into account when deciding on a work placement.
>
> (A. Goode 2007: 317)

Moreover, all communities must have access to the benefits of the scheme (HM Inspectorate of Probation 2004) – something which may not be assumed will simply happen by inviting the public to nominate their preferred tasks.

Tensions and synergies

Throughout this chapter, there has been an emphasis on the way in which the various purposes of CS may find themselves in tension. But there are also synergies. Rehabilitation and reparation may have different emphases, but in practice they are mutually supportive. There is ample evidence (see McIvor 2002) that performing tasks that are of genuine value to the community (reparative) is also effective in reducing reoffending (rehabilitative). This perspective arguably transcends the question of whether the principal beneficiary should be the offender 'or' the community.

An early community service study by Pease and McWilliams discussed by Worrall and Hoy (2005: 120) drew attention to a defining difference between CS and probation: CS instates the offender as a giver rather than a receiver of help. Experiences of reciprocity, gaining trust and the appreciation that may be gained through direct contact with beneficiaries all conduce to successful completion and reduced reoffending (McIvor 2007). Theoretical support for the effectiveness of this experience in reducing reoffending is given by strengths-based approaches to desistance, which is often accomplished and sustained through active agency on behalf of other people (McNeill and Maruna 2007; see also Chapter 9).

Punishment, awarded appropriately and administered fairly, also fits well with the other objectives of the scheme. Especially if worthwhile work is assigned, the punishment of CS can support rehabilitation and reparation. But, as we have seen, a zeal for punishment, as McIvor (2007) has cautioned, can detract from the potential of CS. The very viability of a scheme depends upon the availability of appropriate placements offering the right type of opportunities (something which in itself may come under pressure if the number of required hours continues to increase). A crude interpretation of what a 'demanding' punishment should be like could diminish the quality of placements, reduce access to direct beneficiaries and otherwise compromise the reparative, rehabilitative and reintegrative potential of the scheme.

Here, as in other aspects of penal policy, 'credibility' might be better achieved by a clear and confident affirmation of purposes like rehabilitation and reparation, and by working well towards these objectives, rather than a vain attempt to be 'tough'.

Summary

In this chapter, it has been argued that community service has always tried to incorporate principles of punishment, rehabilitation, reparation and reintegration. Sometimes these objectives have worked in harmony, but there have also been tensions. The extent to which these tensions have constrained the scheme's potential is debatable: an over-emphasis on rehabilitation may have limited CS's impact on the prison population; others would argue that the focus on punishment has undermined its capacity to achieve other, more constructive outcomes.

But while, as we have seen, it is possible to separate out CS's several objectives, in practice schemes have to find a way of incorporating all of them – a scheme that abandoned any one of the objectives under discussion would probably not be recognisable as community service.

Task: Design a community service scheme

Design a range of different community service schemes based on these principles:

1   Community service is a tough and demanding punishment.
2   Community service should do as much as possible to reduce the incidence of reoffending.
3   Community service must involve work of genuine value to the community.
4   Community service should do all it can to promote reintegration and social inclusion.

What tasks would you choose for the schemes? How would offenders be supervised? How would the orders be enforced?

How would you present your scheme in each case to:

- offenders
- victims
- politicians
- sentencers
- the public
- the local community.

How alike are these schemes and in what respects? How different are they from one another?

Further reading

A concise introduction to the topic is A. Goode (2007). McIvor (2007) is an excellent fuller discussion.

12 Probation and prison

The prison casts its long and sombre shadow over many aspects of probation's history, its policies, practices and organisation. Dismay at the sheer pointlessness of sentence after sentence of imprisonment was a stimulus to the development of probation originally. At times, probation has declared the provision of alternatives to imprisonment as its principal purpose and Secretaries of State have often spoken as if the main worth of probation lies in its potential contribution to reducing the prison population – although, as we saw in Chapter 5, any such potential has seldom been realised. In a quest for 'credibility', probation has sometimes attempted to present itself as prison-like in its capacity to punish and to protect the public.

Some probation officers work full-time in prison while, where the offender manager model is in operation, community-based offender managers oversee sentence plans for serving prisoners. Probation has long worked with prisoners during sentence and, for even longer, has offered help and supervision to them after release. (For part of its history the service's name was the Probation and After-Care Service.) Probation staff may be instrumental in the recall to prison of offenders whose release is conditional and indeed the prospect of imprisonment is sometimes among the incentives to comply with a community sentence. The aspiration that prison and probation should work better together has led to radical organisational change. In all these respects, probation's work is moulded by the realities of the prison and by beliefs about what prison could or should be.

In this chapter, then, we shall consider probation and prison. After a brief account of the characteristics of the prison population, not forgetting prisoners held awaiting trial, probation's work with serving prisoners will be discussed, including the work of probation staff inside the prison. Most of the rest of the chapter is about resettlement – the preferred term nowadays for work with people after they have left prison, when many are not yet released from the statutory requirements of their sentence and can be recalled.

The prison

It was suggested in earlier chapters that prison is often the first thing that people think about when they hear the term *punishment*. While offenders should in law only be sent to prison when no other sentence is suitable, while many more convicted offenders are dealt with in other ways and for all its manifest failures to reform, prison remains an icon of the state's response to crime and the standard against which 'alternatives to custody' must prove themselves.

Remand

> On remand, a prisoner is theoretically not yet proven guilty, but in effect he is a prisoner and treated as guilty; his warders have no training in how to deal with him otherwise . . . Innocent or not, he learns the culture of criminals. As one prisoner said, 'I'll never get rid of it, the stink of jail. It's in me, in my skin, in my hair, in my gear. Anyone I meet will know it and smell it. I'll never get shot of it.'
>
> (Smith 1989: 42)

People accused of offences have a legal right to bail unless certain circumstances can be shown to obtain: bail may be refused if offending seems likely, for instance, or if there are substantial concerns that the defendant may fail to attend court as required, or might interfere with the process of justice; and in these cases, defendants are sent to prison to await trial.

On 31 July 2010, 83,962 people were in prison (79,630 men; 4,332 women) in England and Wales. Of these 13,291 were remand prisoners, of whom 8,903 were untried and 4,388 were convicted and awaiting sentence. Thus just over 10 per cent of those in prison are unconvicted. Some will be acquitted, with prospects of compensation remote and no formal support from probation, and perhaps as many as half will eventually receive non-custodial sentences (Haines and Morgan 2007). Proportions of 'pre-trial detainees' are much higher in some other countries (Walmsley 2009).

Remand prisoners are often overlooked in discussions of imprisonment but plainly the usual justifications of punishment cannot apply to those who must be presumed to be innocent. Yet they often experience the worst of conditions, with serious over-crowding and fewer opportunities for meaningful out-of-cell activities than other prisoners (Coyle 2005). Custodial remand can jeopardise employment and accommodation and its negative impact on stabilising factors that might otherwise have been adduced in mitigation may be part of the explanation why those held in prison awaiting trial are more likely to receive a custodial sentence in the end (Haines and Morgan 2007).

Probation has been variably but significantly involved in helping to prevent avoidable remands in custody, by providing information to the court (or perhaps to the Crown Prosecution Service to assure them that bail need not be opposed) or providing services that directly address the grounds for refusing bail (bail support or accommodation). Much of this work is now undertaken by private or independent organisations rather than by probation: probation-run approved premises are primarily now a resettlement facility, with bail accommodation managed in the independent sector. As Octigan (2007: 264) suggests, probation's potential here is insufficiently realised: 'remand services continue to be vulnerable to changes in policy and other priorities have sometimes deflected attention away from their development'. Haines and Morgan (2007) deprecate probation's forced retreat from pre-trial services, insisting that the presumption of innocence, the principle of prison as a last resort and the human and emotional cost of custodial remand all require this to be a much greater priority.

People in prison

> I used to cut myself to try and get attention, and they've had me in straitjackets for that in Holloway. Sometimes I've tried to kill myself, like when I did this scar on my arm. I had a hundred stitches – it goes all the way up, and it was infected as well. I never cut myself on the outside, only in prison. I set my cell on fire because I hate being locked in . . . I couldn't have been trying to kill myself, because as soon as I set it on fire, I rang the bell. But as I was always getting put in my room and ringing the bell they probably thought, 'Oh, she's messing around again.' When they did come, I could have been dead, because all the smoke had got to me . . .
>
> (Joanne in Padel and Stevenson (1988): 156)

Notoriously, numbers of people in prison have been increasing and this is especially marked for women – an increase of 60 per cent over the past decade, compared to 28 per cent for men (Prison Reform Trust 2009). The reasons for this are far from clear. It cannot be explained by increases in the seriousness of their offending: women offend less often and less seriously than men (Gelsthorpe and Morris 2002). The vulnerability and distress experienced by many women in prison has been highlighted by the Corston Report (2007), which also emphasises the need to take account of their troubled lives and experiences of abuse.

Corston too drew attention to the consequences for children of their mothers' imprisonment. The court's first responsibility in taking decisions that affect children is to have regard to their welfare, but this principle has so far insufficiently influenced the sentencing of parents, whose incarceration inevitably has immeasurable consequences for the children (see http://www.familiesoutside.org.uk/).

In June 2008, 27 per cent of people in prison were from a minority ethnic group (compared with about 9 per cent in the general population), just over half of whom are black. The over-representation of black and minority ethnic groups in prison is quite well known; less well known, perhaps is the number of non-national offenders (Bhui 2008 and references there cited). In the last ten years or so, there has been an increase of 144 per cent in the number of foreign nationals in prison and as many as one in five women in prison are from other countries, more than half of them serving (often very long) sentences for drug offences. Other countries too are having the same experiences:

> One day last week I had to sentence a peasant woman from West Africa to 46 months in a drug case. The result for her young children will undoubtedly be, as she suggested, devastating . . . confirming my sense of depression about much of the cruelty I have been party to in connection with the 'war on drugs'

> . . . At the moment . . . I simply cannot sentence another impoverished person
> whose destruction has no discernible effect on the drug trade . . . I am just a
> tired old judge who has temporarily filled his quota of remorselessness.
>
> (US judge, quoted in Doob 1995: 229)

Foreign nationals often have an uncertain right of residence, complicated by their status as offenders. In popular debate, the matter becomes entangled with the politically volatile topics of immigration and deportation. While there has been agitation about the dangers of offenders released who 'should have' been deported, in truth this is an exceptionally vulnerable group of people, whose needs and risks cannot always be reliably managed at the interface between NOMS and the UK Border Agency. Some central probation concepts – reintegration, community, social capital – have a quite different significance for people who may be sent back to countries who may not want them and to which they may have no wish to return. Probation practice in this area is complex and still developing (Hammond 2007).

As noted in Chapter 3, it is often in the overlaps among groups (which figures sometimes fail to capture) that the most extreme disadvantages occur. For example, the chances for mothers to make adequate arrangements for their children are much worse for foreign nationals.

By any criteria, the prison population is a hugely disadvantaged group. The incidence of socio-economic marginalisation, lack of opportunities, inadequate access to services and ill-health is by now well known (Social Exclusion Unit 2002; Prison Reform Trust 2009). Prisoners are several times more likely to be mentally ill and the combination of vulnerabilities, stresses of incarceration and poor conditions lead to a high incidence of self-harm and suicide. Less well known perhaps are the difficulties associated with a 'young but ageing' prison population (Morgan and Liebling 2007) and an emerging recognition that the incidence of learning disability may be much higher than had been realised (Talbot 2008).

The extent to which disadvantage is associated with offending is disputed, although it is hard to think that troubled lives and deprivation are not part of the explanation of some offending careers and it is certain that social disadvantage is an obstacle to desistance. Punitive strategies, however, prefer to withhold the compassion they feel for some victims of some crimes from the many deprived and abused offenders who are serving sentences. As we shall see in Chapter 13, these can turn out to be the same people.

In prison

Figure 12.1 shows the steep increases in the prison population in recent years. An immediate consequence has been severe overcrowding, with pressure on all resources: demand exceeds supply for all facilities – cell space, out-of-cell activities, staff time with prisoners and training/rehabilitative programmes. Prisoners may be moved around the prison estate to ease pressure on the most overcrowded establishments. All of this subverts sentence planning and reduces opportunities for staff to provide purposeful regimes or sometimes even safe and

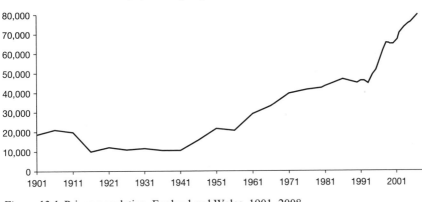

Figure 12.1 Prison population, England and Wales, 1901–2008

decent conditions (Bhui 2007). As was seen in Chapter 5, the greater the size of the population, the larger the number of prisoners likely to be reconvicted after release (Hedderman 2008).

While overcrowding and resource pressures have put the prison estate under enormous strain, Cavadino and Dignan (2007) argue that at the heart of the problem is a *crisis of legitimacy*. The penal system – perhaps prison in particular – is 'morally indefensible' (*ibid*.: 31) and courts, the public, offenders, victims and its own staff are not persuaded of its worth, its effectiveness and the justice of its practices. Prison's difficulties, then, arise from more than a crisis of resources: attempts to reorganise typically fail because these are not problems that are amenable to managerial solutions, but deeply based in moral and political uncertainties about punishment itself and in contradictory ideas of what punishment could and should achieve. (This is an example of how the theoretical models set out in Chapter 1 contribute to our understanding: questions of the moral significance of punishment are illuminated by the expressive model, while questions of social justice can scarcely be discussed without reference to the power model.)

This idea of legitimacy consciously echoes one of the main findings of Lord Woolf's (1991) inquiry into the riots that had taken place in a number of prisons in April 1990. Woolf argued that one of the main reasons for the disturbances was that prisons had been unable to persuade numbers of prisoners that they were being dealt with fairly. He urged prisons to found themselves on three principles: security, discipline (which Morgan later suggested might better be referred to as *good order*) and justice. These principles are inter-related: a just prison will be better ordered than one that is not just; a well-ordered prison will be more secure; the manner in which security and good order are accomplished affects staff and prisoner perceptions of fairness. The quality of relationships between prisoners and prison officers also makes a decisive difference to the legitimacy of the regime and the behaviour of the prisoners (Liebling 2004).

Although there have been changes in the language in which these matters are discussed, there is a clear thread – from the justice that Woolf affirmed, through the idea of legitimacy and the 'decency agenda' (Cavadino and Dignan 2007) to an awareness of the importance of prison's *moral performance* (Liebling 2004) – which recognises the meaning and significance of prison, not just its material characteristics. Again, these debates demonstrate the *expressive* character of criminal justice (Chapter 1) and the limitations of trying to understand prison simply in instrumental terms.

Rehabilitation in prison

One aspect of prisons' legitimacy is that people should go out from prison, if not reformed, at least not 'in an embittered and disaffected state' (Woolf 1991, quoted in Morgan and Liebling 2007: 1112) or posing an even greater risk of reoffending than before. Can prisons, in the nature of the case, achieve their contemporary statement of purpose to 'help [prisoners] lead law-abiding and useful lives in custody and after release' (HM Prison Service n.d.)?

Historically, attempts to effect reform in prison have been through work, schooling, moral influence and discipline (Mathiesen 1990). Yet reformative aspirations have commonly been frustrated: through the process of what Carlen (2002) has termed 'carceral clawback', prison by its very nature militates against constructive rehabilitative work, subordinating other objectives to the imperatives of security and control. Foucault's seminal analysis (1977) too suggests that prison generates power relationships of its own, imposing priorities of security and control that transcend any 'purposes' that may be set for it.

This is by no means to deny the value of much that takes place in prison. Accredited programmes run in prison, for example, have constituted an influential part of the evidence base for effectiveness (Raynor 2004a). While programmes in the community have been found to have better results (see Chapters 6 and 8), effectiveness is also known to be associated with programme completion – something that prisons might, at least in principle, be better placed to ensure. Yet prison is an artificial setting, providing few opportunities to apply and test out learning from programmes in the real world.

> For me, prison was a positive experience. I know – I'm thoroughly convinced – that if I hadn't gone to jail at that time there would have been some sort of disaster waiting for me. Because I was up to my eyeballs in gear, I was taking sulphate, everything to try and blot out my father's death, my job loss, my daughter going, everything. And I didn't care – I became reckless because of it. The crime thing didn't matter to me, it was something that gave me a buzz, this getting involved in crime.
>
> (Milos 'Mish' Biberovic in Devlin and Turney 1999: 117)

There may be times when imprisonment is unavoidable for public protection or to mark the seriousness of a grave offence. There are also times when people's behaviour is so offensive and self-destructive that, at least for a while, there is benefit from the constraint that prison can bring. None of this should be allowed to conceal the destructive effects of prison, not least its capacity to undermine or to destroy almost all the factors known to be associated with desistance. If we consider the 'pathways' (Chapter 8), it is hard to think of one that is not obstructed by a term of imprisonment.

An intrinsic problem is that a total institution effectively precludes inmates' taking responsibility for themselves or for others. There are, however, approaches to imprisonment that try to envisage how this could be different. The European Prison Rules (Council of Europe 2006a) include a principle of *normalisation* – a prisoner's life should be as much like life in the community as possible. Pryor (2001) explores how regimes might change to maximise opportunities to accept responsibility. These include not only personal responsibilities and duties towards dependants, but also the duties of citizenship that members of a community have towards one another (Faulkner 2002).

> Parts of me had changed and for the first time in my life I was thinking not as a victim but as a person who had been responsible for doing things that I shouldn't have. I qualify this by pointing out that whenever I was sentenced in the past for something and came into prison, the humiliation and degradation I met with there made me think of myself as the victim. I hadn't given a shit for the person or deed I was in for, or had any sympathy, as I had been too concerned with my own miseries and misfortunes . . . this unit was allowing me to function responsibly and in order to achieve this one had to think responsibly.
>
> (Boyle 1977: 251)

Jimmy Boyle strikingly contrasts earlier experiences of imprisonment with his time in the Barlinnie Special Unit, but such regimes could not be said to be typical. The tragic irony is that offenders, often denounced by courts for being irresponsible, are put in a position where, typically, they are insulated from all the responsibilities that they need to learn to accept.

It is has been argued that the legitimacy of imprisonment rests at least partly on its capacity to release people who are less likely to reoffend than when they went in. There are ways of developing prison regimes to enable and encourage prisoners to take more responsibility (Pryor 2001) and a number of valuable initiatives that seek to enhance the personal skills offenders will need in order to cope on release. Even so, there are tensions in the very idea of imprisonment – especially the denial of responsibility in a total institution – that militate against these initiatives.

The role of probation

The offender management model envisages a key role for community-based probation staff who, as offender managers, should assess and plan, influencing the individual's experience of prison. This involves close liaison with staff in prison who are in regular contact with the offender. While much of this communication takes place directly with prison officers, the role of seconded probation officers is central. These are probation staff who work in prison, accountable to the governor but also to their employing Trust, who represent probation to the prison and, especially in local prisons, may often act as the link with outside services involved in the resettlement and rehabilitation of short-term prisoners, thus representing the prison to the community.

Probation staff in prison undertake different tasks in different prisons, depending partly on the type of establishment, but also on the governor's conception of their role (Williams 2008). They are typically involved in assessment and planning and contribute to decisions on temporary release, parole and release subject to home detention curfew. They are often part of a larger team who deliver accredited programmes. The days when probation staff were regarded as affable but naive 'welfare' officers, both by prisoners and by staff, have largely gone and there is greater understanding between probation and prison staff and integration in their work. Senior probation officers have often become a key part of the prison management team, even though they continue to work on secondment, assigned roles like 'head of resettlement', in which they may supervise prison staff (Hancock 2007e). Hancock anticipates that the implementation of OMM will increasingly shape the character of the probation prison team, as prisons move to establish offender management units, but this has been an uneven process and many prisoners in effect remain outside of the model.

Resettlement

> Prison culture, it dominates you, it's all around you. Some guys in prison, they climb up on chairs and tables in the cells and look out through the bars at what they can see of the outside world. And they talk of it, and talk of it, but it's never anything else but fantasies and dreams. 'When I get out, when I get out . . .'
>
> ('Andy Reid' in Parker 1991: 110)

In the 1980s and 1990s, the emphasis on community sentences arguably displaced work with former prisoners as a priority for probation. Yet in the past ten years this has changed markedly and resettlement work has attracted initiatives in policy, practice and in research. A joint thematic inspection (HMI Probation /HMI Prisons 2001) urged both agencies to assert the central importance of this work and to collaborate in its implementation. The Social Exclusion Unit Report (2002) was signally influential, drawing attention to the large volume of crime committed by ex-prisoners and linking this with their multiple needs and social exclusion, stimulating an inter-agency, cross-departmental approach to resettlement. And indeed the Carter Report, deploring the 'silos' of prison and probation, found this to be a principal reason to create a National Offender Management Service (see Chapter 14).

The Halliday report spoke of implementing prison and post-release interventions 'seamlessly' and the seamless sentence has become a guiding idea. Yet it is hard to think of a sharper facture in an individual's life – being in prison on one day and in the community the next. All the parameters of behaviour that were considered in Chapter 9 – normative, instrumental, constraint-based and habitual – are all completely different. Routines and constraints have obviously changed; just as plainly, the reasons to behave in particular ways – the costs and benefits of certain courses of action, normative considerations, even the possibility of taking independent action – are entirely altered.

The aspiration is to provide a seamless continuity of service, but can services be abstracted from the context of their provision? Resource shortages and the logistics of managing an overcrowded estate conspire against seamlessness. The term *throughcare* had well expressed this idea of integration, but practice had deteriorated over time (Maguire and Raynor 2006) and the recent political re-emphasis may not be assumed to have been matched by an enhancement in practice. Prisoners report that they value working with the same person during and after the sentence (Raynor and Maguire 2006; Maguire 2007), but role specialisation and costs are making prison visits ever harder to undertake, undermining the relationships that are believed to be so important in the process of desistance (Chapter 9). Again, there are circumstances in which community providers come to pre-release groups and present a market-place of services (Maguire 2007), but many prisoners are some distance from the areas where they will live on release. Continuity of role and of the type of service provided may be the best that can be hoped for, but even this is variably achieved and it is doubtful anyway that this is enough. It seems to be a continuity of personal relationship that matters most (Raynor and Maguire 2006).

This hoped for continuity has a long history – and perhaps a history of disappointment.

> Borstal training falls into two parts. In the first part a lad is trained in custody at an Institution: in the second part he enjoys the comparative freedom of licence or supervision, and is under the training of the Borstal Association. The functions of the two bodies dovetail closely into one another. The one sort of training will fail if the other is badly done.
>
> (Prison Commission 1932: 31)

While this Borstal vision deploys the (better) metaphor of woodwork (*dovetail*) rather than needlecraft (*seam*), the idea is much the same.

Among the most important changes in post-release work has been the change of emphasis from voluntary support to statutory compulsion. Until the Criminal Justice Act 1991, while many serious offenders were supervised compulsorily on parole or life licence, most adult offenders left prison without further obligation and after-care was voluntary. (It was voluntary in the sense that ex-prisoners could choose whether or not to avail themselves of this offered support, though the Probation Rules required services to provide it.) But subsequently all those serving

sentences of more than 12 months became subject to a period of formal supervision and a further period during which the possibility of recall remained. These
are people who did not choose probation involvement and may not be assumed to
be suitable for community supervision (Maguire 2007).

The political imperatives that have shaped these developments have been public
protection and the management of risk posed by former prisoners, but also the
need to deploy early release mechanisms to manage the prison population while
trying to avoid any sense that this is a premature ending of the deserved punishment. Contemporary resettlement often emphasises that the period of licence
following release is *a continuation of the sentence, only in the community.* Here we
have an inversion of the principle of normalisation: instead of prison regimes
aspiring to be like life in the community, the conditions of post-release supervision
strive to be prison-like.

> MAPPA and other arrangements (Chapter 10) are often deployed to manage
> the risks posed by people released from prison. Approved premises
> (Dunkley 2007) constitute one important component of an overall strategy.
> Formerly known as hostels, and often in the past accommodating people
> on bail to avoid custodial remand, premises (approved under Offender
> Management Act 2007 s. 13) are increasingly filled by prisoners believed to
> pose a high risk of serious harm. This provision is especially necessary for
> people who have nowhere else to live. Perhaps because they may not return
> to a former residence, premises often accommodate sex offenders – a
> change in the resident profile that can cause concerns among communities
> and alters the character of the establishment. Approved premises are staffed
> 24 hours a day, require residents to be in by a certain time and seek to
> provide a coherent programme of activities. But they are (emphatically) not
> prisons.

This conception of post-release work leads to an approach to resettlement
characterised by compulsion, tight enforcement and a focus on risk and criminogenic need. One consequence has been the substantial increase in the incidence of
recall to prison: not only reoffending or an assessed increased risk, but also non-
compliance in itself are grounds for recall – with significant inflationary impact
on the prison population (Padfield and Maruna 2006).

The move away from voluntary after-care has entailed the effective withdrawal
of service from short-term prisoners who have high(er) reconviction rates and
high(er) social needs (Maguire 2007). These prisoners had fewer rehabilitative
opportunities in prison, inadequate preparation for release and help with release
plans, and in the community experience exclusion, for example, discrimination in
employment markets and perhaps in finding accommodation. Some medium-term
prisoners too have very short periods of supervision and inadequate support on

release. Resettlement work then concentrates on longer-term prisoners, many of whom do not need it, while the short-termers are denied service (Hough *et al.* 2006).

There is widespread scepticism about the value of short sentences. There is little or no chance to offer prisoners useful rehabilitative interventions. Any respite for the public from their offending is brief – postponement more than prevention. High 'turnover' is resource-intensive, making it difficult for prison to focus on the work of rehabilitation of more serious offenders. Most of the efforts of post-release work are spent on trying to put right problems that have been caused or aggravated by prison itself – for example, loss of accommodation or employment and disruption to personal relationships. Courts, however, continue to impose short sentences. People serving six months or less made up half of all prison receptions in 2007 – more than 90,000 people. The many attempts to change this, most recently through the idea of custody plus (not implemented) (J. Roberts 2007), have all foundered. Changes in law and policy here seem likely.

While approaches to resettlement have typically been evaluated for their effects on reconviction, a more rounded approach recognises the importance of other criteria besides (Lewis *et al.* 2007). After pointing out that the term *resettlement* evokes an often entirely misleading idea of resuming a settled life that was enjoyed before, Maguire (2007) considers several models. A desistance paradigm, for example, might emphasise the strengths and potential of former prisoners, in the belief that through agency and generativity offenders may achieve and sustain desistance (Burnett and Maruna 2006; also Chapter 9). A community model importantly recognises that reintegration calls not only for a reformed ex-offender, but a responsive and receptive community, implying a responsibility to provide accessible services and opportunities to enable offenders to desist.

While punitive strategies may emphasise continuing the sentence in the community, there is a moral basis for resettlement. Robinson and Raynor (2006: 339) urge a conception of rehabilitation that is conceptually distinct from punishment and may even be an 'antidote to punishment's harmful effects', while Lewis (2005) reaffirms a *right to rehabilitation*. Since imprisonment has effectively blocked so many legitimate 'pathways' and closed off so many opportunities, since the state has confined prisoners to the total institution and assumed responsibility for their lives, it incurs weighty corresponding responsibilities towards them (Canton 2010b).

The lexicon of the Council of Europe (see the Glossary in Council of Europe 2010) includes *after-care* which is distinguished from resettlement by its voluntary character, but affirmed as a duty of the state towards those of its members who have completed their sentence and have a right to meaningful opportunities of reintegration.

> I do feel prison's where I belong. There are good days and bad days, but even on the good days that feeling doesn't change . . . if the truth's to be said, I'm beyond the pale of ordinary society and couldn't ever get back inside it again. I don't think I'm properly living in society and never could because I'm not

a fit member of it, I only belong to it in theory, I'd like to put it like that. I'm outside humanity, both in humanity's eyes and mine.

('Philip Derbyshire' in Parker 1991: 167)

As Maguire (2007) notes, different models of resettlement are rarely found in a pure form and typically represent an accommodation among competing conceptions of what is due to people after release. As we have seen, political strategies have reframed this question and replaced it with (legitimate) concerns about public protection, but the extent to which the state and the community has responsibilities to reintegrate, as well as rights against offenders, is insufficiently part of the political debate.

What does this mean for probation? It suggests that the current understanding of practice should be complemented by a perspective that recognises the value of the personal relationship in facilitating change, appreciating that the change process is appropriately led by the ex-prisoner rather than the practitioner, acknowledging that reoffending must be understood as among the vicissitudes of desistance, and developing new skills – especially those of advocacy, representing to the community the ex-prisoner's needs and legitimate aspirations and calling upon their responsibilities (McNeill *et al.* 2005).

The National Action Plan (Home Office 2004b) represents a clear recognition of the social preconditions of effective reintegration. Maguire (2007: 416), however, summarises some of the difficulties, including:

- the sheer scale of the problem – the numbers of ex-prisoners and the extent of their needs;
- questions about how services are to be paid for, especially after a licence period ends;
- resources are likely to be matched to OMM tier (Chapter 7), but many, denied the services they need, will go on to pose an increasing risk;
- can hard-pressed public services give priority to offenders? Priority usually is (arguably should be) given to those in most need and while some offenders are among the neediest, there are many others whose need is quite as great.

Summary

We must not forget that when every material improvement has been effected in prisons, when the temperature has been adjusted, when the proper food to maintain health and strength has been given, when the doctors, chaplains, and prison visitors have come and gone, the convict stands deprived of everything that a free man calls life. We must not forget that all these improvements, which are sometimes salves to our consciences, do not change that position.

(Winston Churchill, Speech to Home Office Supply, July 1910)

Newspapers occasionally incite warm and righteous indignation among their readers with stories of the luxuries of imprisonment. Yet a moment's reflection reveals the truth of Churchill's words: practically everything that is valued in a worthwhile life is lost or jeopardised through imprisonment. In Chapter 9 we saw that it is in the context of a meaningful life that desistance is achieved and sustained: imprisonment is to this extent inherently obstructive of desistance.

In this chapter, we have seen probation's relationship with prison, looked at some of the characteristics of prison and prisoners and considered resettlement. It has been suggested that a different focus – attending to rights to rehabilitation no less than to risks of reoffending – would represent a sounder ethical base for probation's work here. Since this would serve to enhance probation's legitimacy, it would tend to strengthen compliance and may turn out to be more effective even by the criteria of reconviction.

Questions for discussion

- A Home Secretary famously once claimed 'Prison works'. Do you agree?
- Who ought to be in prison?
- What kind of arrangements should be made to support foreign nationals in prison and to prepare for their release?

Further reading

Jewkes (2007) is a valuable collection of papers on many aspects of imprison-ment. Coyle (2005) is very useful. Morgan and Liebling (2007) is a brief but authoritative overview. Statistics about prison and prisoners are well compiled in the Prison Reform Trust (2009). On resettlement, Raynor (2004), Maguire and Raynor (2006), Raynor and Maguire (2006) and Maguire (2007) are strongly recommended. Hucklesby and Hagley-Dickinson (2007) includes many important contributions about resettlement.

13 Victims, probation and criminal justice

This chapter will discuss probation's work with victims of crime. The criminal justice system's historical neglect of victims will first be considered, then the evolution of probation's practice with victims. The sharp political distinction between offenders and victims will be questioned – offenders are often a highly victimised group, although punitive political rhetoric fails to acknowledge this or to take it seriously. The chapter will conclude with some comments about restorative approaches to crime.

Victims and the criminal justice system

Garland (2001) identified the *return of the victim* as one of the characteristics of contemporary criminal justice debate. Yet to a significant extent this is more a first arrival than a return. It is not easy to point to a time when victims' interests were a prominent (much less the main) consideration of a criminal justice system which sets for itself priorities of detection, prosecution, conviction and punishment – all processes that centre on the offender.

Victims contribute to these criminal justice processes, but it seems more accurate to describe their involvement as *in the service of the system*: there is no sense that the system is putting victims first. Joanna Shapland famously likened victims to *peasants* whose interests are disregarded by the agencies of criminal justice, the *fiefs* – independent powerful domains – with quite different concerns and priorities (1988). More recently, Victims' Champion Sara Payne reflected that 'Initiatives which have sought, often effectively, to improve support for victims and witnesses must nonetheless operate within a system which has always had at its heart different objectives than meeting the complete needs of victims' (Payne 2009: 10) and called for a new perspective.

It is not only the formal priorities of the system that may work against the interests of victims. The power model of criminal justice (Chapter 1) helps to explain why, because of systematic differences in power, some crimes and victim experiences are more readily able to command political attention and response. For example, violence against women often fails to gain the political priority that it merits (Fawcett Society 2009). Similarly *hate crime* is typically perpetrated against structurally disadvantaged or oppressed groups – minority ethnic groups, gay and lesbian people, those with a disability – and thus often struggles to gain attention and response.

The idea of secondary victimisation – that victims' experience of criminal justice might be so distressing as to amount to a further abuse – has become familiar. Victims expecting that their dealings with criminal justice would lead to a vindication of their experience have often been sorely disappointed. Concern for the victim is a natural expression of an ethical approach to criminal justice, but, at a political level, the victim has often been recruited by the proponents of a punitive strategy simply to urge more severe punishment – usually with disregard for what victims of crime really want (Christie 2010).

An increasing awareness that the agencies of criminal justice often did not do well by the victims of crime (e.g. Shapland 1998) and the *politicisation* of crime and punishment (Downes and Morgan 1997) led in 1990 to the publication of a 'Victim's Charter', assigning particular responsibilities to agencies and setting out what victims were entitled to expect in their dealings with them. A second (and stronger) Charter was issued in 1996 (Home Office 1996), but the Charters were not well known or extensively used by victims (Williams 2007). In April 2006, the Charter was replaced by a 'Code of Practice' which, for the first time, introduced a legal requirement for criminal justice agencies to provide minimum standards of service to victims of crime. The Code puts emphasis on *informing* victims about the progress of 'their' case – when someone is arrested, charged, bailed and sentenced – as well as providing for an enhanced service for vulnerable and intimidated victims (Criminal Justice System 2006). As we shall see, in the more serious cases, this giving of information continues during an offender's prison term when the probation service has a central role.

There have, then, been determined endeavours over the past twenty years to improve the victim experience of criminal justice. While these have sometimes been initially disappointing (see the fairly bleak review in the White Paper, *Justice for All* (Home Office 2002)), there has been undeniable progress and one inspection found that 81 per cent of victims and witnesses were satisfied with their experience of criminal justice (CJJI 2009). Another inquiry found almost three-quarters (74 per cent) of respondents to be satisfied with the information provided about the criminal justice process (Moore and Blakeborough 2008).

What does society owe to victims?

Should we speak of the needs of victims or their rights? Some rights may be established in statute or in formal commitments like the Code of Practice. The Council of Europe (2006b) has also tried to set out what is due to victims, drawing out the practical implications of the European Human Rights Convention. Victims' most fundamental entitlements have been said:

- to be heard, and treated with dignity, fairness and respect;
- to be provided with information about the criminal justice system and the outcome of their case, and protected from 'secondary victimisation' by criminal justice agencies;

- in certain cases, to be provided with or referred for counselling or support to address the emotional impact of the offence;
- to be protected from further victimisation, especially where there is concern that the same offender might revictimise them (Williams and Goodman 2007: 523–524).

These claims seem relatively uncontroversial – at least in general and in principle – which is not to say that they are easy to achieve in practice. Yet victims' needs are diverse in many other respects. Some may need practical advice or financial compensation, others personal support – for example, counselling. Williams (2007: 323) emphasises the value of reassurance: 'it can be enormously helpful to be told that others react in similar ways and that there is nothing abnormal about their own responses'.

Reactions can include denial, shock, wariness, a loss of trust in other people, fear, rage and shame. This plainly depends upon the nature of the offence(s), the victim's personality and circumstances, the extent to which family or friends can support them. Some people are overwhelmed by crimes that appear to be relatively minor, while others appear resilient to even very serious offences.

The impact of 'the same offence' can differ. Williams (2007: 323) gives the example of assault occasioning actual bodily harm, where circumstances and context can make a substantial difference: 'For example, since women as victims of domestic violence have often suffered numerous assaults before they report this abuse, their experience of victimisation is quite different from that of (say) a young man assaulted outside a pub.' Again, victims of hate crime experience not only discrete (and cumulatively oppressive) episodes of harassment or assault, but a threat to their identity – and to others who share that identity. The appropriate response may accordingly need to be different.

Victims of crime, incidentally, have not been found to be more than averagely punitive in their attitudes – either towards 'their' offender(s) or towards offenders in general (Maruna and King 2004). It may not be assumed that the weighty punishment of offenders must be what victims want, much less that this is all that they need.

Probation and the victims of crime

Pease (1999) reflected that, if a probation service were to be created today, services for victims would be set as a central part of its work. As it is, acquiring responsibilities to victims came late to probation, and, mirroring the difficulties of the wider criminal justice system, it has not always found it easy to accommodate this work within the structures of a service organised to supervise offenders.

It would not be fair to say that probation neglected victims: on the contrary, at a local level, the service often supported local groups and played an influential and honourable part in helping to set up victim support services (Mawby 2007; Williams 2007). Yet this work was often done by a few committed individuals and it was not until the 1990s that the service began to engage thoroughly with its new responsibilities to provide information to victims through *victim contact* (Crawford and Enterkin 2001). Williams (2007: 321) remarks that 'In the probation context, working with victims was new and, for many staff, threatening: some felt that they had trained to work with offenders and saw no need for change.' Perhaps other reasons for probation's diffidence here included an awareness that, in political debate, affirmation of the rights of victims was often translated into an urge for more punitive treatment of offenders.

It should also be noted that until these responsibilities were assigned, probation staff never met victims – not, that is, in their respective roles of probation officer and victim – so that it was possible for probation officers to exclude victims from their professional consciousness in a way that is not possible for, say, police officers, who often have vivid and distressing encounters with the victims of crime.

Even the original Victim's Charter had little impact in many areas: many probation services are said simply to have ignored it (Mawby 2007: 226) and at the best it was implemented incompletely and unevenly. Better supported by policy documents, instructions and guidance, the 1996 Charter extended probation's responsibility. While the original charter had required probation to make contact with the families of victims in cases where the offender had been sentenced to life imprisonment, the 1996 Charter prescribed that when an offender had received a custodial sentence of more than four years (or, in specified circumstances, a shorter term) for a violent or sexual offence, the victim(s) would be contacted (Probation Circular 61/1995). The Criminal Justice and Court Services Act 2000 (s.69) enacted these rights to contact for the first time (Gerty 2007), extending them to victims of violent or sexual offenders who had been sentenced to one year or more. Face-to-face contact should be offered within 56 working days of sentence (Probation Circular 62/2001).

Through this contact, the meaning and implications of the sentence are be explained and the victim asked if they wish to be kept informed about the timing of release and, when release comes to be considered, if there are any particular concerns they feel ought to be taken into account. The information disclosed to the victim is limited to matters that bear on their legitimate interests and their safety. They are informed of significant developments or milestones in the sentence (notably temporary release), but are not, for example, told the name of the prison where the offender is detained.

There are many important considerations here. First, probation's role is to give information, rather than personal support or counselling. Where victims need personal support, the proper course is referral (for example to counselling or psychological services or for legal advice about claiming for criminal injury compensation), requiring sensitive cooperation with victims' organisations. But while probation's role is formally circumscribed in this way, in practice the distinction between informing and listening and, on the other hand, giving active support is not always easy to sustain. Initial contact follows soon after the sentencing decision when distress and fear may still be acute. Victims – who will often be experiencing some of the reactions that were described earlier in this chapter – may well want to talk about this. Gerty (2007: 322) refers to a victim who may need help to articulate fears – 'for example, that a sex offender may persist in harassment or abuse during or after the term of imprisonment'. Contact and dialogue are likely to evoke painful memories and discussion must be managed sensitively. If the victim is in distress or confusion, no probation representative will close the conversation abruptly by insisting upon a rigid role demarcation. As in other probation encounters, the role differentiation that is important to professionals may not necessarily be seen by service users in quite the same way. Victim contact is never just a technical or administrative task, but emotionally demanding, calling for personal sensitivity – and self-awareness – as well as for reliable knowledge of the criminal justice system (Williams and Goodman 2007).

Second, the victim contact worker's role is not limited to giving information, but also involves attending carefully to the victim's views about the circumstances of release and making sure that they are brought to the attention of those who will take the decision. This may lead to additional licence conditions, commonly requirements not to contact the victim and geographical restrictions. There are many challenges here. Approaches to victims near the time of release can be especially difficult if there has been little or no contact (for whatever reason) since the sentence was imposed. Again, victims must be made aware that their views will be taken seriously but will never be decisive. There is a risk that 'victim contact work blurs and confuses the decision-making process and the victim's role therein' (Crawford and Enterkin 2001: 719). The worker must therefore make sure that no unreal expectation is raised that will later give rise to frustration or anger that the victim's views did not determine the outcome.

Since natural justice seems to require that offenders should know why decisions about them are taken – and perhaps enabled to challenge the information on which they are based – hard questions arise about confidentiality. Sometimes submissions might, if disclosed to the offender, compromise the victim's safety. 'Special victim advocates' were appointed whose original responsibility was to protect victims' interests (Gerty 2007). The same considerations arise where the victim discloses potentially sensitive information about the offence(s) which may (perhaps for evidential reasons) not have been available to the court, but which have clear relevance to judgements about risk.

Who should represent the service in making the contact? Should it be the same officer as the offender's supervisor? (Are there role conflicts here?) Or another officer? Or a specialist? Probation areas have used all of these models and there is no clear evidence that one is superior to another. Meanwhile, specialist victim contact staff are increasingly common (Crawford and Enterkin 2001; Williams and Goodman 2007).

Crawford and Enterkin (2001) complain about a lack of coherence in victim services and the inadequate attention given to the place of contact work among other initiatives for victims. Spalek similarly suggests that probation work with victims lacks an explicit or coherent philosophy. Yet, she argues, such a philosophy may be inferred which 'incorporates a de-politicised, consumerist and individualistic notion of the victim' (2003: 218), side-lining radical and politicised responses represented by organisations like *Rape Crisis*, which often pose uncomfortable challenges to the main agencies of criminal justice. Issues of power and of diversity are quite as salient in working with victims as in working with offenders. Spalek's critique also points to the potential influence of the (relatively) new discipline of victimology, which was beginning to offer distinct theoretical approaches to the understanding of victims with different implications for policy and practice (Hoyle and Zedner 2007).

One area where contact work has been criticised is domestic violence (Williams and Goodman 2007). The challenge of undertaking this work well include the context of the offence(s), the prior relationship between victim and offender and the possibility of some kind of continuing contact with attendant risks of further abuse. Here the priority is to reduce the incidence of any repetition and 'contact' may be bound up with continuing work with the victim. The Integrated Domestic Abuse Programme (see Chapter 8) involves support to and consultation with victims. Another example is the use of Multi-Agency Risk Assessment Conferences (MARACs) in response to domestic violence (Robinson 2004). Organisationally, MARAC builds on the achievements of MAPPA (see Chapter 10). Victim participation is central to the management of risk reduction: Robinson and Tregidga (2005) found that victims appreciated a multi-agency approach in helping them to make their own lives safer. Similar approaches have been used to support victims of sexual violence, where the involvement of independent advisers has added to the value of services (Robinson 2009). MARAC and IDAP help victims to safeguard themselves and to contribute actively to the reduction of risk.

Developments in victim contact work have been periodically inspected by HMIP who have variously commented on the need for greater consistency in service provision, the importance of training for staff to do this work well and the value of monitoring race and ethnicity to ensure fair provision (Williams and Goodman 2007). Even so, the achievements of victim contact work in probation should be appreciated: probation has come a long way in a relatively short time and a MORI survey, for example, found that 81 per cent of victims were satisfied with the treatment they received from the Victim Contact Service (National Probation Service 2004).

Victim awareness

Victim contact is not the only aspect of probation's work with victims. The authors of pre-sentence reports are expected to demonstrate 'victim awareness', by considering the impact of offences upon victims, although in many cases they have little direct information on which to base such an assessment. (Probation staff rarely if ever contact victims directly in the course of preparing a PSR.) OASys includes assessment of the offender's recognition of the impact of the offence and supervision may seek to develop this: many groupwork programmes, for example, include specific sessions on victim awareness, sometimes designed in consultation with victim representatives (Williams and Goodman 2007). When serious offenders are considered for early release on licence, as we have seen, probation reports should address victims' safety and concerns.

It is often assumed that offenders who become more aware of the consequences of their offending will become more remorseful and less likely to offend. Yet it is not at all easy to gauge or interpret the offender's degree of remorse (Dominey 2002). For that matter, there is little empirical evidence of a link between remorse and reduced reoffending. Nevertheless, it seems morally fitting that offenders be brought to recognise and accept responsibility for the wrongs that they have done: one of the purposes of punishment is to communicate moral disapproval and to affirm the values offenders have flouted (see Chapter 4; Duff 2007). *How* this may be achieved is another matter. Offenders – though, to be sure, not only criminal offenders – deploy *techniques of neutralisation* (Sykes and Matza 1957) to persuade practitioners, judges, others and commonly themselves that the crime they committed should be mitigated or even absolved. (*They asked for it. There was no real harm done. It was only because of the drink.*) Probation work can and should look to work with this neutralisation to try to strengthen the ethical constraints that may inhibit further offending.

As our consideration of motivation and dealing with resistance suggests, hectoring and scolding are unlikely to enhance victim empathy. Indirect approaches – for example posing scenarios or hypothetical cases and asking offenders to consider effects on victims – can be useful. Restorative approaches (see below) encourage contact between victim and offender where the human consequences of the offence may be made vividly apparent to the offender. Williams and Goodman (2007) offer examples of victims' participating in mediation encounters in prison and/or meeting with prisoners who have committed the types of offence they have themselves experienced.

It is hoped that an appreciation of the distress caused to the victim(s) will occasion empathy and remorse. It should be remembered, however, that there are some offenders whose reaction will be very different and for whom evocation of this distress may even be part of the stimulus to offend. This calls for considerable skill and emotional literacy from the practitioner.

Victims and offenders

Dennis and Shaun – part one

The police are called to a house in a run-down part of an inner city area. Neighbours have heard shouting and banging from next door. They arrive to find Dennis, aged 41, shut up in a kitchen cupboard. The door has been wedged shut from the outside with a broom. Dennis says he has been there in the dark for nearly 24 hours and is plainly in considerable distress. He is taken to hospital, but apart from discomfort and shock he seems otherwise unharmed. He tells the police that three young lads came into his house uninvited. They made him give them drinks and biscuits and then started to tease and torment him. When he asked them to leave, they swore at him and threatened him. They then shut him up in the cupboard. He doesn't know their names, but he thinks they live nearby. Neighbours tell the police that Dennis has lived alone since his mother died last year. They say he is 'none too bright' and they see him as a loner and a bit odd, but 'with no harm in him'.

What reactions do you have when you read this account? How do you think Dennis might be feeling? What initial thoughts do you have about what should now be done to or with the 'three young lads'? How do you think this might be reported in a newspaper?

In political debate, a sharp distinction is typically drawn between offenders and victims and, generally, between the law-abiding majority and the (relatively) few that prey upon them. Spalek (2003) is among those who criticise a mind-set which imagines an 'ideal victim' starkly contrasted with an (equally stereotyped) offender, failing to do justice to the realities of many crimes. Political rhetoric sets the rights and interests of victims and offenders in opposition and a 'balance' must be struck. Yet if the interests of victims and offenders are assumed to be in opposition, as the metaphor of balance implies, every gain for offenders must entail a loss for victims and any claim for the rights of offenders will immediately be regarded with suspicion.

One consequence of this is offenders become *ineligible to be victims*. The Criminal Injuries Compensation Authority (2008) allows that compensation may be reduced or withheld on the basis of the victim's character as indicated by a criminal record. Consider too the claim that people cannot offend while they are in prison. Yet all manner of crimes are committed in prisons, of course (O'Donnell and Edgar 1998) and to deny the importance of this or victim status to the victims of those crimes is quite unjustifiable – and a direct result of a felt need to make offenders and victims exclusive categories. As we shall see, the terms in which this debate is conducted have directly discriminatory consequences for women.

Dennis and Shaun – part two

The police soon identify one of the lads, Shaun (aged 11), who lives just round the corner. He has nothing to say at first. The police emphasise the seriousness of the matter and mention the possibility of a charge of aggravated burglary. Shaun then begins to give a different account. He says that he and his mates had started chatting to Dennis on odd days during the school holidays. Dennis then began to invite them into the house quite often, giving them drinks and snacks. He also gave them cigarettes and sometimes offered them alcohol. On the day of the incident, they had gone in and found him watching a pornographic film. He said they could watch it with him if they wanted to and gave them some strong cider. After they had been watching for a while, Dennis touched one of the boys who became alarmed and then angry. Dennis then left the room. They followed him into the kitchen and shut him in the cupboard.

The other two boys (both aged 10) are soon identified and substantially confirm what Shaun has said, although there is some disagreement about who pushed Dennis into the cupboard and jammed the door.

What reactions do you have when you read this account? How do you think Shaun and the others may be feeling? What initial thoughts do you have about what should now be done to or with Dennis? How do you think this might be reported in a newspaper?

Offenders as victims

There is compelling evidence that offenders are themselves a disproportionately victimised group. The Edinburgh studies of youth transitions and crime (see Smith 2004; McAra and McVie 2007) are finding that young people with criminal records are significantly more highly victimised than those without. An inquiry by Victim Support (2007) confirmed that young people who have been victims of violence may themselves go on to become violent offenders and that those who offend violently may become victims of violence. After all, people whose lifestyles are associated with offending are exposed to considerable risks of victimisation. As Farrall and Maltby put it (2003: 49) 'thieves may experience theft themselves, those who assault others may themselves be assaulted and drug users may receive death threats and attempts on their lives'. Homelessness, for example, is associated with offending (in complex ways) and is also a risk marker for being a victim of violence (BBC 2004). Earlier chapters have considered offenders' characteristic social exclusion and these dimensions are the same for victims.

Rumgay (2004) summarised the strong association between women's involvement as offenders in the criminal justice system and their experiences of victimisation, while Corston (2007) insisted that the offending behaviour of many women can only be understood in the context of a history of abuse. Boswell (1996) showed that the same is true of many – probably most – of the young men who commit grave crimes.

It is likely that experiences of abuse are part of an understanding of the reason why some people offend. There is no inevitable consequence and many victims of serious abuse do not offend. It is important to be aware, however, that the children about whom we are so properly concerned as victims and the young demons we vilify some years later may well be the same people. Probation staff supervising offenders need to be sensitised to the possibility that this is a highly victimised and often vulnerable group, even as they discharge their responsibilities to contribute to public protection (Farrall and Maltby 2003). And when working to enhance victim empathy, it should be borne in mind that 'Some offenders may need to work through issues relating to their own victimisation before they can begin to contemplate putting themselves psychologically into the position of their own victims' (Williams and Goodman 2007: 530).

Restorative justice

Dennis and Shaun – part three

When the boys' account is put to Dennis, he becomes tearful. He says that he had befriended them because he was lonely, but they had taken advantage of him. They often came uninvited and had begun to bully him. They had just let themselves in on that day and laughed at him when he told them to go. He thought they had been drinking, but he strongly denies that he had ever given them any alcohol. When asked about the allegation that he had touched them, he becomes both distressed and angry. He says that they are making up cruel lies to put the blame on him.

Do the categories of victim and offender help us to make sense of this event? What offences may have taken place? What is the community interest in this? What would be the best way of responding to what has taken place? Who if anyone should be cautioned or prosecuted?

The conventional responses of criminal justice call for censure for offenders, sympathy for victims. But while few incidents are as ambiguous as the story of Dennis and Shaun (based on an experience of the author's when a probation officer), there are some occasions where the need to assign the roles of offender and victim – one role to the exclusion of the other – distorts the character of what has actually taken place, loses any sense of context and limits the possibility of resolution.

Restorative justice offers a different 'lens' (Zehr 1990). It sets as its priority making amends for the harms that a crime has caused. While the topic is considered here in our chapter about victims, it should not be seen as 'for' victims any more than it is 'for' offenders. It tries to transcend the political assumption that the interests of victims and offenders are inherently opposed to one another and concentrates on peaceful solutions to the conflicts that crime represents. The community has responsibilities here too, not only because both offender and victim are (typically) members of that community, but also because the crime can be a symptom of problems which the community needs to address, as the concept of community justice recognises (see Chapter 14).

Restorative justice aspires to healing and resolution. An approach that depends upon external control over the offender is inherently limited. Licences, after all, come to an end and so do additional conditions such as non-contact and geographical exclusions. The date of this ending, from the victim's point of view, is arbitrary. By contrast, restorative approaches could enable victims and offenders to negotiate and function in the community in the longer term (Ann Gerty – personal communication).

Restorative practices are not well embedded in contemporary probation. Yet there are examples of excellent practice where probation and other criminal justice agencies have tried to work to restorative principles, even in the most serious cases (Williams 2002). Again, as Williams and Goodman (2007: 562) note:

> youth justice practitioners are working directly and indirectly with victims and issues of victimisation to an unprecedented extent, and this experience will no doubt find its way back into the Probation Service as staff seconded to serve as members of YOTs return to their posts in probation.

The reparative components of community service (Chapter 11) should also be mentioned.

Interestingly, mediation and conciliation have a place in probation's history through family court work, as we saw in Chapter 2. An adversarial approach was recognised to be an inept way of responding to parental dispute and family court welfare officers (until 2001, probation officers) worked to assist parents to work together to find solutions that would enable their children to thrive. Although the number of staff still in the probation service who used to work in that capacity is declining, a preference for conciliation over adversarialism is arguably still part of probation's legacy.

Does restorative justice 'work'? While the findings are expressed with due caution, studies by Shapland *et al.* (2008) are encouraging in terms of reconviction. But here it is essential to ensure that restorative approaches are not simply appropriated as a rehabilitative intervention: this would again be victims in the service of the system. The worth of restorative justice is in the extent to which it achieves the resolution that victims and offenders need and this cannot be captured by reconviction measures alone.

> We should no longer simply ask ourselves 'Are we providing effective treatments?' or 'Are we inflicting consistent punishment?', but should consider whether we are providing opportunities for those involved in and affected by offences to be dealt with in ways that respect their perceptions, responsibilities, needs and potential contribution to setting matters right. The institution of criminal justice then appears not as a set of arrangements for eliminating crime (which it cannot do) but as a system whose outcomes can contribute to a more satisfactory way of living with the consequences of crime.
>
> (Raynor 1985: 142)

Summary

In January 2010, the Minister of Justice, Jack Straw, announced plans to create a new National Victims' Service (Ministry of Justice 2010c). The change of administration in May 2010 and economic recession may well put an end to this idea, at least for the time being. If such a service were to be established, however, it would probably remove victim contact responsibilities from the work of probation. Might that be a good thing? There is little doubt, as we have seen, that probation has sometimes struggled to accommodate victim work within an organisation established to work with offenders. Recent structural developments have done little to ameliorate this. As Williams and Goodman say (2007: 536) 'The National Offender Management Service has been created without much (if any) thought being given to its impact upon victims of crime.' Perhaps a separate organisation, combining victim contact and victim support, would serve better.

On the other hand, for those who feel that criminal justice needs to find another way of responding to crime – some form of vindication of the experience of victims that does not merely license unbridled punitiveness, some way of responding that does not have to involve prosecution and all the unhappy consequences this brings (for victims as well as for offenders) – restorative justice has singular potential. In that case, probation, an organisation that works with victims *and* offenders and in a position to recognise that these are not permanent and exclusive categories could have an influential role in realising that potential.

Questions

- Do you think that the victimisation and abuse that are common in offenders' personal histories explains their own offending? And what are the implications for sentencing these offenders and for working with them?
- Could victim work ever be more than a marginal and under-resourced activity in an organisation centred on public protection and rehabilitation?
- How should restorative justice be evaluated?

Further reading

On victims generally, Walklate (2007) has many useful chapters. Williams and Goodman (2007) offer a succinct and authoritative review of probation work with victims. The collection edited by Williams (2002) has many examples of good practice and valuable insights. The literature on restorative justice is enormous. Good beginnings are Johnstone (2002) and Wright (2008).

14 The local and the national

In this chapter, the organisation and governance of probation will be discussed. There will be a short account of the creation of the National Probation Service and of the National Offender Management Service (NOMS) and the influences that led to these developments. Discussion will then focus on the central vision for NOMS: an integration of prison and probation and an 'opening up of the market' for other service providers, through the mechanism of *contestability*. Both debates raise fundamental challenges about the relationship between the local and the national and about not only what NOMS should do, but *what kind of organisation it ought to be* (Faulkner 2007), prompting similar questions about probation.

The National Probation Service and NOMS

In the early years of the New Labour government a number of inter-related initiatives to modernise the criminal justice system were put in place. Following the Halliday Report's review of sentencing (Home Office 2001) and the *Justice for All* White Paper (Home Office 2002), the sentencing framework was transformed by the Criminal Justice Act 2003 (Chapter 4). The Sentencing Guidelines Council was established to guide the courts in the use of their new powers. What was still to be established was an organisational structure to give effect to the sentences of the court.

While there was a national prison service, the organisational structure of probation may have been thought to be too diffuse and even fragmented. Until 2001, the 54 probation services had been independent bodies corporate. Probation officers had originally been appointed by their local courts. As the services evolved, probation committees, constituted mainly by Justices of the Peace, were not only employers but, through and with the Principal (later Chief) Probation Officer, were responsible for policy and direction. Local authorities were represented on the committees, partly because of the financial contributions they made to probation, but also in recognition of the local interest in and responsibility for the work of the services and their accountability to the communities they served.

There had indeed always been national influences and oversight – a common statutory framework and system of governance, the 'Probation Rules', Home

Office Circulars and Memoranda, Her Majesty's Inspectorate of Probation. The Home Office, from the beginning exercising its influences through exhortation, authoritative advice, regulation and inspection, progressively became first more assertive and then more directive. The first Statement of National Objectives and Priorities in 1984, tighter financial control at national level, the dissemination of National Standards, the requirement to plan and report to prescribed formats, the setting of targets (and the linking of funding to achieve them) and many other disciplines of managerialism all pushed towards a uniformity directed by central government. Even so, at the end of the twentieth century, probation governance remained essentially local.

In 2001 a National Probation Service for England and Wales was created (Criminal Justice and Court Services Act 2000) and its first Director, Eithne Wallis, appointed. Accountable to the Secretary of State, the Director would be able to offer clear leadership to bring about greater consistency and rigour in policy and practice. The emerging confidence that probation now knew *what works* and could deliver interventions to reduce reoffending (see Chapter 6) was an additional impetus towards organisational arrangements that could ensure consistent implementation. Probation's supporters further anticipated that a stronger national presence, embodied by the Director, might increase the political authority of the probation service.

Yet this model was intended at the same time to recognise and value a strong local influence on governance. Committees were superseded by boards which retained a role for local authority representation as well as magistrates and members of the judiciary. The number of areas was reduced from 54 to 42, aligning probation to the same area boundaries of most other criminal justice agencies to facilitate their working together. The value of local partnership was emphasised (Hancock 2007d) – for example, in public protection arrangements and in drug action teams – and probation was to be an influential member of the Local Criminal Justice Boards.

A later director claimed that this 'largely devolved' structure achieved 'significant gains in performance against targets between 2001 and 2006 and can be seen as one of the successes of government during that time' (Hill 2007: 179). Yet even as the new service was consolidating and progressing, further proposals for change were emerging.

In 2003, Patrick Carter was commissioned to carry out a review. This mainly took place inside government, with little wider consultation. His report *Managing Offenders, Reducing Crime: A new approach* (Carter 2003), published in January 2004, had two guiding ideas: one was the need to break down 'silos' between prison and probation; the second was the introduction of what Carter referred to as 'greater contestability, using providers of prison and probation from across the public, private and voluntary sectors' which he felt would lead to a more effective delivery of services (2003: 34). He proposed the creation of a National Offender Management Service and the government accepted the idea enthusiastically (Home Office 2004a), establishing NOMS in 2004 (Knott 2007). We shall look at Carter's two central ideas in turn.

Prison and probation

Since at least the mid-1990s there had been consideration of the possibility of merging the prison and probation services (discussed most fully in the 1998 Home Office review). Responsibility for prisons and probation was combined in a single ministerial portfolio and the expression *correctional services* became increasingly common. The creation of the National Probation Service deferred the question for a while, though, as we have seen, it was soon re-opened – and, at least arguably, well before the new service had had a reasonable opportunity to show that it might be able to achieve what was required.

An influential joint inspection report *Through the Prison Gate* (HMI Probation/ HMI Prisons 2001) challenged the two services to work together more efficiently and effectively, while the Social Exclusion Unit report (2002), drawing attention to the enormous number of offences committed by former prisoners, urged the need for closer working arrangements. Carter emphasised that 'Prison and probation need to be focused on the management of the offender throughout their sentence, driven by information on what works to reduce reoffending' (2003: 25).

While the aspiration to achieve continuity between rehabilitative initiatives in prison and further work after release seems unassailable, this is an idea with a long history of disappointment. Chapter 12 argued that services cannot be abstracted from the context of their provision – and that the context of prison and the community are likely to be critically different. It is true that measures can be introduced to ease the transition and Chapter 12 considered some valuable initiatives. We have also seen that *relational* continuity – especially having the same worker before and after release – is at least as important as continuity in services: this is especially appreciated by people leaving prison and a feature of the best 'through the gate' projects (Raynor and Maguire 2006), though resource and organisational pressures often militate against this (see Chapter 12). Even so, by the time Carter reported, considerable progress was already being made in developing coherent services (Raynor and Maguire 2006). Was merger sufficient or necessary to achieve the enhancements Carter expected?

Organisational merger is certainly not *sufficient* to bring about more efficient and effective ways of working together. Even organisations with a less contested set of objectives can struggle to operate coherently to achieve complex tasks. In attempting to unite prison and probation, there are additional challenges of differences of operational practice, including professional traditions and cultures, that would continue to be problematic even if prison and probation staff could come to feel that in some sense they were part of the same organisation (Burke 2005). Some of the differences are deeply embedded in the respective organisa-tions: probation is community focused, committed to social inclusion and actively manages risk; prison is centrally focused, socially excluding and institutionally risk averse.

The close structural alignment of prison and probation, moreover, leads to the risk that probation will be simply 'taken over' – understood and valued just for its contribution to advancing prison's mission. In particular, probation's policies might be set by contemporary ideas about how best the prison population could be reduced. The highest levels of NOMS have been dominated by people from professional backgrounds other than probation and it is not always apparent who has the experience and knowledge to represent probation in policy and implementation.

Might organisational merger nevertheless be *necessary* to bring about the improvements that Carter envisaged? There are examples, as we have seen in Chapter 1 – and more specifically in Chapter 10 when inter-agency work in the management of risk was considered – of different agencies working well together, drawing on their *complementary* skills, resources and authority. This does not require merger and indeed merger would jeopardise the very achievements that are made possible by the involvement of *different* professional perspectives and disciplines. It is complementary differences that are the defining strength of inter-agency partnerships, which could be attenuated by merger into a single organisation. Nor should the possibility be overlooked that these differences are likely to bring tensions which reflect legitimate differences in agencies' priorities and can be creative rather than dysfunctional.

More radically it could be objected that Carter's vision of breaking down the 'silos' creates new silos of its own, isolating 'correctional services' from community organisations in their implementation of the wider social policies that are known to be strongly associated with reoffending and desistance (see Chapters 8 and 9). The sense of community and an awareness of the organisational context in which probation must function at local level – notably in partnership with the police in public protection – is conspicuously absent in the Carter report. Even if Woolf's ideal of community prisons were to be realised, the prison cannot acquire or work with the necessary sense of place and community that probation needs as an agency of community justice. Crucially too the NOMS vision was likely to distance probation from the courts that it has traditionally served and whose confidence is a precondition of the appropriate use of community orders.

Partnerships and contestability

A second central component of the NOMS vision is the idea of *contestability*, a relatively unfamiliar word that Carter uses interchangeably with *competition* to denote an 'opening up of the market' for other providers of service, from the voluntary and private sectors as well as the public sector. It is claimed that contestability can enhance the quality of public service through the stimulus of competition (S. Goode 2007, though see also Fletcher 2007).

Among the precepts of New Public Management (Chapter 1) are:

- shift to disaggregation of units in the public sector;
- shift to more competition in the public sector;
- stress on private-sector styles of management practice (Raine and Willson 1993: 68).

and Carter's critical scrutiny of the dominant role of the state in 'corrections' was, to this extent, a particular application of a general stance. More specifically, Carter was influenced by his understanding of the effects of market competition on the prison service: 'The introduction of competition has provided a strong incentive for improvements in public sector prisons. The introduction of performance testing has been successful in driving down costs, changing the culture and enabling flexible staffing structures to be introduced' (2003: 24). Yet Liebling (2006) warns against drawing too close a parallel between prison privatisation and contestability in probation services, noting decisive differences between the ostensible problems in the two estates which privatisation and contestability were proposed to resolve. Moreover, Carter's interpretation of the effects of the private sector's involvement with prisons is disputed by others (Burke 2005, Prison Reform Trust 2005, Cavadino and Dignan 2007, Fletcher 2007).

Probation was already actively engaged in any number of creative partnerships with other agencies in the voluntary sector (Hancock 2007d). While such arrangements were complex and often challenging, the principle and the practice have achieved a great deal. The added gains from introducing contestability are far from clear. Instead of probation commissioning services from partners, there is now to be competition with them for work commissioned by the Secretary of State. One immediate consequence would be to turn partners into competitors and, foreseeably, to inhibit the sharing of good practice among service providers who might come to find themselves in competition for business, as well as occasioning much wasteful duplication of provision.

Burke (2005) further warns of the tendency to monopoly, observing that similar initiatives in the health service have not provided the diversity and competition that had been hoped for. Certainly short-term contracts – and the more recent conception of *payment by results*, implying reviewable and relatively short-term arrangements – would favour large organisations with the capacity to make the substantial required investment and absorb the risks of possibly losing business when contracts came to be renewed. Their local, often small-scale character is part of the reason why voluntary organisations are so special and valuable and this is imperilled by contestability.

Again, part of the price that the voluntary sector will be obliged to pay in return for contracted work will be to compromise their independence: they will be expected to deliver to targets set for them and to work as the government requires. This is of course just how markets are intended to work (commissioners buying what they require), but among the reasons why the voluntary sector is so valuable is precisely that it is *not* in the service of government and may indeed often campaign energetically against government policies. The direct commissioning of services by the state jeopardises this invaluable contribution.

Despite Carter's claims, then, it is an ideological position and not a self-evident truth that market competition serves to raise standards. There are certainly sectors where such an effect is discernible, but the experience of the privatisation of probation services does not support the assumption. In a robust critique, Fletcher (2007: 220) concludes that a much clearer consequence of privatisation has been 'driving down the terms and conditions of staff and depressing service delivery standards'. Most fundamentally, Hancock (2007b: 32) argues that Carter fails to recognise that the principal resources needed to protect the public and stop re-offending are not products to be purchased. They are the public services of police, health, employment, education, housing etc. The skills and culture needed to develop partnerships with these services so they can be useful to offenders are worlds away from the consumerist market culture signalled by Carter's view of contestability.

There is an affinity between instrumental conceptions of probation and the move towards contestability. If probation is taken to be (no more than) a set of services to bring about socially desirable ends, then the provider of these services is not of itself important – it would be a matter of judgement about effectiveness and value for money. But it has been argued throughout this book that probation expresses something important about how a community should respond to those of its members who have offended, about how to regard victims and offenders and the responsibilities that the community has towards them. Can these practices be appropriately valued if they are understood as (reduced to) economic transactions?

What of the private and commercial sector? Christie's influential critique of *crime control as industry* is quite as cogent now as when it first appeared in 1991 and his third edition (2000) shows how prescient was his original analysis. There are three particular arguments to adduce here against an extensive involvement of the private sector in the work of criminal justice:

- In law, directors of private companies are required to take account of 'the impact of the company's operations on the community', but this is just one of several considerations when they fulfil their responsibility to act in the way that 'would be most likely to promote the success of the company for the benefit of its members as a whole' (Companies Act 2006, s. 172). These statutory duties may not be assumed to coincide with the wider public interest. Under market provision, accountability may well be restricted to the commissioner, rather than the community to be served, and involve a review of outcomes or, more narrowly, 'results'. But attention to the extent to which an organisation has achieved its intended results could divert attention not only from the processes – which have been argued earlier to matter significantly – but also from other unintended outcomes that a results audit could fail to capture.
- It is in the nature of commerce to expand. Private sector firms will seek to extend their involvement either by diversifying their services and/or by seeking to provide them to increasing numbers of people. This will unavoidably have a net-widening and inflationary effect on the penal system.
- Most fundamentally, however, is an argument about what Michael Sandel (1998, 2009) has called the moral limits of markets. Debate is often conducted on the basis of effectiveness and value for money, but, Sandel argues, there are some domains where the market has no place. The involvement of the market corrupts and distorts the values of the social practices in question. If the value of probation consists in what it represents and embodies about

society's duties towards victims and offenders, then its practices are not things to be bought and sold. Security is not a commodity, rehabilitation not a 'product'.

The local and the national

Are individuals . . . accountable first and foremost to the Government that sets the agenda, to the management that is responsible for their careers, to the customers who create the need for this service, or to the taxpayer who foots the bill?

(John Mackinson, quoted in Faulkner: 2006: 81)

the managerialism to which we have all subscribed for more than half a century is bust. It's all over. Everyone has to be held to account, not to the remote impersonal bureaucracies of Whitehall or town hall, but to each other through decentralised, local, autonomous and diverse structures and institutions, with government merely holding the ring and regulating standards.

(Melanie Phillips, *The Sunday Times*,
10 June 2001, quoted Wargent 2002: 197)

The centralising developments towards a unified correctional service represented by NOMS are in striking contrast to New Labour's initial general approach to crime and disorder. Here the Crime and Disorder Act 1998 carried the standard for the new administration's crime policies. The government appreciated and often emphasised the *local* character of crime and the Act imposed a responsibility on local authorities to take a lead, together with the police, in enhancing community safety. The Act established local Crime and Disorder Reduction Partnerships in which police and local authorities were to be the principal partners. Being 'tough on the causes of crime' meant strengthening communities and called for the active participation of local agencies within and beyond the criminal justice system (Home Office 1999).

As we have seen, the new National Probation Service recognised and valued a strong local character. Even so, the perceived requirement to establish unified and coherent 'correctional services' did not always fit comfortably with the local crime reduction strategy – and indeed sometimes these two agendas seem to have proceeded without much reference to one another. It was not until April 2010 that Probation Boards/Trusts were included as one of the authorities responsible for crime reduction (Policing and Crime Act 2009, s. 108) – 12 years after the 1998 Act had introduced this concept. It is arguable that the creation of the Ministry of Justice aggravated this disjunction. For all its shortcomings, the Home Office has retained a much stronger sense of the local – perhaps because this is so salient to the policies of the police. Even as NOMS kept its tight hold on probation governance, other legislative initiatives (notably the Local Government and Public Involvement in Health Act 2007 s. 104 [2], placing a duty on Probation Boards to engage as partners in local arrangements) were pulling in another direction. While Trust arrangements are said to require connection with 'the local', the specified targets continue to be at odds with this conception of probation: there is a dissonance between the policy statements and the targets against which performance is to be appraised.

The question of the proper allocation of responsibility between local and national levels has become ever more acute. The political imperative to be seen to be controlling crime effectively was believed to call for a strong national lead. Perhaps the more a political party insists that crime can be influenced through the practices of criminal justice, the more direction it may feel it must have over the policies and practices of the criminal justice agencies. Again, national governance should guard against local idiosyncrasy and the unfairness of 'justice by postcode'. Once identified, 'what works' and other aspects of best practice should be adopted everywhere and there must be reliable mechanisms to ensure that this takes place.

At the same time, communities are diverse in many ways, with distinctive social, demographic, cultural, economic and geographical characteristics. Local people understand their communities better than anyone else and local agencies should have the authority to adapt their services to respond accordingly. Not all variation in practice should be seen as inconsistency.

There are, to be sure, some hard questions here. It can probably be agreed that there should be room for services and practices to be developed at a local level within the parameters of a national framework. Yet how these parameters should be set and what degree of latitude should be granted to local areas is still extremely contentious. Beginning with a conception of a rationally organised coherent correctional service, the Labour government constructed a centralised and national governance for probation with some latitude for 'the local'. But another vision could be imagined for probation which starts with the local, framing national policy in ways that not only allow but encourage differences of implementation in acknowledgement of the diversity of communities. This would ground probation work in the idea of community justice.

Community justice

> Community justice . . . explicitly includes the community in criminal justice processes. It is expressly concerned with improving the quality of community life and the capacity of local communities to prevent crime and to effectively respond to criminal incidents when they occur.
>
> (Karp and Clear 2002: 3)

As we saw in Chapter 3, after the government had repudiated social work, community justice emerged as another way of characterising the work of probation. While community justice could represent a guiding and uniting approach for the agencies of criminal justice, its meaning remains contested (Nellis 2000). Clear and Karp (1999) identify four defining characteristics of community justice: operation at neighbourhood level, a focus on problem-solving in response to crimes (Wright 2010), decentralised authority and accountability, and the involvement of local people in the processes of justice. At its heart is the recognition that the origins of offending and responses to it must understand offenders in relation to their community (Clear and Karp 1999).

Community justice starts with the presumption that the crime is a *marker*, a sign of something wrong in the community that its members need to address, and so explicitly includes the community in its responses to crime. Inquiry into crime, then, involves not only an assessment of the individual offender – their vices, weaknesses or criminogenic needs – but also reflection on the nature of the community, including 'the social influences or pressures that make people in one community more likely to offend but people in another community less likely to offend' (Karp and Clear 2002: 2). In this way it focuses attention on localities and 'seeks to develop comprehensive strategies for improving the social environment in which people live' (*ibid.*).

The community justice ideal insists that the community has obligations towards those of its members who have committed offences, as well as claims on them to make amends and to work to desist. Community justice may well include punishment, but, as John Braithwaite (1989) proposed in a very similar context, such punishment should take place against a background of an unqualified acceptance that the offender is a member of the community – one whose standing is for the time being affected by their wrongdoing, but whose restoration to full community membership and participation is willingly anticipated. Community justice, then, represents a framework within which a number of other concepts may be located – social inclusion, reintegration, restorative justice, belief in the possibility of change, the role of social capital in desistance – that constitute many of the values of probation.

Reintegration and reparation are central themes. An objection here, however, is that these approaches depend on kinds of community that no longer exist – not at least in modern Britain (for discussion, see Johnstone 2002). Modes of conflict resolution that may suit pre-modern and 'traditional' communities are ill adapted to the requirements of crime control in modern societies. Communities are diverse, disparate, fragmented and over-dependent on formal agencies and systems to manage their problems. They lack the capacity to act in the manner that community justice calls for.

A possible rejoinder, however, is that taking a collective responsibility here is among the ways in which communities can realise their capacity to unite in positive and cooperative practices. Community justice can achieve not only just outcomes, but an enhanced ability for a community to solve its own problems: it can be both 'a means of achieving criminal justice and a strategy for community building' (Karp and Clear 2002: 27). This includes strengthening community institutions and supporting them in their socialising roles. Harding (2007: 51) puts it well:

> Not only do citizens participate to ensure that local concerns are addressed but citizens' participation is strategic for building community capacity so that

informal mechanisms of crime control can gradually share the burden with the more formal processes of criminal justice services.

Communities are empowered and invigorated through action: it is no good waiting until communities feel confident before initiatives are attempted; rather, they achieve their confidence through their communal practices and this should include taking charge of their own responses to crime and disorder (Brownlee 1998).

People and places

We have seen that even as probation has been part of an emerging community justice sector, governance arrangements have been at risk of distancing it from its community. Probation has continued to work in energetic and creative partnership with local organisations, but the centralising arrangements represented by NOMS, the closure of small neighbourhood offices (mainly for resource reasons) and the decline of home visits (Hancock 2007c) have all been signs of this distancing. This was occurring at precisely a time when scholarship and research were recognising an enhanced role for the community in the processes of desistance (McNeill and Maruna 2007).

In thinking about governance, much depends on whether the starting point is people or places (Clear 2005). The courts and the penal system are bound to focus on individual wrongdoers: the extent to which they can comprehend or deal with the social context of offending is decidedly limited. But criminal justice must be concerned not only with the apportionment of blame and punishment, but must also contribute to reducing offending and reoffending and to managing the consequences of crime – for victim, offender and community. These are tasks that benefit from an initial focus on places rather than people. Karp and Clear (2002: 2) tellingly begin their account of community justice by describing it as *corrections of place*.

This is more than a question of organisational efficiency and effectiveness: a neglected dimension of the debate is how the meaning and significance of probation might be affected by its mode of governance. If probation is to participate in community responses to crime, it must be seen to be in and of its community. The agencies of criminal justice, after all, derive their legitimacy from strong connections with the communities they serve. (This has always been self-evident to the police services.) This calls for:

> not only a sense of identification and understanding between those providing the service and local communities, but also a sense of ownership on the part of local communities themselves. Public confidence in probation is not just a matter of performance compliance and percentage reductions in the rate of re-offending, but in local communities being mobilised by probation to exercise a degree of civic responsibility for the reintegration of offenders in ways that are personal and accountable.
>
> (Harding 2003: 373)

In this sense, probation can be a catalyst as well as a component of community justice. In the process it can rediscover the commitment to social justice that has been less apparent when the political priority of a 'correctional service' has been to try to reduce reoffending through a practice model that concentrates on (and sometimes does not go beyond) individual risks, needs and responsivity (Smith and Vanstone 2002). This question is closely related to public perception and confidence, a persistent worry for probation (Hough 2007). It is the *local* achievement of legitimacy, confidence and accountability that are critical. It is hard to feel much sense of ownership of a large national organisation like NOMS, or to feel that it is in any significant way accountable to you, or to be confident in its practices: it is indeed only likely to become visible through its failures.

Clear (2005) sets out a number of ways in which probation practice could be changed and strengthened by attention to place. Other initiatives chime with this too. The Thames Valley Partnership (http://www.thamesvalleypartnership.org/) is a specific example of how a vision for community justice might be developed. At policy level, the idea of *justice reinvestment* is attracting considerable interest (Allen and Stern 2007; House of Commons Justice Committee 2009). Briefly and roughly, this idea urges diverting some of the enormous sums of money spent on 'corrections' towards an investment into community resources to reduce crime and to respond to it when it does take place. National systems to disburse correctional resources would be substantially displaced by local arrangements devised and implemented by those with the best knowledge of the communities they serve. While this idea is not co-extensive with community justice, the affinities are clear.

Probation trusts

The full realisation of Carter's vision for NOMS awaited the enactment of new legislation. The statutory duty to arrange provision of probation services was the responsibility of local Probation Boards and this constrained the development of contestability. The Offender Management Act 2007 transferred this responsibility to the Secretary of State who was thus empowered to commission services directly. While for the time being only a Probation Trust or other public body may be commissioned to give assistance to courts (mainly pre-sentence reports) (s.4), the Secretary of State may now commission other probation tasks – not only from the public sector providers (Areas now constituted as Trusts (s.5)), but from other sectors besides. Commissioning of services was to take place not only at national level, but also at regional (through the offices of regional Directors of Offender Management) and local area levels (where trusts would commission as well as provide).

In April 2010, after a demanding and rigorous process of demonstrating their suitability, all areas in England and Wales became trusts, some areas merging to form larger trusts, 35 in number. It was anticipated that this status would allow local trusts much greater control over their own affairs, though it is not yet clear how far this has been achieved. One inherent difficulty is trusts remain tightly accountable to NOMS with a proliferation of instructions and targets to respond to.

NOMS continues to influence the management and functioning of trusts and it is not clear how this fits with its role as a commissioner of services.

Many trusts express some frustration that the new arrangements have not brought the degree of independence they had hoped for. An especially vexed matter is that trusts have not been granted 'end of year flexibility': funds may not be carried across from one financial year to the next, restricting budgetary planning year by year, and constraining capacity to compete. A central system of estates management precludes trusts from taking strategic control of premises that used to be their own. There are also concerns about the burden of bureaucracy and the criteria used nationally to evaluate local performance. Commenting on the proposed 'modernising' of the Integrated Probation Performance Framework (IPPF), the Probation Association (2010: 2) described the IPPF as 'an over-detailed regulatory burden' and argued that a revised IPPF should reflect 'trusts' primary focus on delivery of local services to courts, victims and offenders and the increased accountability to local communities'. The argument is that probation trusts are responsible authorities in a collaborative and essentially local endeavour to reduce offending and it is in these terms that their performance should be evaluated. NOMS should therefore align its own expectations with local performance frameworks rather than seeking to impose additional performance criteria and targets of its own.

NOMS has moved from being the central management system for the areas of a national service towards being a commissioner of services. Instructions are now better understood as contractual requirements, but both NOMS and the local trusts are still learning what this new relationship amounts to and what differences it may entail. Meanwhile, many trusts would welcome an opportunity to undertake more direct local commissioning. Again there is tension between the local and the national. A focus on *place* might suggest that commissioning could be done most effectively by local agencies, including consortia of local agencies from a negotiated common conception of the area's challenges. But the prevailing arrangements militate against such possibilities.

There are potential economies of scale for commissioning at regional and national level. Commissioning is a sophisticated skill and it is plausible to think that a smaller number of accomplished commissioners might be well placed to negotiate better deals in the public interest. On the other hand, not all instances of national-level commissioning have been celebrated as an unalloyed success. The Parliamentary Public Accounts Committee described the hugely expensive IT project C-NOMIS as 'a shambles' (BBC 2009). Centralised estates management has attracted some criticism and does not command the confidence of all areas. Fletcher (2007) gives other examples of centrally commissioned private services where costs have been alarming and benefits doubtful.

Crucially localism should encourage probation to see itself as one key organisation in a collective, locally based endeavour. In partnership with health services, education, employment and housing, probation is made to see 'offenders' as patients, as students, as unemployed and homeless people – a more rounded and potentially reintegrative understanding of the users of its services. It is at least arguable that this is a perspective in which pathways to desistance are the focus and which makes rehabilitation and public protection more likely to be achieved than by a sharp but restricted focus on offending behaviour.

There is no doubt that trusts are working with energy and imagination with local organisations to engage with the communities they serve. The questions remain: does NOMS facilitate or inhibit these initiatives and will it trust the trusts?

The position is fast changing, with the coalition government elected in May 2010 and the comprehensive spending review in October 2010. The role of the probation service is again under scrutiny and legislation is anticipated – perhaps to vary the powers of courts and to give effect to an anticipated 'rehabilitation revolution'. While forecasting penal policy is always hazardous, it seems certain that the independent and private sectors will become more extensively involved in the provision of what have traditionally been regarded as 'probation' services and the responsibility and prerogative of the state. How these will be commissioned, implemented and evaluated will be a matter of continuing dispute.

Summary

This chapter has considered the governance of probation. For most of its history, probation services have been led by and accountable to national government, local communities and to the courts. This balance was progressively tipped as central government assumed full financial responsibility and began to see the service as an agency to implement its criminal justice policies. The establishment of NOMS, first in 2004, but especially after its restructuring in 2008, substantially diminished the local influence and the authority of the courts over probation policy and practice.

We have discussed the main components of the NOMS vision and challenged their assumptions and their implications. A merger between prison and probation was neither necessary nor sufficient, created new 'silos' of its own and weakened probation's connections with its communities. Contestability disturbs probation's relationship with its partner organisations, and is likely to favour large organisations, thereby losing some of the most conspicuous strengths of the independent sector. The extensive involvement of the private sector has been argued to be at odds with a wider public interest, to introduce an expansionist and inflationary pressure which is the last thing the penal system needs and to go beyond the *moral limits of the market*. Another – local – vision for probation has been set out, grounded in a conception of community justice, which recognises the authority of local agencies and communities to lead in the management of their problems of crime and disorder. The creation of trusts has been considered too and it has been suggested that some of the potential gains have yet to be realised, as NOMS and trusts are still in the process of understanding their new and quite different role relationships.

These debates may seem dry and inward looking, but they go to the heart of the purpose and philosophy of probation. How probation is organised should, after all, reflect not only what it is trying to achieve, but what it represents and the *kind of organisation that it should be* (Faulkner 2007). NOMS understands probation as an arm of central government. Nevertheless the organisational structures already exist to enable probation to operate as a local service, working in partnerships with local organisations, to motivate offenders and give them the abilities and opportunities that they need to thrive and to develop ways of living in which offending has no place. At the same time, probation will be among those who seek to advocate the interests of victims and offenders to the community of which they are members. In this vision, the presumption is that governance, direction and accountability are local, with central government setting policy parameters which not only permit but encourage variation in response to local differences.

Questions

- What are the main advantages and drawbacks of merging prison and probation into a *correctional services* agency?
- The author is suspicious of the extensive involvement of the commercial sector. Yet public sector agencies can be complacent and self-serving as well. What (if anything) is the difference between public and private sector ambitions?
- Communities are different and need different crime reduction strategies. How worried should we be about 'post code' justice if probation is locally led?

Further reading

A full and authoritative account of the origins of NOMS is to be found in Morgan (2007). The papers collected by Hough *et al.* (2006) remain very relevant and prescient about NOMS developments. Faulkner (2006 and in several other papers) offers many deep and wise insights into these questions.

15 Areas and their staff: working in the probation service

The last chapter considered the emergence of NOMS and the changes in governance, organisation and accountability that have taken place in probation in the past ten years. In this chapter, we move to consider what these developments have entailed for the experience of staff working in the contemporary probation service. The proliferation of criminal justice policy, the development of target-based performance management, practice guidance – and often instruction – have required areas/trusts to set up mechanisms to ensure that their policies are being put into effect. This has led to a tighter management of practice within the organisation itself, with consequences that include changes in staff's understanding of their own work, of the boundaries of their discretion and of their relationship with their managers. These developments have been taking place too at a time of radical organisational change. The chapter begins with a discussion of the discretion, accountability and supervision of staff, moving on to consider the changing size and nature of the workforce and roles within it, before looking at training.

Discretion, accountability and staff supervision

It is conventional to contrast contemporary practice, under the disciplines of modern management, with the vagaries of a past time when probation officers, it is supposed, took their own decisions and service users' experiences were unduly dependent on their officers' preferences. While many stark contrasts between probation's past and present risk oversimplification, it is probably fair to say that, at least until the mid-1980s, practitioners retained considerable latitude about how they undertook their work. The immediate line managers of service delivery staff, senior probation officers, were seen (and saw themselves) more as senior practitioners and consultants than as managers. They filled managerial roles, representing the employer to the member of staff and allocating work, but probation officers mostly worked in accordance with their own understanding of best practice rather than under direction from their manager.

The Statement of National Objectives and Priorities (1984) was a milestone on the way to change. As we saw in the last chapter, this represented a more assertive approach from central government and, in calling for local statements in response, required services to manage practice much more tightly. Financial disciplines, notably the linking of revenue to the meeting of performance targets, were a further push in this direction. But while the principles of management and accountability were being advanced, and while local services began to set out more explicitly what they expected of their staff, there was still very little national practice direction. This changed with the arrival of National Standards for supervision.

National Standards prescribe how offenders are to be supervised and managed, specifying the process and timeliness of allocation of new cases, initial appointment, assessment, frequency of contact, sentence planning and review (Canton and Eadie 2007). They were first issued in 1989 in relation to community service, with a full set of standards promulgated in 1992 to support the implementation of the Criminal Justice Act 1991. They were intended to give an assurance to courts, to service users and to the public about how orders would be implemented. An early study made the interesting discovery that, in relation to the matter of enforcement, for example, practitioners welcomed the clarity and consistency the standards promised. Yet the standards were not implemented strictly and 'Some probation officers indicated that they might ignore any attempt to reduce their discretion in ways which they considered would interfere with productive work with offenders' (Ellis *et al.* 1996: ix). It should be emphasised that standards were never intended to remove discretion, but they were plainly intended to clarify (and limit) its boundaries and successive editions of the standards have circumscribed discretion ever more tightly.

Supporters of standards commend their contribution to enhancing consistency as well as good practice (Hopley 2002). Consistency appears to be both an organisational and an ethical virtue. Service users are entitled to know what they may expect of the organisation, while justice requires that like cases should be treated alike. But justice no less requires that relevant differences must be respected and prescribing a standard experience without regard to the many ways in which offenders and their circumstances may *differ* risks overlooking the diversity of offenders, mistaking sameness for fairness (Canton and Eadie 2008). The tighter the specification of the rules, the less opportunity there will be to accommodate relevant difference. The difficulty for those taking the decision, then, is to determine which differences are relevant: for example, to what extent should personal responsibilities like childcare be taken into account when an appointment is missed? This is the central dilemma around discretion, but it is not resolved by the (bureaucratic-managerial) assumption that treating everyone the same is a guarantee of justice (Chapter 3).

As for their contribution to implementing best practice, National Standards have never been evidenced-based in any significant sense and conformity with these standards, while plausibly a measure of efficiency, is no indication of quality or effectiveness. Their insistence on specific timescales can frustrate best practice: for example it is widely agreed that planning should involve the full participation of the offender (Chapter 7), but the organisational imperative to complete the work quickly brings an avoidable pressure to a complex process. It has been argued more generally that 'As the basis on which staff would be held to account for their practice, Standards had considerable potential, but their decisive importance as targets in performance management, inspection and inquiries have led to a mechanistic and often defensive implementation' (Canton and Eadie 2007: 182).

Managerialism requires mechanisms of control and of assurance that practice is taking place as instructed. But in the nature of the case, this is not easy to achieve. It can happen, then, that managerialism feels a need to translate practice into overt and auditable episodes that it can comprehend. Compliance, for example, is conceptualised as (reduced to) keeping appointments, being at places at times; but compliance should be seen as much more than this (Chapter 9). Audit in support of regulation can deal with events, but struggles with processes. Yet it is often the processes – of assessment, planning, the building of relationships, the iterative assessment of risk – that matter most. That which audit cannot capture ceases to count and in this way an unreflective managerialism can distort the character of practice.

The specification of regulations, of course, cannot in any case guarantee that practitioners will implement them as intended. Lipsky (1980) writes about *street-level bureaucrats* – practitioners who, in reality, have considerable *de facto* discretion because so many of their decisions are effectively invisible from their managers.

The path from policy to practice is never straightforward. Kemshall notes that, between policy and practice stand 'the interpretation and mediation of policies by operational managers, required to balance and implement competing demands within limited resources [and] . . . by frontline workers operating within well-established working practices, ideologies and value bases' (2003: 144). These influences mediate policy implementation: they do not block it. The upshot can be anything between a complete shutting out of the policy and its fulfilment as intended, but is most likely to lead to a qualified – and, as it may be, distorted – implementation. Again, although those processes may be described as *resistance*, it would be a mistake to see this necessarily as obduracy or as deliberate defiance. It may be better seen as a collision, when policy, thought through but often in abstract, encounters the complexity and vicissitudes of real life – a collision which practitioners try to manage with variable ratios of pragmatism and principle as they apply 'policy' to real working challenges. Nor should managers ever forget, in their commitment to put policy into practice, that there is a significant sense in which the policy of the organisation is less what they prescribe than what practitioner staff actually do (Lipsky 1980).

But if there is to be wide discretion and judgement case by case, is there not a risk that practice may deteriorate into unfairness? It is one thing to argue that a service user's experience should be influenced by their own individual characteristics or circumstances, but it should not depend upon the idiosyncrasies of the supervising officer. The best safeguard against this, however, is not the ever-tighter prescription of practice through regulation, but effective accountability.

By *accountability* is here meant a responsibility and willingness to expose one's practice and to explain it. While the need for accountability has been taken to imply reduced discretion, it has been argued that this rests on a misunderstanding:

accountability is in no way incompatible with wide discretion, while assuredly attempts to limit discretion are no guarantee of effective accountability (Canton and Eadie 2008).

Accountability is a precondition of performance management, one of the central components of New Public Management (see Chapter 1). But a fuller under-standing of its value should include accountability not only to managers, but to the courts, the community and especially to service users, who are usually those most affected by practitioners' decisions. This willingness to explain and negotiate with offenders, likely to be mistrusted by proponents of a punitive approach, is a key component of legitimacy. Some requirements of community supervision are non-negotiable (though even in these circumstances decisions should be explained with authority, not implemented oppressively), but principles of shared assessment and planning, of motivation, of building relationships of mutual respect and trust, call for practitioners to set out the reasons for the decisions they intend to take and to attend carefully to the views – and misgivings – of offenders. In this way, the manner of implementation should support the message that the punishment is intended to communicate (Duff 2001).

Accountability, then, ought to be much more than an aspect of managerial discipline, although it includes this: in its fuller sense it is an ethical responsibility (Gelsthorpe 2001) and, through its enhancement of legitimacy and its associated contribution to achieving compliance, an important ingredient of effective practice.

There is a distinction between the accountability of an individual member of staff and, on the other hand, the accountability of an organisation. Formally, staff are accountable to the trust and this is achieved through line management pro-cesses of supervision and scrutiny. Formally, the organisation is accountable to local stakeholders through the trustees and to the government through the chief officer. Organisational accountability is achieved through a variety of statutory and non-statutory processes: for example annual reports, HMIP inspection reports, performance league tables, internal and external audits. At both individual and organisational levels, however, accountability should be understood as a much wider principle than constitutional authority (Faulkner 2006). Again, the last chapter argued that trusts should have the latitude to apply national policy to the distinctive local conditions of their areas; in this chapter, it is argued that individual members of staff should be accorded the discretion they need to undertake their work wisely and well. Not all difference is inconsistency.

Staff supervision should attend to accountability, but also to support and to the continuing professional development of staff (MacLeod 2007). Earlier chapters (especially Chapters 9 and 10) have discussed the emotional demands made upon practitioners and the importance of considered reflective practice. These emotional consequences need to be acknowledged and managed, not only for the well-being of staff but to avoid some of the errors of judgement that can arise from anxiety, denial and wishful thinking. Staff are likely to need opportunities to review their work in dialogue and reflection with a supportive colleague who would not be focused on formal accountability, but rather on enabling them to question their own assumptions and the values that they are bringing to their work. This requires a quiet and unthreatening atmosphere conducive to dialogue and undefensive reflection. This is not the same as a line management function, though it is the responsibility of the line manager to ensure that these opportunities are effectively available. A colleague from another country (personal communication) uses the term *intervision* – to distinguish this process from *supervision*, with its line management connotations, and to emphasise the equality and mutuality among those involved.

Line managers should – and commonly do – also offer leadership and support, representing the organisation to its staff, and modelling the same standards of professionalism and courtesy that should characterise users' experience of the service. Indeed many of the insights about how to work well with offenders have a clear parallel in the requirements for good staff management. Just as an understanding of motivation shows the importance of dialogue and negotiation with offenders and the futility of trying merely to trample on misgivings and resistance, leadership includes the quality of commanding consent through these processes. Bailey *et al.* (2007: 127) suggest that, by contrast, during much of the period of policy, practice and organisational change, 'staff have not been kept well informed and the reasons for some changes are not apparent'. Yet without this level of understanding, effective implementation of policy is likely to be frustrated: staff need an opportunity to question and challenge policy directives if they are to implement them as intended. There is a normative component to this, just as there is to the compliance sought from offenders.

Workforce and roles

Questions about professional discretion and accountability have implications for the profile of probation's workforce. Discretion and judgement are hallmarks of professionalism. Some probation officers have reported that they have felt 'deprofessionalised' by many of the developments in policy and practice in the past ten years: discretion has been eroded and conformity with National Standards emphasised; technical instruments to assess risk and need have been feared by some to have displaced the need for professional judgement; tightly prescribed modes of intervention have been stipulated and have, at least until recently, tended to suppress attention to the personal relationships which have been probation's traditional means of effecting change (Robinson and Burnett 2007; Bailey *et al.* 2007).

Some of these anxieties may be misplaced: as has been argued, judgement is indispensable to the wise deployment of assessment instruments and relationships continue to be paramount. But if probation is taken – even if *mistaken* – to be work that is susceptible to regulation, that practitioners need do no more than follow procedures and routines, then the character of the workforce inevitably comes into question.

Oldfield and Grimshaw (2010) reviewed recent changes to probation's budget, workload and workforce. 2001 to 2006–7 was a time of growth: there was a real terms increase in budget of 21 per cent (although this has declined sharply in the period of economic recession). In the same period, the number of community penalties increased by 27 per cent. The number of staff involved in delivering or supporting work with offenders increased by nearly a third between 2002 and 2007. But at the same time the number of qualified probation officers rose by just 12 per cent, with numbers of trainee probation officers falling quite sharply. In about the same period, numbers of senior support staff increased by 22 per cent and managerial staff by nearly 80 per cent.

Among service delivery staff, the marked increase has been in the numbers of probation service officers (PSOs) – a 53 per cent increase over the relevant period. Viewed over a longer term, the change is even more marked: in 1997 there were 1,919 in the service, but by 2006 there were 7,247 (Oldfield and Grimshaw 2010: 20, Table 11). So while the workforce has increased in size, its character has changed markedly.

Appointed from the early 1960s, PSOs were originally known as *ancillaries* and undertook a number of practical tasks that did not require a probation officer's level of training or remuneration (Ferguson 2007). While PSO has never been formally a trainee grade, many probation officers nowadays have worked in that role before their qualifying training or in equivalent grades as community service assistants or staff in approved premises.

PSOs may be described as 'paraprofessionals' and the emergence of comparable roles has characterised several other professions, including social work, policing (Police Community Support Officers) as well as health and education services. In probation certainly, and no doubt in all these other occupations, there have been controversies over role boundaries. Bailey *et al.* (2007) found a widespread recognition that role boundaries were being eroded. Some PSOs welcomed new challenges, but others felt that both training and salary were inadequate for the responsibilities expected of them.

PSOs are often required to take on tasks that call for considerable skill and responsibility: they are extensively involved in interventions, for example. They also work as offender managers and, while this is expected to be with offenders in the lower tiers of the offender management model, risk is not static and PSOs need to be able to elicit, interpret, recognise and respond to indications of increasing levels of risk. There continue to be significant differences between areas about how this works out in practice; questions have been raised in Parliament (see, for example, Hansard 11 November 2009: Column 498W), receiving answers that barely conceal government uncertainty on the matter. PSO training remains variable, with local examples of excellent training – for example the Certificate in Criminal Justice – which is not yet available to all (Dominey 2010). The new training framework (see below) is intended to solve this problem.

Case administrators constitute another vital part of the workforce. Sound administration is appropriately valued within the OMM and is clearly essential to the task of 'keeping things on course and on time' (NOMS 2006: 41). Administrators are in charge of data collection and management, administration and communication within and beyond the offender management unit. In some places, too, case administrators are having direct contact with offenders, raising important questions about their distinctive training needs (Knight and Stout 2009).

There is also a 'long and honourable history' (Henson 2007: 326) of volunteers working in the probation service. At best, volunteers represent the responsibility of the community towards those of its members who have offended and can contribute influentially to reintegration and social inclusion. Their commitment can be all the more appreciated because it is willingly given by people who do not carry the formal authority of staff of the service.

At the same time, volunteers should advance the objectives of probation, including public protection, and offenders need to know the boundaries of their befriending role. Probation has a responsibility to ensure the suitability of people to undertake such work which is likely to involve careful recruitment, training and supervision. Subject to appropriate tests of personal suitability, people who have criminal records can contribute valuably, for example as 'peer mentors', drawing on their own experiences to understand some of the predicaments that offenders face and bringing perspectives, insights and perhaps a credibility with offenders that professional staff may lack. Among the benefits of such work is its contribution to people's own desistance: taking responsibility, personal agency and accomplishment for the benefit of other people are often influential components of a 'good life' (Chapter 9).

Education and training

Training has naturally been influenced by changes in conception of probation's work. It would indeed be possible to write a history of training, mapping its developments against changing understandings of probation's character and purposes. But as we saw in Chapter 2, that approach risks exaggerating change and concealing continuities. For example, for the first probation officers, a sound and trustworthy character was necessary. But these are the kind of people the service still hopes to employ. Can such personal qualities be acquired or developed through training? What sort of training? And especially if they are *not* the kind of quality that can be instilled through training, how can it be ensured that entrants have them? While not always framed in these terms, such questions have been a persistent challenge.

Are qualities of good character and personal integrity enough? Writing in 1914 in the first ever book in England to be dedicated to the work of probation, Cecil Leeson argued that officers needed a good grounding in social and economic science. It is noteworthy, however, that he did not relate this directly to the requirements of the job – to what it takes to do the work – so much as to the 'habit of mind which such studies produce' (quoted by Nellis 2001: 379). Education was first valued, then, not only or even mainly, for its direct instrumental contribution to the knowledge and skills needed to practise, but for less specific influences upon character and intellect. This is a reminder that debates about training reflect varying understandings not only of probation but also of the purpose and value of higher education.

As probation became more conscious of its needs for skills, a witness to a Departmental Committee in 1922 wanted to combine university education with 'practical training under regular officers' – a combination of theory and practice which came to be characteristic of probation and social work training (Bochel 1976). That committee did not give general endorsement to the idea of a university education for probation officers, seeing probation more as a vocation – and perhaps deterred by the financial implications of a graduate status that was then associated mainly with senior professions. But it is at this time that probation consolidated and developed its relationship with universities. By the 1930s, the Home Office had established a scheme 'for a small number of selected candidates with a period of practical training under experienced probation officers' – and also offered the chance to obtain a university qualification in social science (Bochel 1976: 113). Graduates had only to attend to practice, while non-graduates had studies to undertake as well.

There are many recurring themes in probation training debates. As early as the 1930s, questions arising included:

- What is the role of higher education in training?
- How ought practice and study to be combined?
- How are staff to be given sufficient time for study? What other tensions are there in combining the roles of employee and student?
- What is the relevance of previous life and educational experience and how should it be valued in training? And to what extent should such experiences offer exemption from the normal curriculum or put people on a 'fast track'?

All these questions echo in today's debates.

A Departmental Committee in 1936 insisted all probation officers should be trained before appointment, though in practice the service continued to appoint people without such training ('direct entrants' – Haxby 1978: table p. 59). Direct entry became less common as probation consolidated its relationship with higher education. In 1971 the Central Council for Education and Training in Social Work (CCETSW) was established and developed the Certificate of Qualification in Social Work (CQSW). By 1981 there were more than 75 courses in universities and polytechnics with probation options, many of them eligible for places sponsored by the Home Office (Pillay 2000: 15). By 1984 it had become a require-ment that probation officers should hold the CQSW: universities, regulated by CCETSW, led and governed the curriculum and students undertook practice placements in a range of settings (by no means only in probation).

A new Diploma in Social Work (DipSW), was introduced in 1989, with a much sharper focus on demonstrable skills and competences. The Home Office sought a tighter control over the curriculum and many generic social work courses intro-duced specific probation 'streams'. In 1994 came the rejection of social work training, reflecting the more punitive characterisation of probation practice advanced by the government, with an accompanying suggestion that skills could be acquired in and through practice without the benefit of higher education.

After an uncomfortable period of uncertainty in the mid-1990s, with the DipSW no longer required but with nothing yet to take its place, the New Labour government of 1997 moved quickly to introduce the Diploma in Probation Studies (DipPS). This was a dedicated qualification that combined academic study at honours degree level with a period in practice where practice skills were acquired, developed and assessed by experienced and appropriately trained probation officers known as practice development assessors. These staff were pivotal in enabling trainee probation officers to integrate their university learning with their practice – an integration which was a hallmark of the DipPS and arguably its most impressive achievement (Bailey *et al.* 2007).

For all its strengths, a fair criticism of the DipPS is that it provided high quality training only to aspiring probation officers. Other grades of staff, especially though not only PSOs, were expected to undertake increasingly responsible and sophisticated work, often without training of sufficient quality or assessment of their ability. Knight and Stout (2009) explored the training needs of the wider workforce and argued cogently for higher education in the training not only of probation officers but of other staff as well. They concluded that the skills and responsibilities of PSOs are commensurate with a higher education level of training. At the same time, they asserted the need to retain and clarify role boundaries: 'Providing appropriate training for PSOs should be a way of preparing them to carry out their current role better, it should not provide a rationale for continuing to pass increasing amounts of the work of probation officers onto their PSO colleagues' (Knight and Stout 2009: 281).

A new training framework was introduced in 2010. A qualified probation officer still requires an honours degree, but this can be gained incrementally within a framework that offers a tiered curriculum, matching the tiers of the offender management model, in which staff will receive training commensurate with their responsibilities (Knight and Stout 2009; Burke 2010). While it plainly makes sense to align a vocational curriculum with the needs of the job, Burke (2010: 46) warns of the risk that such developments could result in 'a fragmented system of training in which knowledge is subservient to practice requirements'.

Other aspects of staff development that remain incompletely addressed include continuing professional development. No post-qualifying framework exists and while some universities offer Master's level opportunities, most training takes place within the service itself and is sometimes not much more than briefing staff in new requirements and procedures. Management training too is patchy and, while there are undoubtedly better examples, some management training courses have been experienced as overly generic and insufficiently applied to the distinctive skills and responsibilities of managing probation.

Knowledge, skills and values

One approach to curriculum planning – and one which informed the design of the DipPS as well as the new framework – is to consider the knowledge, skills and values required to work well in probation. Many chapters in this book bear on this, but a short summary is given below.

Knowledge includes an understanding of human motivation and the processes of change, drawn perhaps from psychology; an appreciation of the wider social context of offending and desistance and the significance of social and penal policies, calling for insights from sociology, social policy and criminology; and a sufficient and reliable knowledge of the law and policy which probation implements. Since probation aspires to be evidence-led, staff also need to be able to appraise evidence and interpret critically the inferences that are drawn from research. As well as drawing upon better-established academic disciplines, probation's proliferation of policies and practices has also generated distinctive areas of study – for example around assessment and risk.

One of the influences on a curriculum should be the perception of what experienced staff have found that they need to do their work. In an instructive study of *skills*, comparing a Canadian province and an English probation area, Bracken found that in both jurisdictions *coping with offender emotions*, *interpersonal communication* and *interviewing* skills were especially highly valued by staff and concluded (2003: 112) that 'This would seem to suggest that working with offenders still necessitates a firm grounding in the skills of establishing good relationships with offenders that can be the foundation for further work.' This also emphasises the importance of reflection, self-awareness and emotional literacy, since interpersonal skills are never reducible to processes and techniques.

The *values* of probation were discussed in Chapter 3 where it was argued that values should guide and infuse all aspects of practice, not merely stand as declaratory expressions of good intent. *How* this is to be done is a challenge for both study and practice. Chapter 3 insisted, for example, that anti-discrimination requires *knowledge* (of the processes and practices that give rise to unfairness – often in ways that are far from obvious – and the consequences of discrimination), *self-awareness* and *an ethical commitment to justice*.

While a curriculum should be shaped by the knowledge, skills and values that staff need to work well, there remains the elusive question of personal qualities – for example, resilience, patience, emotional literacy, self-awareness and an ability to relate to a broad range of (often difficult) people with confidence and demonstrating a positive but a realistic belief in their potential. Such qualities include skills, but are not merely skills and are central to the work of probation. It is not easy to see these qualities as part of a curriculum, to see how they could be taught or assessed. No doubt they can be developed in practice, by taking feedback and through honest self-reflection, but there are hard questions here for those responsible for staff education and training.

At the same time, staff must be able to respond to changes and this may present challenges that go beyond a contemporary understanding of the required knowledge, skills and values. Findings from inspections too and from serious further offence inquiries are often an occasion to look critically at training. That said, many 'failures' in practice can be more plausibly attributed to inadequate resourcing or to failures of implementation and management than to shortcomings in training (Knight and Stout 2009). Again, while it is entirely reasonable for employers to expect staff to be well prepared as beginning practitioners when they qualify, they have a continuing responsibility to support their staff in practice through supervision and to provide opportunities for professional development. The new framework sharpens this expectation on employers: the distinction between *qualified* and *unqualified* staff is superseded by the framework, which prepares people to undertake work appropriate to their level of responsibility. But the exercise of this responsibility is a matter for the organisation as a whole and not just the individual practitioner.

Staff motivation and morale

Annison *et al.* (2008: 262) brought together a number of studies that show that for 'applicants [sc. to probation] and probation students, helping and challenging people to change is the single most influential factor in their career choice'. It is likely that this would have been true of successive generations of probation staff, but instructive to note that this type of motivation has persisted throughout political attempts to change the perception of probation and in particular to emphasise its punitive and controlling character at the expense of helping. Working with people continues to be what many officers find most rewarding, while the amount of paperwork, bureaucracy and time at the computer are frustrating. Annison *et al.* urge a perspective on training that recognises that staff have a special insight into what they need to do the job well and that managerialism and audit can distort this. It appears that there is an uncomfortable dissonance between staff's motivation, and their own perception of what they need to do to undertake their work well and, on the other hand, the imperatives of a target-driven and managerial culture (see also Eadie and Winwin Sein 2005).

The pace and nature of change in probation in recent years have left some staff uncertain and anxious. While the integration of service that NOMS is felt to represent is welcomed by many, the implications of contestability and its impact upon people's employment has inevitably occasioned anxiety. Staff express confusion about their roles and professional identities, while the values that attracted staff into the profession are felt to be under threat. There is a general sense of 'change fatigue' (Robinson and Burnett 2007: 318) and that policy changes have sometimes been driven through without adequate regard for the understanding or support of the staff most affected. There have been predictable consequences for morale, stress, staff absence through sickness and indeed staff retention in a troubled service (Farrow 2004; Eadie and Winwin Sein 2005). Robinson and Burnett (2007) pointedly conclude that at a time when there is renewed attention to interpersonal and relationship skills in working with offenders, the question of *who* is to work with them face to face is undecided and there are understandable anxieties that the organisation itself is at risk of being experienced as a constraint on the realisation of best practice.

Technicality and indeterminacy

Many of the matters reviewed in this chapter hinge on the question of the extent to which probation should be seen as a technical activity or as intrinsically indeterminate (Robinson 2003c). If probation is seen as practice that can be prescribed – through regulation, National Standards, instruments of assessment, specified 'manualised' interventions – then discretion can be tightly circumscribed and the basis and criteria of accountability precisely set; staff supervision could be focused and determinate; staff training would be task-oriented and concentrate on ensuring that staff know what is expected of them and how they are to achieve it.

But if probation is taken to be indeterminate, to call for judgement, reflection and emotional literacy, this sets different parameters for discretion and account-ability. Robinson (2003c – and in many of her other papers) has shown that probation is not reducible to technicality and that in practice staff do not and cannot simply apply prescribed schedules and routines. As we saw in earlier chapters, probation requires considered judgement. The proper implementation of National Standards involves an appreciation of their purpose and value and a willingness to recognise when effectiveness and fairness call for a departure from the presumptions of standards; risk assessment and management require not only judgements about instantiation (Chapter 7) but also for an understanding of what assessment instruments can and cannot determine and their contribution to a wise decision; every relationship has unique characteristics and interpersonal trans-actions are not susceptible to routine prescription. It is not that there is no place for technicality, but probation is not and could not be merely technical. Yet its recent preoccupation with trying to stipulate best practice, to enhance consistency and to bind discretion could easily mislead people into a misunderstanding of its character and a consequent scepticism about the need for sophisticated training.

Another theme in a history of probation training, then, is an uncertainty about the character of the work. Should probation officers be functionaries, doing as they are told? (Part of the discipline of working in an organisation is the requirement to advance that organisation's policies and practices.) Or should they be professional, thinking for themselves and making principled judgments? (The attempt to implement policy, notoriously, generates unforeseen and sometimes perverse consequences which practitioners are well placed to discern and to inform managers about how policy might be improved.) This debate has implications for the role of higher education, which traditionally encourages reflection, criticism and independent thought. But 'Critical thinkers can find themselves in uncom-fortable positions within a service that increasingly requires compliance and conformity to national standards and procedures' (Bailey *et al.* 2007: 122).

Summary

This chapter has considered a number of aspects of working in the probation service. It explored discretion and accountability, trying to distinguish between them and challenging the view that strong accountability entails tightened discretion. Discussion then turned to the roles in the work force, education and training. A theme throughout has been the rejection of any idea that probation is amenable to regulation and the precise prescription of practice. Working well with diversity, complexity and the common challenge of trying to work purposefully in circumstances of uncertainty call for openness, reflection and emotional literacy, as well as for the support and guidance of colleagues. Such characteristics are not easily reducible to a set of practice skills or performance competences.

If the best probation practice requires judgement, flexibility and appropriate recognition of difference, the organisation should be so structured as to support its staff in achieving this. As it is, it has sometimes seemed to staff that their work has had to conform to the precepts of management, its targets and its disciplines of inspection and audit. It is as if the needs of organisation have led and shaped the character of the work to which staff and users must adapt, rather than the organisation being structured to support best practice.

Questions

- How can fairness be ensured if officers can exercise wide discretion?
- Has the distinction between probation officers and probation service officers had its day? What should be the difference between these roles and how should the role boundary be defined?
- Relationships seem to be key to effective work, but to what extent can these skills be learned? How?

Further reading

Faulkner (2006) is full of important ideas relevant to the themes of this chapter, especially on the matter of accountability. Bailey *et al.* (2007) is a brief but insightful discussion. See also Robinson (2003c).

16 Some international perspectives

This chapter considers probation in other countries. It begins with a brief account of the other jurisdictions of the United Kingdom and goes on to consider some aspects of contemporary probation in Europe. A number of influences have brought it about that policy and practice developed in one country have been 'transferred' to others and these processes will also be discussed. These accounts are instructive not only for their own sake but for the light that they shed, through comparison and contrast, upon probation in England and Wales.

The jurisdictions of the United Kingdom

Wales

England and Wales are a single jurisdiction. The Government of Wales Act 1998 created a National Assembly whose authority was increased by a further Act (2006) setting in motion 'the incremental acquisition of primary law-making powers' (Drakeford 2010: 138). Authority over the work of probation is not devolved, however, nor foreseeably is it likely to be, remaining the domain of the UK Ministry of Justice, and NOMS covers Wales as well as England.

Drakeford (2010) instructively discusses the implications of the Welsh Assembly for youth justice. While authority for youth justice is also not devolved, most of the agencies who staff the youth offending teams are the responsibility of the Assembly. This has entailed complex and sometimes delicate negotiations to manage tensions between the Assembly's priorities and those of the Youth Justice Board. As Drakeford goes on to show, the resulting strategy includes elements that are significantly different from the priorities of Westminster – including some resistance to the punitivism that has characterised much English policy.

While the position of probation is not the same as youth justice, many of the agencies with whom probation must work in partnership, in matters of public protection and in the provision of services to offenders, take direction from the Assembly. On 1 April 2010 the four probation areas/trusts across Wales combined to form the Wales Probation Trust and this could enhance the possibility of a distinct identity for Welsh probation. Drakeford argues that the political traditions of Wales are more supportive of social democratic and welfare principles than some other parts of the UK. Since socio-political factors are a significant influence on a country's penal culture (Cavadino and Dignan 2006a, 2006b), it is possible to anticipate an increasing divergence between England and Wales, with the priorities of a strengthened and more confident Assembly increasingly influencing the policy, but still more the practices, of probation in Wales.

Northern Ireland

O'Mahony and Chapman (2007: 155) begin their account of probation in Northern Ireland by pointing to its 'unique historical development, the civil conflict and the peace process [which] have all forced probation to examine its relationship to the state, to offenders and to communities'. This has made for instructive differences between probation in Northern Ireland and in England and Wales, for all their many similarities.

Probation is delivered through the Probation Board for Northern Ireland (PBNI). Originally created in 1982, PBNI is now part of the Department of Justice, established in April 2010. Stout (2007) identifies training and community development as the principal differences between PBNI and the areas/trusts of England and Wales. As in Scotland, and indeed many other European countries, PBNI requires its probation officers to be trained in social work and the professional affiliation of staff, often powerfully shaped by their training, is among the influences on their interpretation and implementation of policy. For all that the delivery of *what works* and the management of high risk offenders are now policy priorities for PBNI, as they are for NOMS, staff's professional education and background could lead to differences in understanding, interpretation and implementation in practice.

PBNI's relationship to the communities it serves is especially interesting and must be understood in the context of probation's development during the period of conflict. The 'Black Report', the 1979 review which was the origin of PBNI, had strongly emphasised the need to work in partnership with its communities (O'Mahony and Chapman 2007). The political focus on civil conflict, moreover, meant that working with offenders did not attract the same level of government attention or involvement as in England. At the same time, the period of conflict was marked by political disaffection, suspicion of or hostility towards the state and a lack of confidence in the normal systems of criminal justice to respond to crime. If probation could establish itself as a partner of the community rather than an agency of the state, these factors could provide 'a space in which the Probation Board in partnership with the voluntary sector and the community could create a range of interventions with people who offend' (Chapman and O'Mahony 2007: 100).

The origins of much offending were manifestly embedded in the communities and the conflicts and could not plausibly be interpreted simply as the misbehaviour of a few. While the British government was determined to 'depoliticise' participation in civil disorder and to characterise it as crime, conventional rehabilitative or social work interventions were clearly inappropriate and likely to be rejected anyway. Even so, prisoners, whatever the reason for their incarceration, and others prosecuted and sentenced continued to have a range of welfare needs, which probation was willing to try to meet, finding respect for its work, its integrity and its independence (Chapman and O'Mahony 2007).

Stout (2007) gives several examples of programmes delivered in partnership with community agencies, including the Inclusive Model of Partnership Against Car Crime (IMPACT), the Course for Drink Drive Offenders (CDDO) and Men Overcoming Domestic Violence (MODV). It appears that these initiatives emerged more from the communities' own identification of their problems – for example the dangers of 'joy-riding' in West Belfast (Chapman and O'Mahony 2007) – than from a centrally led agenda to implement those programmes which the government had decided most needed to be delivered. So while English probation too has developed partnership approaches, it is arguable that these Northern Ireland projects were less a matter of probation engaging community organisations to help it in 'its' work, more that community-based organisations sought probation support and funding to find solutions of their own.

Restorative justice practice is also of especial interest. In Northern Ireland as in England, this practice is often welcomed and has become common in working with young offenders in particular. But conciliation and other principles of restorative justice have been part of the communities' own healing processes (sometimes as an alternative to paramilitary punishment) and some local initiatives have been viewed with suspicion because of their political origins and connections (O'Mahony and Chapman 2007). On the other hand, especially in the lead up to the peace process, the state was not seen as an even-handed peacemaker. As we saw in Chapter 13, restorative justice calls for the involvement of the community, but this must have a different significance when the community itself is so fractured and some of the 'conflicts' between offenders and victims mirror deeper and wider divides.

As Northern Ireland moved towards political resolution of its conflicts, the findings of research and aspirations for evidence-based practice, to which Northern Irish probation made an important contribution, influenced policy here as in England and Wales. The Good Friday Agreement (1998) led to a review of criminal justice practice throughout Northern Ireland. One consequence was the opening up of the work of PBNI to inspection and scrutiny, changing the Board's internal culture (Chapman and O'Mahony 2007).

PBNI still allocates a significant part of its budget to community development and works closely with a range of statutory, community and voluntary organisations. The Corporate Plan (PBNI 2008: 19) affirms 'The need for the organisation to fully engage with the community in the delivery of services and continue to input to prevention and diversion.' Even so, PBNI is becoming less central in community safety work, which is now more likely to be led by other agencies and resourced in other ways. O'Mahony and Chapman (2007: 173) anticipate that PBNI, as part of the Department of Justice, will increasingly be accountable to the Northern Ireland Assembly and may 'follow the English model for probation rather than continue to develop a specifically Northern Irish approach'. An emphasis on public protection and closer relationships with the prison service might displace the innovative work undertaken in close partnership with the community.

The relationship between the local and the national and (what is not quite the same thing) the relationship between the community and the state shape the character of probation practice. This has been markedly different in Northern Ireland and continues to evolve as 'the state' and communities change following the peace process.

Scotland

In many respects, Scottish and English practices in working with offenders are, again, very similar. Yet Scotland has a distinct legal system, with its own court structure and sanctions for dealing with offenders (Whyte 2007). There is no probation service in Scotland, the work instead being undertaken by *criminal justice social workers* employed by local authorities (McIvor and McNeill 2007, on which the following account heavily relies). There used to be a probation service in Scotland – there was an office in Glasgow as early as 1905 – but for much of the twentieth century Scottish courts were reluctant to use probation, at least for adult offenders, calling into question the viability of a separate service.

The Kilbrandon Report (1964) led to an integration of probation and after-care into local authority generic social work departments. Even if this was as much a pragmatic reorganisation as an affirmation of welfare in working with offenders, this organisational basis may be part of the explanation for Scotland's ability to resist the punitivism that characterised policy in England. As McIvor and McNeill (2007: 136) put it 'probation in Scotland was never required to negotiate the ideological traverse towards punishment in the community' and policy continued to be characterised by an emphasis on social inclusion, rehabilitation and welfare as much as punishment and public protection.

A drawback in the organisational arrangements, however, was that it became difficult for criminal justice social work to hold its place among the priorities of social work departments, already pressed to meet their responsibilities in child care and protection, and to gain the confidence of the criminal courts. In 1991, National Objectives and Standards were promulgated and at the same time central government became responsible for the funding of criminal justice social work, ring-fencing this revenue against other claims. This changed (and tightened) lines of accountability as well as leading to the establishment of specialist units, specific training and the development of distinctive criminal justice skills. Scottish researchers meanwhile – notably Gill McIvor and her colleagues – were influential in developing insights into effective practice, including community service, and significantly contributed to the development of practice in England as well (for example McIvor 1990, 1992).

In 1996 local government reorganisation created many more authorities, leaving some criminal justice social work departments unviably small. The response was to combine authorities into a smaller number of sturdier groupings, retaining a strong local identity but benefiting from economies of scale. A further more recent development has been the creation of Community Justice Authorities (CJAs), enacted by the Management of Offenders (Scotland) Act 2005, which came into effect in April 2006. These authorities include not only the usual agencies of criminal justice, but also victim services, health services and other organisations from the statutory and voluntary sectors. Each CJA began by drawing up a strategic plan for its area: resources were then to be deployed accordingly and the results monitored and evaluated.

In May 2006, a National Strategy was published to guide the work of the CJAs. But while central government offers a strategic lead, governance in Scotland is much less centralised. This may be among the reasons why Scotland has stopped short of the organisational changes made in England and Wales: in particular, Scotland has found little support for combining the Scottish prison service with criminal justice social work services into a single correctional agency – though this was proposed by the Scottish Labour Party before the 2003 parliamentary election. Scotland's local base, represented by the CJAs, its associated willingness to allow other agency perspectives to contribute to strategy, and its tight organisational connections with social work have militated against any absorption of probation into a correctional agency dominated by prison. These factors have also helped Scotland to resist the dominance of punishment and control in penal debate. If in England it has sometimes seemed that rehabilitation and social inclusion matter just to the extent that they contribute to public protection, in Scotland they have been seen not only as of equal value, but as mutually supportive and inter-dependent purposes.

In an insightful comparative study, Robinson and McNeill (2004) found that practitioners in Scotland were able to draw on policy commitments to social work and inclusion to interpret the newer political emphasis on public protection and accommodate it into their understanding of their work. England's stark disavowal of social work makes that much harder to achieve and creates a tension for some practitioners between policy imperatives and a professional commitment to rehabilitation and reintegration as valuable for their own sake, not only for their contingent contribution to reduced reoffending.

Scotland continues to affirm the importance of offenders' social inclusion. Since the election in 2007 of a minority Scottish National Party administration, policy developments have put a particular emphasis on reparation and *payback* – not in the punitive and shaming sense evoked in the Casey report (2008: see further Chapter 11), but with a recognition that wrongdoing calls for making amends. This can be achieved in a number of ways and, rather than seek to align payback with punishment, there is a strong rehabilitative and inclusive connotation in Scottish policy thinking: notably, 'the notion of paying back by turning one's life around represents a very neat, if underdeveloped, reframing of engagement in rehabilitation as an act of reparation' (Munro and McNeill 2010: 227).

At the same time, McIvor and McNeill (2007: 143) have pointed to a policy shift towards 'an increasing preoccupation with the effective management of offender risk'. As in England, prisoners with longer sentences have been subject to increasingly rigorous forms of surveillance after release and the recognition of the importance of resettlement for shorter-term prisoners too could bind criminal justice social work and prison closer together in their common objectives of public protection (Munro and McNeill 2010).

It is both instructive and ironic to note that, in Scotland as in Northern Ireland, the growth of devolved political authority has in many respects moved policy and organisation *closer* to that of England. Reciprocally, however, it is possible to anticipate that probation in England and Wales could develop in ways that have been adumbrated in Scotland and Northern Ireland – specifically, grounding strategy locally could lead to a community-focused, inter-agency response to crime and criminal justice, like the Scottish CJAs. As was argued in Chapter 14, one plausible future for English probation would be that responsible local agencies rather than the political imperatives of central government should determine strategy and that governance arrangements should support that development.

Probation in Europe

Europe is an increasingly significant context for probation in England and Wales. Although European probation continues to take a wide range of forms, with different organisational structures, agency responsibilities tasks and policy priorities, the European probation agencies are becoming more alike, as a comparison of the first and second editions of the compendium of probation systems in Europe reveals (van Kalmthout and Derks 2000; van Kalmthout and Durnescu 2008). One stimulus to these developments has been policy transfer (see below). Others include the work of the Council of Europe and the forum for exchange of ideas and good practice constituted by the *Conférence Permanente Européenne de la Probation* (CEP). In January 2010 the Council of Europe adopted European Probation Rules which attempt to set standards for member states, grounded in the shared ethical principles of the European Convention on Human Rights (see Canton 2010b).

Van Kalmthout and Durnescu (2008: 19–20) identify 33 specific tasks undertaken by probation staff across Europe. Some of these are common to almost all of the 33 countries covered (e.g. preparing a pre-sentence report is a probation task in all but 4 countries; community service in all but 1). Some tasks are undertaken in just a few countries, while others again ('mediation/victim support') are undertaken in several countries but not in several others.

Walters (2003) usefully identified several themes and trends in European probation, which are still apparent now. Among these is a move 'From Welfare to Corrections', a tendency in almost all countries away from social work concepts and values and towards an alignment with the goals of other criminal justice agencies – notably, risk management, public protection and punishment (van Kalmthout and Derks 2000). At the same time, however, 'it is clear that the job of providing guidance, care and assistance is still the most important one of probation services' (*ibid*.: 17) and many services continue to characterise their work as a type of social work and provide social work training for staff.

Another trend is a 'more scientific' approach to practice. Assessment instruments (Chapter 7), effective practice research, cognitive behavioural approaches and the use of accredited programmes are being taken up in most European jurisdictions. Many of these initiatives originated in Canada and have come to Europe, often via England.

In almost all of the probation systems of Western Europe, practice has historically centred on the offender. Over time, it has become essential, ethically and politically, to respond to victims. Austria, Belgium, Norway and parts of Germany have made considerable progress in developing victim–offender mediation and other restorative approaches, but many jurisdictions have struggled to accommodate victim-centred work in an essentially offender-centred organisation (see Chapter 13). Some of the newer services – for example, in the Czech Republic, Latvia and Turkey – have tried to establish principles of reparation and mediation in the foundations of their organisation. The Czech Republic is a particularly interesting example: here the service is called the Probation and Mediation Service. In England, the focus of response to an offence is the offender; in the Czech Republic, the 'unit of intervention' is, so far as possible, the relationship between the offender, the victim and the community, recognising the rights and responsibilities of each. In addition to many other advantages, this recognition of the rights of victims gives services greater credibility and commands the trust of the public.

Voluntary organisations, often the ancestors of state probation provision, remain extensively involved in many jurisdictions. The Salvation Army, for example, is of central importance to probation work in the Netherlands. Services also use volunteers in different ways. In many southern European countries, there is extensive participation of volunteers – with their connections to community organisations, formal and informal – in working with offenders. At best, such practices represent the involvement of the community in working with offenders and promote social inclusion.

In most parts of Europe, probation aspires to provide alternatives to custody and several European countries have looked to find ways of managing very severe prison overcrowding by developing probation systems. As we have seen in Chapter 4, however, the evidence that the provision of 'alternatives' is effective in reducing the prison population is very tenuous. Common challenges include:

- Gaining the confidence of the public, politicians and judiciary. The familiar problem in England – that probation is not always well understood and struggles to establish itself as a credible response to offending – is still more of a challenge in many other countries, especially where probation is new or emerging.
- Meeting the needs of non-nationals, including new communities. With so much movement of people on the Continent, there is a large and growing challenge to develop policies and practices that genuinely meet the needs of people in this position. Some central probation concepts – *reintegration, community, social capital* – have a quite different significance for them.
- Improving quality of service to victims. Probation must acknowledge legitimate concerns about victims even as it rejects a necessary opposition

between the rights of offenders and victims and repudiates punishment as the best way of vindicating a victim's experience.

- Trying to make sure that tougher community sanctions and enforcement do not lead to more imprisonment. Greater demands, together with tighter enforcement, could lead to an increased incidence of breach which, perversely, could in turn increase the prison population (Chapter 9; Padfield and Maruna 2006 Canton and Eadie 2005).
- Responding to popular punitiveness (Snacken 2010). Crime, notoriously, can become a focus for all kinds of other concerns, including economic and social stresses. It is hard to predict how punitive attitudes will be affected by current economic recession and its social consequences, but they may well intensify if crime rises or is perceived as an increasing threat.

A stimulus towards harmonisation is the implementation of a new European Union Framework Decision which will allow for the transfer, in certain circumstances, of probation supervision from one jurisdiction to another – typically where an offender convicted in another country is returned to their own country for supervision (Canton 2009c). The significance of this agreement goes even beyond the enormously important problem that it seeks to address. This is the first time that a probation measure has had such binding significance for so many countries. In order for the framework to achieve its potential, the member states of the EU will need to learn much more about and find confidence in each other's probation practices. Whether or not this will lead to greater assimilation of practice – and whether this is a desirable thing – are interesting questions.

Probation in other countries

If practice is diverse in Europe, it is naturally still more multifarious in other parts of the world. While studies of comparative criminal justice are flourishing (Nelken 2007), comparative probation scholarship is underdeveloped. One challenge is trying to find out if like is being compared with like: the term probation is used in both England and in the USA, for example, but practices are very different in fundamental ways (Bracken 2007). Equally there are countries that do not have a probation service, but nevertheless undertake work with which instructive comparisons (and exchange of ideas) can still be made with England.

The author was involved in exploring the introduction of probation in a transitional democracy in eastern Europe. This country had no probation service, but there was a system of early release from prison and this included supervision, both by police and by staff from the penitentiary department. These staff did not see their work as providing help, but as monitoring and control. Yet their work brought them into contact with people who were manifestly struggling and in need of help. As decent people, they responded to this with kindness, encouragement, referral to agencies that could provide help – work that in practice is indistinguishable from 'probation'. For that matter, there may be experiences of probation in other countries that are experienced as little more than monitoring or control.

Broadly, there are many social, economic and cultural factors that shape the character and organisations of criminal justice and of probation more specifically. These include:

- Social policy. The importance of social capital in desistance (Chapter 9) and probation's dependence on other agencies of civil society suggest that wider social policy will support or, as it may be, undermine the work of probation. Countries vary considerably in their view of what is due to convicted offenders, the extent to which this can be managed by the state (alone or even at all), the role of civil society and community in criminal justice. There are questions too about the relationship between the state and the community: that the criminal justice agencies of the state are in the service of the community is not the legacy of many countries.

- Political economy. Recent important work by Cavadino and Dignan (2006a, 2006b) has emphasised a strong association between penal policy and political economy. Applying a broad categorisation to the political economies of twelve contemporary capitalist societies – neo-liberal, conservative corporatist, social democratic, oriental corporatist – they argue a compelling case for the influence of political economy on punitiveness and rates of imprisonment, with direct implications for probation practice.

- Criminal justice institutions and practices. These may be competitors or allies to probation. Opportunities and constraints presented by probation's place in a mutually influential network of agencies may shape its character significantly. One example is probation's contribution to sentencing: in many countries the prosecution proposes the sentence to the court. This makes for a very different context for the contribution of a pre-sentence report. Stronger and better established professions will at least mediate the implementation of probation policy and can subvert it decisively.

- Technology and commerce. Technology is increasingly a feature of modern penality in many ways (Mair 2001), from the processing and exchange of information to electronic monitoring. The manner in which information is collected and processed can reciprocally influence the way in which the penal subject is understood (Aas 2004). Technological capacity and infrastructure constrain the potential of an agency and its practices and shape their development. This consideration is linked too to commercial markets, as private enterprise become increasingly, though variably, involved in penal practices that have traditionally been the prerogative of the state (Christie 2000).

- Research. Even if penal practice is rarely determined by research, research findings may lend support to (or discourage) policy initiatives. The findings of research are more or less influential in determining policies in different countries.

- Pressure groups, networks, public opinion. The support or opposition of a pressure group can make a significant difference to the political context in which probation operates. Similarly, the manner in which the media represent probation can plainly make a difference to public support and understanding.

These are among the determinants of the policies and practices of probation in different countries. There is naturally much more to be said about the way in which these factors operate – how, as Garland puts it, such broad social characteristics and influences are specifically 'translated into the folkways of the [penal] field' (Garland 2001: 24). But these several influences act and interact in often unpredictable ways to shape and direct the policies and practices of probation.

Policy transfer

European probation has a long tradition of international dialogue and debate (Vanstone 2008). This has no doubt always stimulated exchanges of policy and practice. More recently, however, there have been more deliberate attempts to take systems and practices from one country to another. Notably the transitional democracies of eastern Europe, influenced by their legacies of large prison populations but also by their aspirations to enhance principles of democracy and human rights, have been keen to learn from the achievements – and perhaps also from the mistakes – of longer-established probation services.

Twinning projects and other alliances, for example through EU PHARE projects, have also been the occasion for policy and practice transfer. The *Strengthening Transnational Approaches to Reducing Re-offending* (STARR) project (London probation area, 2009) is another recent initiative to enable effective practices to be taken from one country to another. England has been involved in many of these initiatives (Canton 2009b), and the Scandinavian countries, Switzerland and other jurisdictions have also been influential 'exporters' in furthering these developments (Walters 2003).

Nor should it be forgotten that England has been an 'importer' as well. We have seen that probation practice in Canada and the USA influenced developments in England and there is a ready exchange of research and scholarship among the countries of the UK, North America, Australia and New Zealand. Political priorities with direct and sometimes radical consequences for probation have originated in the USA and stimulated similar developments elsewhere (Jones and Newburn 2007): a clear example is the dominance of risk and the idea of lengthy incapacitative sentences as a means of reducing crime. In probation, not only research insights into effective practice but specific programmes as well were imported from Canada and the US (notably the influential *Reasoning and Rehabilitation* designed by Robert Ross).

The circumstances which conduce to successful transfer – and indeed what would count as success here – are explored in Canton (2006; 2009b). The idea presumably is not to take English probation to another place but to foster the development of local forms of practice. But to what extent can a programme be adapted culturally without compromising programme integrity? Risk instruments, especially actuarial ones, are grounded in statistical correlations that may not be assumed to hold true everywhere. For example, OGRS (see Chapter 7) is based on a set of factors that may not hold true elsewhere. (Age at first conviction will vary, evidently, not only according to the age of criminal responsibility but also with differences in responses to crime committed by young people, similarly with age at first custodial sentence etc.)

There are also examples of second-hand transfer where an instrument already modified (and as it may be attenuated or compromised) has been exported again in that revised form – and then subsequently modified for another country (Bauwens and Snacken 2010). The extent to which practices can be adapted without prejudice to their integrity is insufficiently understood and may not be taken for granted. Generally, if, as has been suggested earlier in the chapter, the character and structure of probation is shaped by a wide range of inter-related influences, policy and practice transfer will always be mediated by these factors (Canton 2006; 2009b). Bluntly *what works here* cannot be assumed to be *what works there*.

Summary

Probation is not a 'thing' to be taken or left but a set of ideas and possibilities to be used creatively and strategically to solve local problems of criminal justice . . . a framework into which locally feasible and desirable solutions may be fitted.

(Robert Harris, 1995: 207)

Just as history gives 'distance' and hence a perspective to understand contemporary practice, so the study of probation in other countries can be instructive not only for its own sake, but also because of its potential to expose taken-for-granted characteristics of our own practices and institutions – and allow them to be seen in a different and often clearer way.

Our brief review of practice in the United Kingdom shows how probation in geographically proximate and culturally similar jurisdictions can nevertheless develop in significantly different ways – even if the differences may seem less apparent than the similarities, especially when comparisons are made between the UK and other countries. Across Europe, too, despite influences towards common purposes and practices and 'globalising' tendencies, marked differences nevertheless remain. As Cavadino and Dignan put it (2006a: 452): 'however many factors we incorporate into our theory, it will still not give us the whole story. Individual nations, and their cultures, histories and politics, can be just as quirky and esoteric as individual human beings.'

Harris's insight (quoted above) does not mean that 'anything goes'. There will be different ideas about the particular tasks and values that set the parameters of probation. It should be noted, however, that the very first Basic Principle of the European Probation Rules affirms relationships as the medium by which probation seeks to bring about change: it is arguable that representatives of many different countries regarded this as perhaps the single important characteristic that their probation agencies had in common. Many criminal justice agencies affirm public protection and crime reduction, but what makes probation distinctive is its values and its commitment to particular ways of effecting change – and its rejection of some other means.

Perhaps the essence of probation, then, is to be found less in its tasks or organisation than in its values. A belief in the possibility of personal change and characteristically (if not necessarily inevitably) scepticism about the efficacy of punishment seem to be values that are definitive of probation. Probation makes statements – however qualified and even compromised – about the place of punishment, about the possibility of change and about social inclusion.

Finally, while we have mostly been concerned with the way in which broader social factors mould the character of probation, this chapter should not end without mention of the reciprocal influence probation may have on society. As an authoritative social institution, probation represents and gives expression to values that go to make a society the kind of society that it is and this is part of the reason why its values matter.

Questions

- The author suggests that 'in Scotland as in Northern Ireland, the growth of devolved political authority has in many respects moved policy and organisation *closer* to that of England'. Why do you think this might be?
- Consider the factors that are identified as shaping probation in different countries (page 219): can you add to these? Are some factors more influential than others?
- Is policy transfer a form of imperialism – of powerful countries attempting to impose their own preferred practices on to others? If so, how much does this matter?

Further reading

For Northern Ireland, see Chapman and O'Mahony (2007), O'Mahony and Chapman (2007); see also http://www.cjsni.gov.uk/. For Scotland, see McIvor and McNeill (2007), McNeill and Whyte (2007), McNeill and Munro (2010). See also http://www.cjsw.ac.uk/cjsw/CCC_FirstPage.jsp. The website of the Scottish Centre for Crime and Justice Research (http://www.sccjr.ac.uk/) is an extremely useful resource.

For Europe, van Kalmthout and Durnescu (2008) must be the starting point. See also the CEP website (http://www.cep-probation.org/) and the Council of Europe website (http://www.coe.int/t/e/legal_affairs/legal_co-operation/prisons_and_alternatives/).

Probation Round the World (Hamai *et al.* 1995) is rather dated, but still contains many insights and much useful information.

Afterword: probation's futures

It was suggested at the beginning that the trajectory of penal policy has been determined by three strategies and the interactions among them. They have been returned to in most of our chapters, where their manifestations and implications for different aspects of probation's policies and practices have been discussed. Foreseeably these strategies will continue to exert their influence and to interact, with inherently unpredictable consequences.

It is likely that punitivism (our first identified strategy) will, at the least, continue to make politicians very wary of exposing themselves to accusations that they are 'soft on crime'. That said, in the 2010 general election, law and order was much less prominent an issue than it has been for many elections past. Debate on this matter was relatively muted and the political parties did not conspicuously invoke the popular punitivism that has so influenced – and perhaps distorted – criminal justice debate in the past 30 years. Nevertheless, enthusiasm for punishment is a light sleeper and it may be that some proposals for sentencing reform or some terrible events will reawaken it and return punishment to the centre of political debate.

It must also be remembered that 'fears expressed about crime are actually a convenient and socially-approved kind of metaphor through which [people] can articulate . . . a much more complex sense of restlessness and anxiety' (Taylor 1998: 23). Recession and hardship are likely to evoke anxieties of this type and it may well be that offenders will be called upon to play their time-honoured role of scapegoat. If the punitive strategy were the only influence (which it never is), it might be possible to anticipate increased levels of punishment and higher rates of imprisonment. Probation might be forced to present itself to a doubting public as prison-like in its capacity both to punish and to protect the public and valued mostly for its (uncertain) contribution to reducing the prison population.

Our second strategy (managerialism) has encumbered probation as an organisation with a range of performance targets, usually relating to output measures, and an associated tight stipulation about how practice should be undertaken. It has been argued that these processes have sometimes failed to understand the character of practice and, in trying to shape practice to that which audit can capture, have distorted it. The early pronouncements of the coalition government do suggest a willingness to liberate public organisations from many of these burdens. But an audit culture, in the name of accountability and 'quality assurance', is deeply embedded in most aspects of contemporary governance, regularly frustrating aspirations to shake off bureaucracy. There are also some controls over probation that central government seems reluctant to give up. For probation, a sharp question is: *will trusts be trusted* and allowed the latitude to develop their work in the context of locally determined priorities, commissioning and resource allocation?

The third strategy recognises the ethical significance of penal practices and understands probation as more than just an agency for delivering services and outcomes. Criminal justice is more than crime control or the administration of punishment, but stands as an authoritative representation of how a society regards those of its members who have been victims and offenders, their rights and responsibilities and the duties of society towards them. While the introduction suggested that this has often been more a constraint on the excesses of the other two strategies than a 'strategy' in its own right, the book has shown many of the ways in which its influence is apparent. Among the contemporary manifestations are a renewed interest in the importance of relationships in working with offenders, a recognition of the association between social exclusion and reoffending and the occasional attempt to assert a *right to rehabilitation*. Again, restorative justice has the ambition to transcend the idea that the rights of offenders and victims are necessarily in opposition and to seek solutions that maximise the interests of both. Community justice (Chapter 14) and justice reinvestment (Allen and Stern 2007; House of Commons Justice Committee 2009) are other concepts that challenge the instrumental effects of conventional approaches, while also appreciating the wider meaning and significance of crime and justice.

There are signs of political change, as the government disavows the dependence on imprisonment that has been so long prominent in penal policy (Clarke 2010). But it is far from clear that the government's solution is to look first or mainly to probation. Just as crime and desistance are more compellingly influenced by wider social, demographic and economic considerations than by the practices of criminal justice, so too the strategies of penal policy function in a broader socio-political context. Carter's report commended an increased involvement of the independent and commercial sectors in the provision of services that had until then been considered to be the prerogative and responsibility of the state. Economic difficulties and an ideological conception of the proper role of the state could lead now to a redefined and as it may be diminished role for probation. It is for this reason that probation needs to affirm its value with clarity, confidence and integrity.

This book has tried to make a case for an ethical understanding of probation practice. At an organisational level, this entails a local foundation for its work, with local agencies and communities actively involved in crime reduction and in responding to offences and their consequences (Chapter 14). Probation's contribution includes not only the coherent management of services and interventions, as envisaged by the offender management model, but the advocacy of the legitimate interests and rights of offenders, including fair access to the services enjoyed by other members of the community (McNeill *et al.* 2005).

At an individual level, the book has argued for an appreciation of the human character of interactions between probation staff and those with whom they work, affirming the significance of relationships as well as methods and techniques. Probation is involved with complex processes of engagement and change and is much more than a matter of the diligent application of assessment instruments, standardised interventions and the following of prescribed routines.

Throughout this book, then, the attempt has been made to advance an ethical and humanistic understanding of probation. Probation sets for itself some instrumental objectives – especially the rehabilitation of offenders, the protection of the public and the reduction of the prison population. Its contribution to these worthy objectives is considerable, though also often contestable and contingent. Interestingly, it may turn out that an ethical focus and foundation will help probation better to achieve its instrumental purposes. A clear affirmation of the value of probation is much more likely to enhance its credibility and therewith its legitimacy than uncertain and disputable claims about its instrumental achievements. Again, the respect and concern for the individual involved at individual level will tend to enhance legitimacy and increase compliance, bringing opportunities for effective interventions to take place.

Yet whatever its achievements and potential, it is not only in these terms that probation should be understood and valued. Its value lies too in what it stands for, the values it expresses – conspicuously the values of social inclusion and a belief in the possibility of change. As probation enters yet another debate about its future, it needs to affirm its values and its social significance and to speak confidently about the kind of organisation that it aspires to be.

Notes

Chapter 3

1   Public authorities have a statutory duty to assess the impact of their policies and practices to guard against unfair discrimination. These Equality Impact Assessments consider whether (existing or anticipated) provision does (or may) affect people differently, and if so, whether this is to their unfair disadvantage. NOMS and the National Probation Service routinely assess initiatives in this manner.

Chapter 4

1   It is to be noted that sometimes the word punishment refers to any sentence of the court and the term is used in this sense throughout this chapter. But sometimes, as in this section of the Act, punishment is distinguished as just one kind of sentencing rationale or characteristic – usually a retributive one – and distinguished from other sentences like those with a rehabilitative or reparative character.

Chapter 5

1   This number may have fallen slightly in recent years (Oldfield and Grimshaw 2010), although identifying trends is complicated by changes in the rules for counting (Ministry of Justice 2008a).

Chapter 7

1   It should be emphasised that the distinction between clinical and actuarial is not the same as that between unstructured and structured: as we shall see, OASys is not, for the most part, actuarial (although it does incorporate an actuarial scale), but it is certainly structured.

2   Clinical assessment is sometimes referred to as first generation, actuarial as second. A fourth generation of assessment instruments is now envisaged that will further tighten the connections between assessment and the supervision plan, enhancing the potential for assessment to inform and guide supervision and intervention (Bonta and Andrews 2007; Bonta and Wormith 2007). Brown warns against the assumption, implicit in this metaphor, that this is a linear progress: these approaches should rather be seen as 'differences in the underlying conception of what can be held to constitute risk' (Brown 2000: 95).

Chapter 10

1 The emergence of risk to its present salience in probation practice has been thoroughly discussed elsewhere (Kemshall 2000, 2003; Kemshall and Wood 2007; Robinson, 2001, 2002, 2003; Oldfield, 2002).
2 This is the first time in this chapter that we encounter the persistent problem of a low base rate. Grave crimes are rare and for that reason the actuarial information is insufficient to generate reliable assessments. It is at least partly for this reason that almost all actuarial instruments are more successful at 'predicting' reconviction than serious harm. Tuddenham (2000) neatly explains why, the less likely an occurrence, the greater the proportion of false positives who will be included in any attempt to make an actuarial assessment.
3 For structured clinical assessment, see Kemshall (2001). I have avoided using the term here because I want to refer not to a specific instrument, but to a general approach that is systematic (but not actuarial), individualised and action-guiding. In practice, it seems likely that this is an approach that practitioners draw on, especially in the highest risk cases.

Chapter 11

1 There is no longer any such sentence as community service in England and Wales. As this chapter explains, the terms have changed over time to reflect different conceptions of primary purpose. The expression community service is used here because it is so well known and understood, in this country and internationally, and because it denotes an underlying continuity in what this work has been and what it should aspire to be.

References

Note: DPOM = Canton, R. and Hancock, D. (eds) (2007) *Dictionary of Probation and Offender Management*, Cullompton: Willan.
All Internet sites accessed November 2010 unless otherwise indicated.

Aas, K. F. (2004) 'From narrative to database: technological change and penal culture', *Punishment & Society* 6 (4): 379–393.

Advisory Council on the Penal System (ACPS) (1970) *Non-Custodial and Semi-Custodial Penalties* (London: HMSO).

Akhurst, M., Brown, I. and Wessely, S. (n.d.) *Dying for Help: Offenders at Risk of Suicide*, West Yorkshire Probation Service.

Aldridge Foundation (2008) *The User Voice of the Criminal Justice System.* Available online at: http://www.aldridgefoundation.com/user_voice.

Allen, R. and Stern, V. (eds) (2007) *Justice Reinvestment: A New Approach to Crime and Justice.* Available online at: http://www.kcl.ac.uk/depsta/law/research/icps/downloads/justice-reinvestment-2007.pdf.

Andrews, D. and Bonta, J. (2010) 'Rehabilitating criminal justice policy and practice', *Psychology, Public Policy, and Law* 16 (1): 39–55.

Andrews, D., Bonta, J. and Hoge, R. (1990) 'Classification for effective rehabilitation: rediscovering psychology', *Criminal Justice and Behavior*, 17 (1): 19–52.

Annison, J. (2006) 'Style over substance: a review of the evidence base for the use of learning styles in probation', *Criminology & Criminal Justice*, 6 (2): 239–257.

Annison, J., Eadie, T. and Knight, C. (2008) 'People first: probation officer perspectives on probation work', *Probation Journal*, 55 (3): 259–271.

Ansbro, M. (2006) 'What can we learn from serious incident reports?', *Probation Journal*, 53 (1): 57–70.

Apiafi, J. (2007) 'Education: skills for life', in DPOM.

Ashcroft, A. (2007) 'Cycle of change', in DPOM.

Ashworth, A. (2007) 'Sentencing', in M. Maguire, R. Morgan and R. Reiner (eds) *The Oxford Handbook of Criminology* (4th edn), Oxford: Oxford University Press.

Ashworth, A. and Zedner, L. (2008) 'Defending the criminal law: reflections on the changing character of crime, procedure, and sanctions', *Criminal Law and Philosophy* 2: 21–51.

Bailey, R. (1995) 'Helping offenders as an element in justice' in D. Ward and M. Lacey (eds) *Probation: Working for Justice*, London: Whiting and Birch.

Bailey, R. (2007) 'Offender perception', in DPOM.

Bailey, R., Knight, C. and Williams, B. (2007) 'The probation service as part of NOMS in England and Wales: fit for purpose', in L. Gelsthorpe and R. Morgan (eds) *Handbook of Probation*, Cullompton: Willan.

Ballucci, D. (2008) 'Risk in action: the practical effects of the youth management assessment', *Social and Legal Studies,* 17 (2): 175–197.

Bandura, A. (1989) 'Social cognitive theory', in R. Vasta (ed.) *Annals of Child Development*, 6 *Six Theories of Child Development*: 1–60, Greenwich, CT: JAI.

Barry, M. (2000) 'The mentor/monitor debate in criminal justice: what works for offenders', *British Journal of Social Work*, 30: 575–595.

BBC (2004) *Homeless Face More Violent Crime* (16 December). Available online at: http://news.bbc.co.uk/1/hi/uk/4099727.stm.

BBC (2007) Fear 'stops child development' (28 October). Available online at: http://news.bbc.co.uk/1/hi/education/7062545.stm.

BBC (2009) *Probation Work in 'Chronic' State* (22 November). Available online at: http://news.bbc.co.uk/1/hi/england/london/8371175.stm.

Bauwens, A. and Snacken S. (2010) 'Modèles de guidance judiciaire: sur la voie d'un modèle intégré?, Congrès: sécurité avant tout? Chances et dangers du risk assessment dans les domaines de l'exécution des sanctions et de la probation', Paulus-Akademie, Zürich, 3–4 September 2009, 1: 93–107. Stämpfli Verlag AG Bern, Switzerland.

Bean, P. (1976) *Rehabilitation and Deviance*, London: Routledge.

Bearne, B. (2007) 'Pre-sentence report (PSR)', in DPOM.

Bennett, J. (2008) *The Social Costs of Dangerousness: Prison and the Dangerous Classes*, London: Centre for Crime and Justice Studies. Available online at: http://www.crimeand justice.org.uk/dangerousness.html.

Bhui, H. S. (1999) 'Race, racism and risk assessment', *Probation Journal*, 46 (3): 171–181.

Bhui, H. S. (2006) 'Anti-racist practice in NOMS: reconciling managerialist and professional realities', *Howard Journal* 45 (2): 171–190.

Bhui, H. S. (2007) 'Prisons', in DPOM.

Bhui, H. S. (2008) 'Foreign national prisoners', in Y. Jewkes and J. Bennett (eds) *Dictionary of Prisons and Punishment,* Cullompton: Willan.

Biestek, F. (1961) *The Casework Relationship*, London: Unwin University Books.

Bochel, D. (1976) *Probation and After-Care: Its Development in England and Wales*, Edinburgh: Scottish Academic Press.

Boeck, T. (2007) 'Social capital', in DPOM.

Bonta, J. and Andrews, D. (2007) *Risk-Need-Responsivity Model for Offender Assessment and Rehabilitation*. Available online at: http://www.publicsafety.gc.ca/res/cor/rep/risk_ need_200706-eng.aspx.

Bonta, J. and Wormith, S. (2007) 'Risk and need assessment', in G. McIvor and P. Raynor (eds) *Developments in Social Work with Offenders, Research Highlights in Social Work 48*, London: Jessica Kingsley.

Bonta, J., Bourgon, G., Rugge, T., Scott, T., Yessine, A., Gutierrez, L. and Li, J. (2010) 'The strategic training initiative in community supervision: risk-need-responsivity in the real world', Public Safety Canada. Available online at: http://198.103.108.123/res/ cor/rep/2010-01-rnr-eng.aspx.

Bonta, J., Hanson, K. and Law, M. (1998) 'The prediction of criminal and violent recidivism among mentally disordered offenders: a meta-analysis', *Psychological Bulletin*, 123 (2): 123–142.

Bottoms, A. (1977) 'Reflections on the renaissance of dangerousness', *Howard Journal*, 16: 70–96.

Bottoms, A. (1983) 'Neglected features of contemporary penal systems', in D. Garland and P. Young (eds) *The Power to Punish*, Aldershot: Gower.

Bottoms, A. (1987) 'Limiting prison use: experiences in England and Wales', *Howard Journal* 26: 177–202.

Bottoms, A. (1995) 'The philosophy and politics of punishment and sentencing', in C. Clarkson and R. Morgan (eds) *The Politics of Sentencing Reform*, Oxford: Oxford University Press.

Bottoms, A. (2001) 'Compliance and community penalties', in A. Bottoms, L. Gelsthorpe and S. Rex (eds) *Community Penalties: Change and Challenges*, Cullompton: Willan.

Bottoms, A. (2004) 'Empirical research relevant to sentencing frameworks', in A. Bottoms, S. Rex and G. Robinson (eds) *Alternatives to Imprisonment: Options for an Insecure Society*, Cullompton: Willan.

Bottoms, A. (2007) 'Bifurcation' in DPOM.

Bottoms, A. and McWilliams, W. (1986) 'Social enquiry reports twenty-five years after the Streatfeild Report' in P. Bean and D. Whynes (eds) *Barbara Wootton: Social Science and Public Policy – Essays in Her Honour*, London: Routledge.

Bottoms, A. and Stelman, A. (1988) *Social Inquiry Reports: A Framework for Practice Development*, Aldershot: Gower.

Bottoms, A., Shapland, J., Costello, A., Holmes, D. and Muir, G. (2004) 'Towards desistance: theoretical underpinnings for an empirical study', *Howard Journal* 43 (4): 368–389.

Boyle, J. (1977) *A Sense of Freedom*, London: Pan.

Bracken, D. (2003) 'Skills and knowledge for contemporary probation practice', *Probation Journal* 50 (2): 101–114.

Bracken, D. (2007) 'Probation in the USA and Canada', in DPOM.

Braithwaite, J. (1989) *Crime, Shame and Reintegration*, Cambridge: Cambridge University Press.

Brantingham, P. and Faust, L. (1976) 'A conceptual model of crime prevention', *Crime & Delinquency*, 22 (3): 284–296.

Bridges, A. (2007) 'Employment, training and education (ETE)', in DPOM.

Brody, S. (1976) *The Effectiveness of Sentencing: A Review of the Literature*, Home Office Research Study No. 35, London: Home Office.

Brooker, C., Syson-Nibbs, L., Barrett, P. and Fox, C. (2009) 'Community managed offenders' access to healthcare services: report of a pilot study', *Probation Journal*, 56 (1): 45–59.

Brown, M. (2000) 'Calculations of risk in contemporary penal practice', in M. Brown and J. Pratt (eds) *Dangerous Offenders: Punishment and Social Order*, London: Routledge.

Brownlee, I. (1998) *Community Punishment: A Critical Introduction*, Harlow: Longman.

Bryant, M., Coker, J., Estlea, B., Himmel, S. and Knapp, T. (1978) 'Sentenced to social work?', *Probation Journal*, 25 (4): 110–114.

Burke, L. (2005) *From Probation to National Offender Management Service: Issues of Contestability, Culture and Community Involvement*, London: NAPO.

Burke, L. (2010) 'No longer social workers: developments in probation officer training and education in England and Wales', *Revista de Asistenta Sociala* (Social Work Review), IX (3/2010): 39–48 (Romania).

Burnett, R. (2004) 'To reoffend or not to reoffend: the ambivalence of convicted property offenders', in Shadd Maruna and Russ Immarigeon (eds) *After Crime and Punishment: Pathways to offender reintegration*, Cullompton: Willan.

Burnett, R., Baker, K. and Roberts, C. (2007) 'Assessment, supervision and intervention: fundamental practice in probation', in L. Gelsthorpe and R. Morgan (eds) *Handbook of Probation*, Cullompton: Willan Publishing.

Burnett, R. and Maruna, S. (2006) 'The kindness of prisoners: strengths-based resettlement in theory and in action', *Criminology & Criminal Justice* 6 (1): 83–106.

Burnett, R. and McNeill, F. (2005) 'The place of the officer–offender relationship in assisting offenders to desist from crime', *Probation Journal*, 52 (3): 221–242.

Busfield, J. (2002) 'Psychiatric disorder and individual violence: imagined death, risk and mental health policy', in A. Buchanan (ed.) *Care of the Mentally Disordered Offender in the Community*, Oxford: Oxford University Press.

Calverley, A., Cole, B., Kaur, G. and Lewis, S. (2004) *Black and Asian Offenders on Probation*, Home Office Research Study 277, London: Home Office.

Canton, R. (1995) 'Mental disorder, justice and censure', in D. Ward and M. Lacey (eds.) *Probation: Working for Justice*, London: Whiting and Birch.

Canton, R. (1993) 'Trying to make sense of it all', *NAPO News*, London: NAPO.

Canton, R. (2005) 'Risk assessment and compliance in probation and mental health practice', in B. Littlechild and D. Fearns (eds) *Mental Disorder and Criminal Justice: Policy, Provision and Practice*, Lyme Regis: Russell House.

Canton, R. (2006) 'Penal policy transfer: a case study from Ukraine', *Howard Journal*, 45 (5): 502–520.

Canton, R. (2007) 'Probation and the tragedy of punishment', *Howard Journal*, 46 (3): 236–254.

Canton, R. (2008a) 'Working with mentally disordered offenders', in S. Green, E. Lancaster and S. Feasey (eds) *Addressing Offending Behaviour: Context, Practice, Values*, Cullompton: Willan Publishing.

Canton, R. (2008b) 'Counterblast: can audits assess good practice in the enforcement of community penalties?', *Howard Journal*, 47 (5): 529–533.

Canton, R. (2009a) 'Nonsense upon stilts? Human rights, the ethics of punishment and the values of probation', *British Journal of Community Justice*, 7 (1): 5–22.

Canton, R. (2009b) 'Taking probation abroad', *European Probation Journal* 1 (1): 66–78.

Canton, R. (2009c) 'Contemporary probation in Europe: some reflections', *EuroVista* 1 (1): 2–9.

Canton, R. (2010a) 'Not another medical model: Using metaphor and analogy to explore crime and criminal justice', *British Journal of Community Justice*, 8 (1): 40–57.

Canton, R. (2010b) 'European probation rules: what they are, why they matter', *EuroVista* 1 (2): 62–71.

Canton, R. and Eadie, T. (2004) 'Social work with young offenders', in M. Lymbery and S. Butler (eds) *Social Work Ideals and Practice Realities*, Basingstoke: Macmillan.

Canton, R. and Eadie, T. (2005) 'From enforcement to compliance: implications for supervising officers', *Vista* 9 (3): 152–158.

Canton, R. and Eadie, T. (2007) 'National Standards', in DPOM.

Canton, R. and Eadie, T. (2008) 'Accountability, legitimacy, and discretion: applying criminology in professional practice', in B. Stout, J. Yates and B. Williams (eds) *Applied Criminology*, London: Sage.

Canton, R. and Hancock, D. (eds) (2007) *Dictionary of Probation and Offender Management* (DPOM), Cullompton: Willan Publishing.

Canton, R. and Yates, J. (2008) 'Applied criminology', in B. Stout, J. Yates and B. Williams (eds) *Applied Criminology*, London: Sage.

Carlen, P. (2002) 'Women's imprisonment: Models of reform and change', *Probation Journal* 49 (2): 76–87.

Carter, P. (2003) *Managing Offenders, Reducing Crime: A New Approach,* London: Home Office.

Casey, L. (2008) *Engaging Communities in Fighting Crime*, London: Cabinet Office. Available online at: http://www.cabinetoffice.gov.uk/media/cabinetoffice/corp/assets/publications/crime/cc_full_report.pdf.

Cavadino, M. and Dignan, J. (2006a) 'Penal policy and political economy', *Criminology and Criminal Justice,* 6 (4): 435–456.

Cavadino, M. and Dignan, J. (2006b) *Penal Systems: A Comparative Approach*, London: Sage.

Cavadino, M. and Dignan, J. (2007) *The Penal System: An Introduction* (4th edn), London: Sage.

Cavadino, M., Crow, I. and Dignan, J. (1999) *Criminal Justice 2000: Strategies for a New Century*, Winchester: Waterside Press.

Chapman, T. and Hough, M. (1998) *Evidence-Based Practice*, London: Home Office.

Chapman, T. and O'Mahony, D. (2007) 'Youth and criminal justice in Northern Ireland', in G. McIvor and P. Raynor (eds) *Developments in Social Work with Offenders, Research Highlights in Social Work 48*, London: Jessica Kingsley.

Cherry, S. (2005) *Transforming Behaviour: Pro-social Modelling in Action,* Cullompton: Willan.

Cherry, S. (2007a) 'Prosocial modelling', in DPOM.

Cherry, S. (2007b) 'Solution-focused work', in DPOM.

Christie, N. (2000) *Crime Control as Industry: Towards Gulags, Western Style* (3rd edn), London: Routledge.

Christie, N. (2004) *A Suitable Amount of Crime*, London: Routledge.

Christie, N. (2010) 'Victim movements at a crossroad', *Punishment & Society*, 12 (2): 115–122.

Chui, W. H. (2003) 'What works in reducing reoffending: principles and programmes', in W. H. Chui and M. Nellis (eds) *Moving Probation Forward: Evidence, Arguments and Practice*, Harlow: Pearson Education.

CJJI (Criminal Justice Joint Inspection) (2009) *Report of a Joint Thematic Review of Victim and Witness Experiences in the Criminal Justice System*. Available online at: http://www.hmcpsi.gov.uk/index.php?id=47&docID=885.

Clark, C. (2000) *Social Work Ethics: Politics, Principles and Practice*, Basingstoke: Macmillan.

Clarke, K. (2010) 'The Government's vision for criminal justice reform', speech to the Centre for Crime and Justice Studies, London. Available online at: http://www.justice.gov.uk/sp300610a.htm.

Clear, T. (2005) 'Places not cases? Re-thinking the probation focus', *Howard Journal* 44 (2): 172–184.

Clear, T. and Karp, D. (1999) *The Community Justice Ideal: Preventing Crime and Achieving Justice*, Oxford: Westview Press.

Cohen, S. (1985) *Visions of Social Control*, Cambridge: Polity Press.

Compton, B. and Galaway, B. (1984) *Social Work Processes* (3rd edn), Chicago Ill.: Dorsey Press.

Cornish, D. and Clarke, R. (eds) (1986) *The Reasoning Criminal: Rational Choice Perspectives on Criminal Offending*, New York: Springer-Verlag. Available online at: http://www.popcenter.org/library/reading/?p=reasoning.

Corston, J. (2007), *The Corston Report: A Review Of Women With Particular Vulnerabilities In The Criminal Justice System*, London: Home Office. Available online at: http://www. homeoffice.gov.uk/documents/corston-report/.

Council of Europe (2006a) *Recommendation Rec. (2006)2 of the Committee of Ministers to member states on the European Prison Rules*, (Adopted by the Committee of Ministers 11 January 2006). Available online at: https://wcd.coe.int/ViewDoc.jsp?id=955747 (accessed November 2010).

Council of Europe (2006b) *Recommendation Rec (2006) 8 of the Committee of Ministers to member states on assistance to crime victims*. Available online at: https://wcd.coe.int/ ViewDoc.jsp?id=1011109&Site=CM.

Council of Europe (2010) *Recommendation CM/Rec (2010)1 of the Committee of Ministers to Member States on the Council of Europe Probation Rules* (adopted by the Committee of Ministers 20 January 2010). Available online at: https://wcd.coe.int/ViewDoc. jsp?id=1575813&Site=CM&BackColorInternet=C3C3C3&BackColorIntranet=EDB02 1&BackColorLogged=F5D383.

Cowe, F. (2007a) 'Self-harm', in DPOM.

Cowe, F. (2007b) 'Suicide', in DPOM.

Coyle, A. (2005) *Understanding Prisons: Key Issues in Policy and Practice*, Maidenhead: Open University Press.

Craissati, J. and Sindall, O. (2009) 'Serious further offences: an exploration of risk and typologies', *Probation Journal* 56 (1): 9–27.

Crawford, A. (2007) 'Crime prevention and community safety', in M. Maguire, R. Morgan and R. Reiner (eds) *The Oxford Handbook of Criminology* (4th edn), Oxford: Oxford University Press.

Crawford, A. and Enterkin, J. (2001) 'Victim contact work in the probation service: paradigm shift or Pandora's box?', *British Journal of Criminology*, 41:707–725.

Criminal Injuries Compensation Authority (2008) *The Criminal Injuries Compensation Scheme*. Available online at: http://www.cica.gov.uk/en-gb/Can-I-apply/.

Criminal Justice Joint Inspection (2009) *Prolific and Other Priority Offenders: A Joint inspection of the PPO Programme*. Available online at: http://www.justice.gov.uk/ inspectorates/hmi-probation/docs/ppo_thematic_report_-rps.pdf.

Criminal Justice System (2006) *Code of Practice for Victims of Crime 2006*. Available online at: http://www.direct.gov.uk/prod_consum_dg/groups/dg_digitalassets/@dg/@ en/documents/digitalasset/dg_073647.pdf.

Critcher, C. (1975) 'Structures, cultures and biography', in S. Hall and T. Jefferson (eds) *Resistance through Rituals: Youth Subcultures in Post-War Britain,* London: Hutchinson.

Davies, K., Lewis, J. Byatt, J., Purvis, E. and Cole, B. (2004) *An Evaluation of the Literacy Demands of General Offending Behaviour Programmes*, Home Office Research Findings 233, London: Home Office. Available online at: http://www.homeoffice.gov. uk/rds/pdfs04/r233.pdf.

Davies, M. (1969) *Probationers in their Social Environment*, Home Office Research Study No. 2, London: Home Office.

Debidin, M. (2007) 'O-DEAT (OASys Data Evaluation And Analysis Team)', in DPOM.

Debidin, M. (ed.) (2009) *A Compendium of Research and Analysis on the Offender Assessment System (OASys) 2006–2009*, Ministry of Justice Research Series 16/09. Available online at: www.justice.gov.uk/research-analysis-offender-assessment-system. pdf.

Devlin, A. and Turney, B. (1999) *Going Straight: After Crime and Punishment*, Winchester: Waterside Press.

Dominey, J. (2002) 'Addressing victim issues in pre-sentence reports', in B. Williams (ed.) *Reparation and Victim-Focused Social Work*, London: Jessica Kingsley.

Dominey, J. (2007) 'Responsivity', in DPOM.

Dominey, J. (2010) 'Work-based distance learning for probation practice: doing the job properly', *Probation Journal* 57 (2): 153–162.

Doob, A. (1995) 'The United States Sentencing Commission Guidelines: if you don't know where you are going, you might not get there', in C. Clarkson and R. Morgan (eds) *The Politics of Sentencing Reform*, Oxford: Oxford University Press.

Dorling, D., Gordon, D., Hillyard, P., Pantazis, C., Pemberton, S. and Tombs S. (2008) *Criminal Obsessions: Why Harm Matters More Than Crime* (2nd edn), London: Centre for Crime and Justice Studies. Available online at: http://www.crimeandjustice.org.uk/harmandsocproject.html.

Dowden, C. and Andrews, D. (2004) 'The importance of staff practice in delivering effective correctional treatment: a meta-analytic review of core correctional practice', *International Journal of Offender Therapy and Comparative Criminology*, 48 (2): 203–214.

Downes, D. and Morgan, R. (1997) 'Dumping the "hostages to fortune"? The politics of law and order in post-war Britain', in M. Maguire, R. Morgan and R. Reiner (eds) *The Oxford Handbook of Criminology* (2nd edn), Oxford: Oxford University Press.

Downes, D. and Morgan, R. (2007) 'No turning back: the politics of law and order into the millennium', in M. Maguire, R. Morgan and R. Reiner (eds) *The Oxford Handbook of Criminology* (4th edn), Oxford: Oxford University Press.

Drake, D., Muncie, J. and Westmarland, L. (eds) (2010) *Criminal Justice: Local and Global*, Cullompton: Willan in association with Open University.

Drakeford, M. (2007) 'Poverty', in DPOM.

Drakeford, M. (2010) 'Devolution and youth justice in Wales', *Criminology and Criminal Justice*, 10 (2): 137–154.

Duff, A. (2007) 'Punishment as communication', in DPOM.

Duff, R. A. (2001) *Punishment, Communication and Community*, Oxford: Oxford University Press.

Dunbar, I. and Langdon, A. (1998) *Tough Justice: Sentencing and Penal Policies in the 1990s*, Oxford: Blackstone Press.

Dunkley, E. (2007) 'Approved premises', in DPOM.

Eadie, T. and Willis, A. (1989) 'National standards for discipline and breach proceedings in community service: an exercise in penal rhetoric?', *Criminal Law Review*, June: 412–419.

Eadie, T. and Winwin Sein, S. (2005) 'When the going gets tough, will the tough get going? Retaining staff during challenging times', *Vista* 10 (3): 171–179.

Easton, S. and Piper, C. (2005) *Sentencing and Punishment: The Quest for Justice,* Oxford: Oxford University Press.

Ellis, T., Hedderman, C. and Mortimer, E. (1996) *Enforcing Community Sentences,* Home Office Research Study No.158, London: Home Office.

Farrall, S. (2002) *Rethinking What Works with Offenders: Probation, Social Context and Desistance from Crime*, Cullompton: Willan.

Farrall, S. (2007) 'Desistance studies vs. cognitive-behavioural therapies: Which offers most hope for the long term?', in DPOM.

Farrall, S. and Calverley, A. (2006) *Understanding Desistance from Crime: Theoretical Directions in Resettlement and Rehabilitation*, Maidenhead: Open University Press.

Farrall, S. and Maltby, S. (2003) 'The victimisation of probationers', *Howard Journal* 42 (1): 32–54.

Farrall, S., Mawby, R. and Worrall, A. (2007) 'Prolific/persistent offenders and desistance', in L. Gelsthorpe and R. Morgan (eds) *Handbook of Probation*, Cullompton: Willan.

Farrington, D. (2007) 'Criminal careers', in DPOM.

Farrow, K. (2004) 'Still committed after all these years. Morale in the modern day probation service', *Probation Journal* 51 (3): 206–20.

Farrow, K., Kelly, G. and Wilkinson, B. (2007) *Offenders in Focus: Risk, Responsivity and Diversity*, Bristol: Policy Press.

Faulkner, D. (2002) 'Prisoners as citizens', *British Journal of Community Justice* 1 (2): 11–19.

Faulkner, D. (2006) *Crime, State and Citizen* (2nd edn), Winchester: Waterside Press.

Faulkner, D. (2007) 'Social exclusion', in DPOM.

Fawcett Society (2009) *Engendering Justice – from Policy to Practice: Final Report of the Commission on Women and the Criminal Justice System*. Available online at: http://www.fawcettsociety.org.uk/index.asp?PageID=933 .

Ferguson, K. (2007) 'Probation service officers', in DPOM.

Finkelhor, D. (1986) *A Sourcebook on Child Sexual Abuse*, New York: Sage.

Fitzmaurice, C. and Pease, K. (1986) *The Psychology of Judicial Sentencing*, Manchester: University of Manchester Press.

Fleet, F. and Annison, J. (2003) 'In support of effectiveness: facilitating participation and sustaining change', in W. H. Chui and M. Nellis (eds) *Moving Probation Forward: Evidence, Arguments and Practice*, Harlow: Pearson Longman.

Flegg, D. (1976) *Community Service: Consumer Survey 1973–1976*, Nottingham: Nottinghamshire Probation and After-Care Service.

Fletcher, H. (2007) 'Privatization', in DPOM.

Floud, J. and Young, W. (1981) *Dangerousness and Criminal Justice*, London: Heinemann.

Foucault, M. (1977) *Discipline and Punish: The Birth of the Prison*, Harmondsworth: Penguin.

Frude, N., Honess, T. and Maguire, M. (2009) CRIME-PICS II Manual. Available online at: http://www.crime-pics.co.uk/cpicsmanual.pdf.

Garland, D. (1985) *Punishment and Welfare: A History of Penal Strategies*, Aldershot: Gower.

Garland, D. (1990) *Punishment and Modern Society: A Study in Social Theory*, Oxford: Oxford University Press.

Garland, D. (2001) *The Culture of Control: Crime and Social Order in Contemporary Society*, Oxford: Oxford University Press.

Gelsthorpe, L. (2001) 'Accountability: difference and diversity in the delivery of community penalties', in A. Bottoms, L. Gelsthorpe and S. Rex (eds) *Community Penalties: Changes and Challenges*, Cullompton: Willan.

Gelsthorpe, L. (2001) 'Critical decisions and processes in the criminal courts', in E. McLaughlin and J. Muncie (eds) *Controlling Crime* (2nd edn), London: Sage in association with Open University.

Gelsthorpe, L. (2006) 'The experiences of female minority ethnic offenders: the other "other"', in S. Lewis, P. Raynor, D. Smith and A. Wardak (eds) *Race and Probation*, Cullompton: Willan.

Gelsthorpe, L. (2007) 'Dealing with diversity', in G. McIvor and P. Raynor (eds) *Developments in Social Work with Offenders, Research Highlights in Social Work 48*, London: Jessica Kingsley.

Gelsthorpe, L. (2007) 'Probation values and human rights', in L. Gelsthorpe and R. Morgan (eds) *Handbook of Probation*, Cullompton: Willan.

Gelsthorpe, L. and Hedderman, C. (eds) (1997) *Understanding the Sentencing of Women*, Home Office Research Study 170, London: Home Office.

Gelsthorpe, L. and Morris, A. (2002) 'Women's imprisonment in England and Wales: a penal paradox', *Criminal Justice* 2 (3): 277–301.

Gelsthorpe, L. and Raynor, P. (1995) 'Quality and effectiveness in probation officers' reports to sentencers', *British Journal of Criminology* 35 (2): 188–200.

Gelsthorpe, L. and Rex, S. (2004) 'Community service as reintegration: exploring the potential', in G. Mair (ed.) *What Matters in Probation*, Cullompton: Willan.

Gelsthorpe, L., Sharp, G. and Roberts, J. (2007) *Provision for Women Offenders in the Community*, London: Fawcett Society. Available online at: http://www.fawcettsociety. org.uk/documents/Provision%20for%20women%20offenders%20in%20the%20community (1).pdf.

Gerty, A. (2007) 'Victim contact', in DPOM.

Goode, A. (2007) 'Unpaid work', in DPOM.

Goode, S. (2007) 'Contestability', in DPOM.

Gorman, K. (2001) 'Cognitive behaviourism and the Holy Grail: the quest for a universal means of managing offender risk', *Probation Journal*, 48 (1): 3–9.

Grapes, T. (2007) 'Offender management', in DPOM.

Griffin, J. (2008) *On Human Rights*, Oxford: Oxford University Press.

Grounds, A. (1991) 'The mentally disordered offender in the criminal process: some research and policy questions', in K. Herbst and J. Gunn (eds) *The Mentally Disordered Offender*, Oxford: Butterworth-Heinemann.

Grounds, A. (1995) 'Risk assessment and management in clinical context', in J. Crichton (ed.) *Psychiatric Patient Violence: Risk and Relapse*, London: Duckworth.

Guardian (2010) 'Former chief inspector says Labour left 'dysfunctional' prison service in crisis', *The Guardian* (24 May). Available online at: http://www.guardian.co.uk/ society/2010/may/24/prisons-policy-labour-crisis-probation.

HM Inspectorate of Probation (2000) *Towards Race Equality: Thematic Inspection*, London: Home Office.

HM Inspectorate of Probation (2004) *Towards Race Equality: Follow-up Inspection Report*. Available online at: http://www.justice.gov.uk/inspectorates/hmi-probation/docs/ towardsraceequality04-rps.pdf.

HM Inspectorate of Probation (2010) *HM Inspectorate of Probation: A Short History*. Available online at: http://www.justice.gov.uk/inspectorates/hmi-probation/docs/ History_of_HMI_Probation-rps.pdf.

HM Prison Service (n.d.) *Statement of Purpose*. Available online at: http://www.hmprison service.gov.uk/abouttheservice/statementofpurpose/.

HMI Probation/HMI Prisons (2001) *Through the Prison Gate*, London: HMI Probation and HMI Prisons. Available online: http://www.justice.gov.uk/inspectorates/hmi-prisons/ docs/prison-gate-rps.pdf.

Hagell, A. and Newburn, T. (1994) *Persistent Young Offenders,* London: Policy Studies Institute.

Haines, K. and Morgan, R. (2007) 'Services before trial and sentence: achievement, decline and potential', in L. Gelsthorpe and R. Morgan (eds) *Handbook of Probation*, Cullompton: Willan.

Hamai, K., Villé, R., Harris, R., Hough, M. and Zvekic, U. (eds) (1995) *Probation Round the World*, London: Routledge.

Hammond, N. (2007) 'Deportation', in DPOM.

Hancock, D. (2007a) 'Accredited programmes in common use', in DPOM.

Hancock, D. (2007b) 'Carter Report', in DPOM.

Hancock, D. (2007c) 'Home visits', in DPOM.

Hancock, D. (2007d) 'Partnerships', in DPOM.

Hancock, D. (2007e) 'Prison probation teams', in DPOM.

Hancock, D. (2007f) 'Prolific and other priority offenders', in DPOM.

Hannah-Moffat, K (1999) 'Moral agent or actuarial subject: risk and Canadian women's imprisonment', *Theoretical Criminology* 3 (1): 71–94.

Hannah-Moffat, K. (2005) 'Criminogenic needs and the transformative risk subject: hybridizations of risk/need in penality', *Punishment and Society* 7 (1): 29–51.

Harding, J. (ed.) (1987) *Probation and the Community: A Practice and Policy Reader*, London: Tavistock.

Harding, J. (2003) 'Which way probation? A correctional or community justice service?', *Probation Journal*, 50 (4): 369–373.

Harding, J. (2007) 'Community justice', in DPOM.

Harper, G. and Chitty, C. (eds) (2005) *The Impact of Corrections on Re-offending: A Review of 'What Works'*, (3rd edn), Home Office Research, Development and Statistics Directorate. Available online at: http://www.homeoffice.gov.uk/rds/pdfs04/hors291.pdf.

Harris, R. (1980) 'A changing service: the case for separating "care" and "control" in probation practice', *British Journal of Social Work*, 10 (2): 163–184.

Harris, R. (1995) 'Reflections on comparative probation', in K. Hamai, R. Villé, R. Harris, M. Hough and U. Zvekic (eds) *Probation Round the World*, London: Routledge.

Haxby, D. (1978) *Probation: A Changing Service*, London: Constable.

Hearnden, I. and Millie, A. (2004) 'Does tougher enforcement lead to lower conviction?', *Probation Journal*, 51 (1): 48–59.

Hedderman, C. (2006) 'Keeping a lid on the prison population – will it work', in M. Hough, R. Allen and U. Padel (eds) *Reshaping Probation and Prisons: The New Offender Management Framework*, Bristol: Policy Press.

Hedderman, C. (2007) 'Past, present and future sentences: what do we know about their effectiveness?', in L. Gelsthorpe and R. Morgan (eds) *Handbook of Probation*, Cullompton: Willan Publishing.

Hedderman, C. (2008) 'Building on sand: why expanding the prison estate is not the way to "secure the future"', *Centre for Crime and Justice Studies Briefing Paper* No. 7. Available online at: http://www.crimeandjustice.org.uk/buildingonsand.html.

Hedderman, C. and Gelsthorpe, L. (eds) (1997) *Understanding the Sentencing of Women*, Home Office Research Study 170, London: Home Office.

Hedderman, C. and Hough, M. (2004) 'Getting tough or being effective: what matters?', in G. Mair (ed.) *What Matters in Probation,* Cullompton: Willan.

Henson, G. (2007) 'Volunteers', in DPOM.

Hine, J., McWilliams, B. and Pease, K. (1978) 'Recommendations, social information and sentencing', *Howard Journal,* 17: 91–100.

Heidensohn, F. and Gelsthorpe, L. (2007) 'Gender and crime', in M. Maguire, R. Morgan and R. Reiner (eds) *The Oxford Handbook of Criminology* (4th edn), Oxford: Oxford University Press.

Hilder, S. (2007) 'Anti-discriminatory practice', in DPOM.

Hill, R. (2007) 'National Probation Service for England and Wales', in DPOM.

Hodgett, V. (2007) 'Multi-Agency Public Protection Arrangements (MAPPAs)', in DPOM.

Holden, L. (2007) 'Offender Assessment System (OASys)', in DPOM.

Hollin, C., McGuire, J., Palmer, E., Bilby, C., Hatcher, R. and Holmes, A. (2002) *Introducing Pathfinder Programmes into the Probation Service: An Interim Report*, Home Office Research Study 247. Available online at: http://rds.homeoffice.gov.uk/rds/pdfs2/hors247.pdf.

Holt, P. (2000) *Case Management: Context for Supervision,* Leicester: De Montfort University.

Home Office (1990a) *Crime, Justice and Protecting the Public*, Cm 965, London: HMSO.

Home Office (1990b) *Partnership in Dealing with Offenders in the Community*, London: Home Office.

Home Office (1990c) *Victim's Charter: A Statement of the Rights of Victims of Crime,* London: Home Office.

Home Office (1996) *The Victim's Charter: A Statement of Service Standards for Victims of Crime.* Available online at: http://www.homeoffice.gov.uk/documents/victims-charter?view=Binary.

Home Office (1998) *Prisons – Probation Review – Final Report: Joining Forces to Protect the Public*, http://webarchive.nationalarchives.gov.uk/+/http:/www.homeoffice.gov.uk/docs/pprcont.html

Home Office (1999) *National Crime Reduction Strategy*, London: Home Office

Home Office (2001) *Making Punishments Work, The Report of a review of the Sentencing Framework for England and Wales. (Halliday Report)* –http://www.homeoffice.gov.uk/documents/halliday-report-sppu/

Home Office (2002) *Justice for All*, White Paper, Presented to Parliament by the Secretary of State for the Home Department, the Lord Chancellor and the Attorney General, CM 5563. Available online at: http://www.cjsonline.gov.uk/downloads/application/pdf/CJS%20White%20Paper%20-%20Justice%20For%20All.pdf.

Home Office (2004a) *Reducing Crime, Changing Life.* Available online at: http://www.probation.homeoffice.gov.uk/files/pdf/master%2020pp%20BB.pdf

Home Office (2004b) *Reducing Re-offending: National Action Plan.* Available online at: http://www.probation.homeoffice.gov.uk/files/pdf/NOMS%20National%20Action%20Plan.pdf

Home Office and Ministry of Justice (2009) *Integrated Offender Management: Government Policy Statement*, London: Home Office.

Homes, A., Walmsley, K. and Debidin, M. (2005) *Intensive Supervision and Monitoring Schemes for Persistent Offenders: Staff and Offender Perceptions*, Home Office Development and Practice Report No. 41. Available online at: http://rds.homeoffice.gov.uk/rds/pdfs05/dpr41.pdf.

Hood, R. (1992) *Race and Sentencing*, Oxford: Oxford University Press.

Hood, R. and Shute, S. (2000) *The Parole System at Work: A Study of Risk Based Decision-making*, Home Office Research Study 202. Available online at: http://www.homeoffice.gov.uk/rds/pdfs/hors202.pdf.

Hopley, K. (2002) 'National Standards: defining the service', in D. Ward, J. Scott and M. Lacey (eds) *Probation: Working for Justice* (2nd edn), Oxford: Oxford University Press.

Hough, M. (1996) *Drugs Misuse and the Criminal Justice System: A Review of the Literature.* DPI Paper 15, London: Home Office.

Hough, M. (2007) 'Public attitudes towards probation', in DPOM.

Hough, M. and Mitchell, D. (2003) 'Drug-dependent offenders and *Justice for All*', in M. Tonry (ed.) *Confronting Crime: Crime Control Policy under New Labour,* Cullompton: Willan.

Hough, M., Allen, R. and Padel, U. (eds) (2006) *Reshaping Probation and Prisons: The New Offender Management Framework*, Bristol: Policy Press.

House of Commons Justice Committee (2009) *Cutting Crime: The Case for Justice Reinvestment*, First Report of Session 2009–10. Available online at: http://www.publications.parliament.uk/pa/cm200910/cmselect/cmjust/94/94i.pdf

Howard, P., Francis, B., Soothill, K. and Humphreys, L. (2009) *OGRS 3: The Revised Offender Group Reconviction Scale*. Available online at: http://www.justice.gov.uk/oasys-research-summary-07-09-ii.pdf.

Hoyle, C. and Zedner, L. (2007) 'Victims, victimization, and criminal justice', in M. Maguire, R. Morgan and R. Reiner (eds) *The Oxford Handbook of Criminology* (4th edn), Oxford: Oxford University Press.

Hucklesby, A. and Hagley-Dickinson, L. (2007) *Prisoner Resettlement: Policy and Practice*, Cullompton: Willan.

Hudson, B. (1996) *Understanding Justice*, Buckingham: Open University Press.

Hudson, B. (2001) 'Punishment, rights and difference: defending justice in the risk society', in K. Stenson and R. Sullivan (eds) *Crime, Risk and Justice: The Politics of Crime Control in Liberal Democracies*, Cullompton: Willan.

Hudson, B. (2005) 'Beyond punishment: rights and freedoms', *Criminal Justice Matters*, No. 60: 4–5.

Hudson, B. and Bramhall, G. (2005) 'Assessing the "other": constructions of "Asianness" in risk assessments by probation officers', *British Journal of Criminology*, 45: 721–740.

Hudson, J. (2007) 'Motivation', in DPOM.

Hull, G., Scott, P. and Smith, B. (eds) (2003) *All the Women Are White, All the Blacks Are Men: But Some Of Us Are Brave: Black Women's Studies*, New York: The Feminist Press at CUNY.

Jewkes, Y. (2007) *Handbook on Prisons*, Cullompton: Willan.

Johnstone, G. (2002) *Restorative Justice: Ideas, Values, Debates,* Cullompton: Willan.

Jones, T. and Newburn, T. (2007) *Policy Transfer and Criminal Justice: Exploring US Influence over British Crime Control Policy*, Maidenhead: Open University Press.

Karp, D. and Clear, T. (2002) (eds) *What is Community Justice: Case Studies of Restorative Justice and Community Supervision*, London: Sage.

Karstedt, S. (2002) 'Emotions and criminal justice', *Theoretical Criminology*, 6 (3) 299–317.

Karstedt, S. and Farrall, S. (2007) *Law-abiding Majority? The Everyday Crimes of the Middle Classes*, London: Centre for Crime and Justice Studies. Available online at: http://www.crimeandjustice.org.uk/opus45/Law_abiding_Majority_FINAL_VERSION.pdf

Kemshall, H. (2001) *Risk Assessment and Management of Known Sexual and Violent Offenders: A Review of Current Issues*. Available online at: http://www.homeoffice.gov.uk/rds/prgpdfs/prs140.pdf.

Kemshall, H. (2003) *Understanding Risk in Criminal Justice*, Maidenhead: Open University Press.

Kemshall, H. (2007) 'Risk assessment and risk management', in DPOM.

Kemshall, H. and Canton, R. (2002) *The Effective Management of Programme Attrition*, Leicester: De Montfort University. Available online at: http://www.dmu.ac.uk/faculties/hls/research/commcrimjustice/commcrimjus.jsp.

Kemshall, H. and Maguire, M. (2001) 'Public protection, partnership and risk penality: the multi-agency risk management of sexual and violent offenders', *Punishment and Society*, 3 (2): 237–264.

Kemshall, H. and Wood, J. (2007a) 'High-risk offenders and public protection', in L. Gelsthorpe and R. Morgan (eds) *Handbook of Probation*, Cullompton: Willan.

Kemshall, H. and Wood, J. (2007b) 'Beyond public protection: an examination of community protection and public health approaches to high-risk offenders', *Criminology and Criminal Justice*, 7 (3): 203–222.

Kemshall, H., Canton, R. and Bailey, R. (2004) 'Dimensions of difference', in A. Bottoms, S. Rex and G. Robinson (eds) *Alternatives to Imprisonment: Options for an Insecure Society*, Cullompton: Willan Publishing.

Kemshall, H., Mackenzie, G., Wood, J., Bailey, R. and Yates, J. (2005) *Strengthening Multi-Agency Public Protection Arrangements (MAPPAs)*. Available online at: http://www.homeoffice.gov.uk/rds/pdfs05/dpr45.pdf.

Kendall, K. (2004) 'Dangerous thinking: a critical history of correctional cognitive behaviouralism', in G. Mair (ed.) *What Matters in Probation*, Cullompton: Willan.

Killias, M., Aebi, M. and Ribeaud, D. (2000) 'Does community service rehabilitate better than short-term imprisonment? Results of a controlled experiment', *Howard Journal* 39 (1): 40–57.

King, M. (1981) *The Framework of Criminal Justice*, London: Croom Helm.

Knight, C. (forthcoming) 'Soft skills for hard work: using emotional literacy to work effectively with sex offenders', in J. Brayford, F. Cowe and J. Deering (eds) *Sex Offenders: Punish, Help, Change or Control?: Theory, Policy and Practice Explored*, Routledge.

Knight, C., Dominey, J. and Hudson, J. (2008) '"Diversity": contested meanings and differential consequences', in B. Stout, J. Yates and B. Williams (eds) *Applied Criminology*, London: Sage.

Knight, C. and Stout, B. (2009) 'Probation and offender manager training: An argument for an integrated approach', *Probation Journal* 56 (3): 269–283.

Knott, C. (2007) 'National Offender Management Service (NOMS)', in DPOM.

Lacey, N. (1994) 'Introduction: making sense of criminal justice', in N. Lacey (ed.) *A Reader on Criminal Justice*, Oxford: Oxford University Press.

Laming, H. (2009) 'The Protection of Children in England: A Progress Report'. Available online at: http://publications.education.gov.uk/default.aspx?PageFunction=product details&PageMode=publications&ProductId=HC+330.

Liebling, A. (2004) *Prisons and their Moral Performance: A Study of Values, Quality and Prison Life*, Oxford: Oxford University Press.

Levitt, S. and Dubner, S. (2006) *Freakonomics: A Rogue Economist Explores the Hidden Side of Everything*, London: Penguin.

Lewis, S. (2005) 'Rehabilitation: headline or footnote in the new penal policy?', *Probation Journal*, 52 (2): 119–135.

Lewis, S., Maguire, M., Raynor, P., Vanstone, M. and Vennard, J. (2007) 'What works in resettlement? Findings from seven Pathfinders for short-term prisoners in England and Wales', *Criminology and Criminal Justice* 7 (1): 33–53.

Liebling, A. (2006) 'Lessons from prison privatisation for probation', in M. Hough, R. Allen and U. Padel (eds) *Reshaping Probation and Prisons: The New Offender Management Framework*, Bristol: Policy Press.

Lipsky, M. (1980) *Street-Level Bureaucracy: Dilemmas of the Individual in Public Services*, New York: Russell Sage.

Loader, I. (2005) 'The affects of punishment: emotions, democracy and penal politics', *Criminal Justice Matters*, 60 (1): 12–13.

Loader, I. (2007) 'Has liberal criminology lost?' Eve Saville Memorial lecture, Centre for Crime and Justice Studies. Available online at: http://www.crimeandjustice.org.uk/opus253.html.

Loader, I. and Sparks, R. (2002) 'Contemporary landscapes of crime, order and control: governance, risk and globalisation', in M. Maguire, R. Morgan and R. Reiner (eds) *The Oxford Handbook of Criminology* (3rd edn), Oxford: Oxford University Press.

Lurigio, A. and Carroll, J. (1985) 'Probation officers' schemata of offenders: content, development, and impact on treatment decisions', Journal of Personality and Social Psychology 48 (5): 1112–1126.

Mackenzie, G. (2007) 'Risk of harm', in DPOM.

MacLeod, K. (2007) 'Staff supervision', in DPOM.

Macpherson, W. (1999) *The Stephen Lawrence Inquiry: Report of an Inquiry by Sir William Macpherson of Cluny advised by Tom Cook, the Right Reverend Dr John Sentamu, Dr Richard Stone, Presented to Parliament by the Secretary of State for the Home Department by Command of Her Majesty*, Cm 4262-I. Available online at: www. archive.official-documents.co.uk/document/cm42/4262/4262.htm.

Maguire, M. (2007) 'The resettlement of ex-prisoners', in L. Gelsthorpe and R. Morgan (eds) *Handbook of Probation*, Cullompton: Willan.

Maguire, M. and Raynor, P. (2006) 'How the resettlement of prisoners promotes desistance from crime: Or does it?', *Criminology and Criminal Justice*, 6 (1): 19–38.

Maguire, M., Kemshall, H., Noaks, L., Wincup, E. and Sharpe, K. (2001) *Risk Management of Sexual and Violent Offenders: The Work of Public Protection Panels*. Available online at: http://rds.homeoffice.gov.uk/rds/prgpdfs/prs139.pdf.

Mahaffey, H. (2009) 'Restorative justice at the heart of the youth community', in W. Taylor, R. Earle and R. Hester (eds) *Youth Justice Handbook: Theory, Policy and Practice*, Cullompton: Willan in association with The Open University.

Mair, G. (2001) 'Technology and the future of community penalties', in A. Bottoms, L. Gelsthorpe and S. Rex (eds), *Community Penalties: Change and Challenges*, Cullompton: Willan.

Mair, G. (2004) 'The origins of what works in England and Wales: a house built on sand?', in G. Mair (ed.) *What Matters in Probation*, Cullompton: Willan.

Mair, G. and Canton, R. (2007) 'Sentencing, community penalties and the role of the probation service', in L. Gelsthorpe and R. Morgan (eds) *Handbook of Probation*, Cullompton: Willan Publishing.

Mair, G. and May, C. (1997) *Offenders on Probation*, Home Office Research Study 167, London: Home Office.

Mair, G. and Mills, H. (2009) *The Community Order and the Suspended Sentence Order Three Years On: The Views and Experiences of Probation Officers and Offenders*, London: Centre for Crime and Justice Studies. Available online at: http://www.crime andjustice.org.uk/publications.html.

Mair, G., Burke, L. and Taylor, S. (2006) 'The worst tax form you've ever seen? Probation officers' views about OASys', *Probation Journal* 53 (1): 7–23.

Malik, S. (2007) 'Drugs', in DPOM.

Mann, S. (2007) 'Interventions', in DPOM.

Mantle, G. (2007) 'Mediation', in DPOM.

Martin, A. (2007) 'Learning disabilities', in DPOM.

Maruna, S. (2000) *Making Good: How Ex-convicts Reform and Rebuild their Lives*, Washington: American Psychological Association.

Maruna, S. and King, A. (2004) 'Public opinion and community penalties', in A. Bottoms, S. Rex and G. Robinson (eds) *Alternatives to Imprisonment: Options for an Insecure Society*, Cullompton: Willan.

Mathiesen, T. (1990) *Prison on Trial: A Critical Assessment*, London: Sage.

Matza, D. (1964) *Delinquency and Drift*, New York: Wiley.

Mawby, R.I. (2007) 'Public sector services and the victim of crime', in S. Walklate (ed.) *Handbook of Victims and Victimology*, Cullompton: Willan.

McAra, L. and McVie, S. (2007) *Criminal Justice Transitions*, Centre for Law and Society, University of Edinburgh. Available online at: http://www.law.ed.ac.uk/file_download/ publications/3_676_criminaljusticetransitions.pdf.

McConville, M., Sanders, A. and Leng, R. (1991) *The Case for the Prosecution: Police Suspects and the Construction of Criminality*, London: Routledge.

McCulloch, C. (2004) 'Through the eyes of a missionary: probation one hundred years on', *Vista* 9 (3): 148–151.

McGuire, J. (2001) *Cognitive-Behavioural Approaches – An Introduction to Theory and Research*. Available online at: http://www.justice.gov.uk/inspectorates/hmi-probation/ docs/cogbeh1-rps.pdf.

McGuire, J. (2002) 'Multiple agencies with diverse goals', in A. Buchanan (ed.) *Care of the Mentally Disordered Offender in the Community*, Oxford: Oxford University Press.

McGuire, J. (2005) 'Is research working? Revisiting the research and effective practice agenda', in J. Winstone and F. Pakes (eds) *Community Justice: Issues for Probation and Criminal Justice*, Cullompton: Willan.

McGuire, J. (2007a) 'Programmes for Probationers', in G. McIvor and P. Raynor (eds) *Developments in Social Work with Offenders, Research Highlights in Social Work 48*, London: Jessica Kingsley.

McGuire, J. (2007b) 'Cognitive-behavioural', in DPOM.

McGuire, J. and Priestley, P. (1985) *Offending Behaviour: Skills and Stratagems for Going Straight*, London: Batsford.

McGuire, J. and Priestley, P. (1995) 'Reviewing "what works": past, present and future', in J. McGuire (ed.) *What Works: Reducing Reoffending – Guidelines from Research and Practice*, Chichester: Wiley.

McIvor, G. (1990) *Sanctions for Serious or Persistent Offenders: A Review of the Literature*, Social Work Research Centre, University of Stirling.

McIvor, G. (1992) *Sentenced to Serve*, Aldershot: Avebury.

McIvor, G. (1998) 'Jobs for the boys? Gender differences in referral to community service', *Howard Journal* 37 (3): 280–290.

McIvor, G. (2002) *What Works in Community Service?*, CJSW Briefing, Criminal Justice Social Work Development Centre for Scotland. Available online at: http://www.cjsw. ac.uk/cjsw/files/Briefing%20Paper%206_final.pdf.

McIvor, G. (2004) 'Service with a smile? Women and community "punishment"', in G. McIvor (ed.) *Women Who Offend*, Research Highlights in Social Work 44, London: Jessica Kingsley.

McIvor, G. (2007) 'Paying back: unpaid work by offenders', in G. McIvor and P. Raynor (eds) *Developments in Social Work with Offenders, Research Highlights in Social Work 48*, London: Jessica Kingsley.

McIvor, G. and McNeill, F. (2007) 'Probation in Scotland: past, present and future', in L. Gelsthorpe and R. Morgan (eds) *Handbook of Probation*, Cullompton: Willan.

McIvor, G., Murray, C. and Jamieson, J. (2004) 'Desistance from crime: is it different for women and girls?', in S. Maruna and R. Immarigeon (eds) *After Crime and Punishment: Pathways to Offender Reintegration*, Cullompton: Willan.

McNeill, F. (2003) 'Desistance-focused probation practice', in W. H. Chui and M. Nellis (eds) *Moving Probation Forward: Evidence, Arguments and Practice*, Harlow: Pearson Education.

McNeill, F. (2006) 'A desistance paradigm for offender management', *Criminology & Criminal Justice*, 6 (1): 39–62.

McNeill, F. (2009) *Towards Effective Practice in Offender Supervision*, Scottish Centre for Crime and Justice Research. Available online at: http://www.sccjr.ac.uk/pubs/Towards-Effective-Practice-in-Offender-Supervision/79.

McNeill, F. and Burnett, R. (2005) 'The place of the officer–offender relationship in assisting offenders to desist from crime', *Probation Journal*, 52 (3): 221–242.

McNeill, F. and Maruna, S. (2007) 'Giving up and giving back: desistance, generativity and social work with offenders', in G. McIvor and P. Raynor (eds) *Developments in Social Work with Offenders, Research Highlights in Social Work 48*, London: Jessica Kingsley.

McNeill, F., Batchelor, S., Burnet, R. and Knox, J. (2005) *21st Century Social Work: Reducing Re-offending: Key Practice Skills*, Glasgow: Glasgow School of Social Work. Available online at: http://www.scotland.gov.uk/Publications/2005/04/21132007/20080.

McNeill, F. and Whyte, B. (2007) *Reducing Reoffending: Social Work and Community Justice in Scotland*, Cullompton: Willan.

McWilliams, W. (1983) 'The mission to the English police courts –1876–1936', *Howard Journal* 22 (3): 129–147.

McWilliams, W. (1985) 'The mission transformed: professionalisation of probation between the wars', *Howard Journal* 24 (4): 257–274.

McWilliams, W. (1986) 'The English probation system and the diagnostic ideal', *Howard Journal* 25 (4): 41–60.

McWilliams, W. (1987) 'Probation, pragmatism and policy', *Howard Journal* 26 (2): 97–121.

McWilliams, W. (1989) 'Community service national standards: practice and sentencing', *Probation Journal* 36 (3): 121–126.

Mead, J. (2007) 'Serious further offences', in DPOM.

Merrington, S. (2006) 'Is more better? The value and potential of intensive community supervision', *Probation Journal,* 53 (4): 347–360.

Merrington, S. and Hine, J. (2001) *A Handbook for Evaluating Probation Work with Offenders*. Available online at: http://www.justice.gov.uk/inspectorates/hmi-probation/docs/whole-rps.pdf.

Merrington, S. and Stanley, S. (2007) 'Effectiveness: who counts what?', in L. Gelsthorpe and R. Morgan (eds.) *Handbook of Probation*, Cullompton: Willan.

Miller, W. and Rollnick, R. (1991) *Motivational Interviewing*, New York: Guilford Press.

Ministry of Justice (2008a) 'Offender Management Caseload Statistics 2007', London: Ministry of Justice. Available online at: http://www.justice.gov.uk/publications/prison andprobation.htm.

Ministry of Justice (2008b) *The Offender Management Guide to Working with Women Offenders*. Available online at: http://noms.justice.gov.uk/news-publications-events/publications/guidance/OM-Guide-Women (accessed August 2010).

Ministry of Justice (2009a) 'Public have their say on how criminals payback', 30 March 2009. Available online at: http://www.justice.gov.uk/news/newsrelease300309a.htm.

Ministry of Justice (2009b) *Criminal Justice Group Business Plan 2009/10: Improving the criminal justice system*. Available online at: http://www.justice.gov.uk/cjg-business-plan-09-10ii.pdf.

Ministry of Justice (2009c) *The Correctional Services Accreditation Panel Report 2008–2009*. Available online at: http://www.justice.gov.uk/publications/docs/correctional-services-report-20080-09.pdf.

Ministry of Justice (2009d) *Offender Management Caseload Statistics 2008*, London: Ministry of Justice. Available online at: http://www.justice.gov.uk/publications/prison andprobation.htm.

Ministry of Justice (2010a) *Ministry of Justice: Draft Structural Reform Plan*. Available online at: http://www.justice.gov.uk/about/docs/moj-structural-reform-plana.pdf.

Ministry of Justice (2010b) *Offender caseload management statistics 2009*. Available online at: http://www.justice.gov.uk/prisonandprobation.htm.

Ministry of Justice (2010c) *National Victims' Service*. Available online at: http://www.justice.gov.uk/news/speech270110a.htm.

Monahan, J. (2004) 'The future of violence risk management', in M. Tonry (ed.) *The Future of Imprisonment*, New York: Oxford University Press.

Moore, B. (1996) *Risk Assessment: A Practitioner's Guide to Predicting Harmful Behaviour*, London: Whiting and Birch.

Moore, L. and Blakeborough, L. (2008) *Early Findings from WAVES (Witness and Victim Experience Survey): Information and Service Provision*, Ministry of Justice Research Series 11/08. Available online at: http://www.justice.gov.uk/publications/witness-victim-experience-survey.htm.

Moore, R. (2007) *Adult Offenders' Perceptions of their Underlying Problems: Findings from the OASys Self-assessment Questionnaire*, Home Office Findings 284. Available online at: http://rds.homeoffice.gov.uk/rds/pdfs07/r284.pdf.

Moore, R., Howard, P. and Burns, M. (2006), 'The further development of OASys: realising the potential of the offender assessment system', *Prison Service Journal* 167: 36–42.

Morgan, R. (2007) 'Probation, governance and accountability', in L. Gelsthorpe and R. Morgan (eds) *Handbook of Probation*, Cullompton: Willan.

Morgan, R. and Smith, A. (2003) 'The Criminal Justice Bill 2002: the future role and workload of the National Probation Service', *British Journal of Community Justice*, 2 (2): 7–23.

Morgan, R. and Liebling, A. (2007) 'Imprisonment: an expanding scene', in M. Maguire, R. Morgan and R. Reiner (eds) *The Oxford Handbook of Criminology* (4th edn), Oxford: Oxford University Press.

Morton, S. (2009) *Can OASys Deliver Consistent Assessments of Offenders? Results from the Inter-rater Reliability Study*, Ministry of Justice Research Summary 1/09. Available online at: www.justice.gov.uk/oasys-research-summary-01-09.pdf.

Mulrenan, U. (2007) 'Supporting people', in DPOM.

Munro, M. and McNeill, F. (2010) 'Fines, community sanctions and measures in Scotland', in H. Croall, G. Mooney and M. Munro (eds) *Criminal Justice in Scotland*, Cullompton: Willan.

Murray, H. and Kluckhohn, C. (1953) *Personality in Nature, Society, and Culture*, New York: Knopf.

Napo (2009) *Literacy, Language and Speech Problems amongst Individuals on Probation or Parole*. Available online at: http://www.napo.org.uk/about/news/news.cfm/news id/40.

National Audit Office (2004) *Delivering Public Services to a Diverse Society*. Available online at: http://www.nao.org.uk/publications/0405/delivering_public_services.aspx.

National Centre for Social Research (n.d.) *Offender Management Community Cohort Study*. Available online at: http://www.natcen.ac.uk/study/offender-management-community-cohort-study-.

National Offender Management Service (NOMS) (2006) *The NOMS Offender Management Model 1.1*, London: Home Office.

National Offender Management Service (2009) *MAPPA Guidance 2009 Version 3.0*. Available online at: http://www.lbhf.gov.uk/Images/MAPPA%20Guidance%20(2009) %20Version%203%200%20_tcm21-120559.pdf.

National Probation Directorate (2003) *A Brief Introduction to Enhanced Community Punishment* (2nd edn), London: Home Office.

National Probation Service (2004) *Views of the Probation Victim Contact Scheme*, London: Home Office.

National Probation Service (2005) *Visible Unpaid Work*, Probation Circular: PC 66/2005.

National Probation Service (2007) *PC 13/2007 – Introduction of a New Skills Screening Tool: First Move – Initial Skills Checker*. Available online at: http://www.probation. homeoffice.gov.uk/files/pdf/PC13%202007.pdf.

National Probation Service (2008a) *Annual Report 2007-2008*, London: Ministry of Justice.

National Probation Service (2008b) *Snapshot of Unpaid Work 2008*. London: Ministry of Justice.

National Probation Service (n.d.) *Interventions: A Guide to Interventions in the National Probation Service*. Available online at: http://www.probation2000.com/documents/ A%20Guide%20to%20Interventions%20in%20the%20NPS.pdf.

Nelken, D. (2007) 'Comparing criminal justice', in M. Maguire, R. Morgan and R. Reiner (eds) *The Oxford Handbook of Criminology* (4th edn), Oxford: Oxford University Press.

Nellis, M (1995) 'Probation values for the 1990s', *Howard Journal*, 34 (1): 19–44.

Nellis, M. (2000) 'Creating community justice', in S. Ballintyne, K. Pease and V. McLaren (eds), *Secure Foundations: Key Issues in Crime Prevention, Crime Reduction and Community Safety*, London: Institute for Public Policy Research.

Nellis, M. (2001) 'The Diploma in Probation Studies in the Midland region: celebration and critique after the first two years', *Howard Journal* 40 (4) 377–401.

Nellis, M. (2007a) 'Humanising justice: the English probation service up to 1972', in L. Gelsthorpe and R. Morgan (eds) *Handbook of Probation*, Cullompton: Willan.

Nellis, M. (2007b) 'Probation values', in DPOM.

Nellis, M. and Gelsthorpe, L. (2003) 'Human rights and the probation values debate', in W. H. Chui and M. Nellis (eds) *Moving Probation Forward: Evidence, Arguments and Practice*, Harlow: Pearson.

Newburn, T. (2007) *Criminology*, Cullompton: Willan.

Nietzsche, F. (1887) *On the Genealogy of Morality: A Polemic*, ed. and trans. by M. Clark and A. Swenson (1998), Indianapolis: Hackett.

O'Connell, B. (2005) *Solution-focused Therapy* (2nd edn), London: Sage.

O'Donnell, I. and Edgar, K. (1998) 'Routine victimisation in prisons', *Howard Journal* 37 (3): 266–279.

Octigan, M. (2007) 'Remand services', in DPOM.

Oldfield, M. (2002) *From Welfare to Risk: Discourse, Power and Politics in the Probation Service*, Issues in Community and Criminal Justice Monograph 1, London: Napo.

Oldfield, M. (2007) 'Risk society', in DPOM.

Oldfield, M. and Grimshaw, R. (2010*) Probation Resources, Staffing and Workloads 2001–2008* (rev. edn), London: Centre for Crime and Justice Studies. Available online at: http://www.crimeandjustice.org.uk/probationspendingrevisedstructure.html.

O'Mahony, D. and Chapman, T. (2007) 'Probation, the state and community – delivering probation services in Northern Ireland', in L. Gelsthorpe and R. Morgan (eds) *Handbook of Probation*, Cullompton: Willan.

Padel, U. and Stevenson, P. (1988) *Insiders: Women's Experience of Prison*, London: Virago, 1988.

Padfield, N. and Maruna, S. (2006) 'The revolving door at the prison gate: exploring the dramatic increase in recalls to prison', *Criminology & Criminal Justice,* 6 (3): 329–352.

Parker, T. (1991) *Life after Life: Interviews with Twelve Murderers*, London: Pan.

Partridge, S. (2004) *Examining Case Management Models for Community Sentences,* Home Office Online Report 17/04. Available online at: http://rds.homeoffice.gov.uk/rds/pdfs04/rdsolr1704.pdf.

Payne, S. (2009) *Redefining Justice: Addressing the Individual Needs of Victims and Witnesses.* Available online at: www.justice.gov.uk/sara-payne-redefining-justice.pdf.

Pease, K. (1999) 'The probation career of Al Truism', *Howard Journal*, 38 (1): 2–16.

Pease, K., Billingham, S. and Earnshaw, I. (1977) *Community Service Assessed in 1976*, Home Office Research Study No. 39, London: HMSO.

Peay, J. (1982) '"Dangerousness" – ascription or description?', in P. Feldman (ed.) *Developments in the Study of Criminal Behaviour: Volume 2: Violence,* Chichester: John Wiley.

Peay, J. (1997) 'Mentally disordered offenders', in M. Maguire, R. Morgan and R. Reiner (eds) *The Oxford Handbook of Criminology* (2nd edn), Oxford: Oxford University Press.

Phillips, C. and Bowling, B. (2007) 'Ethnicities, racism, crime and criminal justice', in M. Maguire, R. Morgan and R. Reiner (eds) *The Oxford Handbook of Criminology* (4th edn), Oxford: Oxford University Press.

Philp, M. (1985) 'Michel Foucault', in Q. Skinner (ed.) *The Return of Grand Theory in the Human Sciences*, Cambridge: Cambridge University Press.

Pillay, C. (ed.) (2000) *Building the Future: The Creation of the Diploma in Probation Studies*, London: NAPO.

Priestley, P., McGuire, J., Flegg, D., Hemsley, V. and Welham, D. (1978) *Social Skills and Personal Problem Solving. A Handbook of Methods*, London, Tavistock.

Prins, H (1995) *Offenders, Deviants or Patients?* (2nd edn) London: Routledge.

Prins, H. (1999) *Will they do it again? Risk Assessment and Management in Criminal Justice and Psychiatry,* London: Routledge.

Prison Commission (1932) *The Principles of the Borstal System*, London: Home Office.

Prison Reform Trust (2005) *Private Punishment: Who Profits?* Available online at: http://www.prisonreformtrust.org.uk/Portals/0/Documents/private%20punishment%20who%20profits.pdf.

Prison Reform Trust (2009) *Bromley Briefings Prison Factfile.* Available online at: http://www.ws3.prisonreform.web.baigent.net/subsection.asp?id=685.

Probation Association (2010) *Probation Trusts in Partnerships: The New Local Performance Context.* Available online at: (http://probationassociation.co.uk/media/6141/probation%20in%20partnerships%20-%20think%20local%20update%20no.1.pdf.

Probation Board for Northern Ireland (PBNI) (2008) Corporate Plan 2008–2011. Available online at: http://www.pbni.org.uk/archive/Publications/Decision%20making/consultation%20docs/cp0811draft.pdf.

Prochaska, J. and DiClemente, C. (1992) 'In search of how people change: applications to addictive behaviors', *American Psychologist* 47 (9): 1102–1114.

Quinney, R. and Trevino, A. (2001) *The Social Reality of Crime*, New Jersey: Transaction.

Pryor, S. (2001) *The Responsible Prisoner*. Available online at: http://www.justice.gov.uk/ inspectorates/hmi-prisons/docs/the-responsible-prisoner-rps.pdf.

Rack, J. (2005) *The Incidence of Hidden Disabilities in the Prison Population: Yorkshire and Humberside Research*, Egham, Surrey: Dyslexia Institute.

Radzinowicz, L. and Hood, R. (1990) *The Emergence of Penal Policy in Victorian and Edwardian England*, Oxford: Oxford University Press.

Raine, J. (2007) 'Managerialism', in DPOM.

Raine, J. and Willson, M. (1993) *Managing Criminal Justice*, London: Harvester Wheatsheaf.

Ramell, P. (2007) 'Her Majesty's Inspectorate of Probation', in DPOM.

Rawls, J. (1972) *A Theory of Justice*, New York: Oxford University Press.

Raynor, P. (1980) 'Is there any sense in social inquiry reports?', *Probation Journal* 27: 78–94.

Raynor, P. (1985) *Social Work, Justice and Control*, Oxford: Blackwell.

Raynor, P. (2004a) 'Rehabilitative and reintegrative approaches', in A. Bottoms, S. Rex and G. Robinson (eds) *Alternatives to Prison: Options for an Insecure Society*, Cullompton: Willan.

Raynor, P. (2004b) 'Opportunity, motivation and change: some findings from research on resettlement', in R. Burnett and C. Roberts (eds) *What Works in Probation and Youth Justice: Developing Evidence-based Practice*, Cullompton: Willan.

Raynor, P. (2006) 'The probation service in England and Wales: modernised or dehumanised', *Criminal Justice Matters* 65 (1): 26–27.

Raynor, P. and Maguire, M. (2006) 'End-to-end or end in tears? Prospects for the effectiveness of the National Offender Management Model', in M. Hough, R. Allen and U. Padel (eds) *Reshaping Probation and Prisons: The New Offender Management Framework*, Bristol: Policy Press.

Raynor, P. and Rex, S. (2007) 'Accreditation', in G. McIvor and P. Raynor (eds), *Developments in Social Work with Offenders, Research Highlights in Social Work 48*, London: Jessica Kingsley.

Raynor, P. and Robinson, G. (2009) *Rehabilitation, Crime and Justice*, Basingstoke: Palgrave Macmillan.

Raynor, P. and Vanstone, M. (2002) *Understanding Community Penalties: Probation, Policy and Social Change*, Buckingham: Open University Press.

Raynor, P. and Vanstone, M. (2007) 'Towards a correctional service', in L. Gelsthorpe and R. Morgan (eds) *Handbook of Probation*, Cullompton: Willan.

Raynor, P., Kinch, J., Roberts, C. and Merrington, S. (2000) *Risk and Need Assessment in Probation Services: An Evaluation,* Home Office Research Study 211, London: Home Office.

Reiman, J. (1990) *The Rich Get Richer and the Poor Get Prison: Ideology, Class and Criminal Justice* (3rd edn), New York: Macmillan.

Rex, S. (1999) 'Desistance from offending: experiences of probation', *Howard Journal*, 38 (4): 366–383.

Rex, S. (2005) *Reforming Community Penalties*, Cullompton: Willan.

Rex, S. and Gelsthorpe, L. (2002) 'The role of community service in reducing offending: evaluating Pathfinder Projects in the UK', *Howard Journal*, 41 (4): 311–325.

Rex, S. and Gelsthorpe, L. (2004) 'Using community service to encourage inclusive citizenship', in R. Burnett and C. Roberts (eds) *What Works in Probation and Youth Justice: Developing Evidence-based Practice*, Cullompton: Willan.

Rex, S., Gelsthorpe, L., Roberts, C. and Jordan, P. (2004) *Crime Reduction Programme An Evaluation of Community Service Pathfinder Projects Final Report 2002*, Home Office Occasional Paper No. 87. Available online at: http://rds.homeoffice.gov.uk/rds/pdfs2/occ87.pdf (accessed June 2010).

Rice, M. (1990) 'Challenging orthodoxies in feminist theory: a black feminist critique', in L. Gelsthorpe and Al. Morris (eds) *Feminist Perspectives in Criminology*, Milton Keynes: Open University Press.

Roberts, C. (2004) 'Offending behaviour programmes: emerging evidence and implications for practice', in R. Burnett and C. Roberts (eds) *What Works in Probation and Youth Justice: Developing Evidence-based Practice*, Cullompton: Willan.

Roberts, C. (2007) 'Assessment instruments', in DPOM.

Roberts, J. (2002) 'Women-centred: the West Mercia community-based programme for women offenders', in P. Carlen (ed.) *Women and Punishment: The Struggle for Justice*, Cullompton: Willan.

Roberts, J. (2007) 'Custody plus, intermittent custody and custody minus', in DPOM.

Robinson, A. (2004) *Domestic Violence MARACs (Multi-Agency Risk Assessment Conferences) for Very High-Risk Victims in Cardiff, Wales: A Process and Outcome Evaluation*. Available online at: http://www.cardiff.ac.uk/socsi/contactsandpeople/academicstaff/Q-S/dr-amanda-robinson-publication.html.

Robinson, A. (2009) *Independent Sexual Violence Advisors: A Process Evaluation*, Home Office Research Report 20. Available online at: http://rds.homeoffice.gov.uk/rds/pdfs09/horr20.pdf.

Robinson, A. and Tregidga, J. (2005) *Domestic Violence MARACS (Multi-Agency Risk Assessment Conferences) for Very High-Risk Victims in Cardiff, Wales: Views from the Victims*. Available online at: http://www.cardiff.ac.uk/socsi/contactsandpeople/academicstaff/Q-S/dr-amanda-robinson-publication.html.

Robinson, G. (2002) 'Exploring risk management in probation practice: contemporary developments in England and Wales', *Punishment and Society* 4 (1): 5–25.

Robinson, G. (2003a) 'Implementing OASys: lessons from research into LSI-R and ACE', *Probation Journal*, 50 (1): 30–40.

Robinson, G. (2003b) 'Risk and risk assessment', in W. H. Chui and M. Nellis (eds) *Moving Probation Forward: Evidence, Arguments and Practice*, Harlow: Pearson Longman.

Robinson, G. (2003c) 'Technicality and indeterminacy in probation practice: a case study', *British Journal of Social Work*, 33 (5): 593–610.

Robinson, G. (2005) 'What works in offender management', *Howard Journal*, 44 (3), 307–318.

Robinson, G. and Burnett, R. (2007) 'Experiencing modernization: frontline probation perspectives on the transition to a National Offender Management Service', *Probation Journal*, 54 (4): 318–337.

Robinson, G. and Crow, I. (2009) *Offender Rehabilitation*, London: Sage.

Robinson, G. and McNeill, F. (2004) 'Purposes matter: examining the "ends" of probation', in G. Mair (ed.) *What Matters in Probation*, Cullompton: Willan.

Robinson, G. and McNeill, F. (2008) 'Exploring the dynamics of compliance with community penalties', *Theoretical Criminology*, 12 (4): 431–449.

Robinson, G. and Raynor, P. (2006) 'The future of rehabilitation: what role for the probation service?', *Probation Journal* 53 (4): 334–346.

Ross, C., Polaschek, D. and Ward, T. (2008) 'The therapeutic alliance: a theoretical revision for offender rehabilitation', *Aggression and Violent Behavior* 13: 462–480.

Rotman, E. (1994) 'Beyond punishment', in R. A. Duff and D. Garland (eds) *Reader on Punishment,* Oxford: Oxford University Press.

Ruck, S. K. (ed.) (1951) *Paterson on Prisons: The Collected Papers of Sir Alexander Paterson*, London: Frederick Muller.

Rumgay, J (2003) 'Partnerships in the probation service', in W. H. Chui and M. Nellis (eds) *Moving Probation Forward: Evidence, Arguments and Practice*, Harlow: Pearson Longman.

Rumgay, J. (2004) 'Dealing with substance-misusing offenders in the community', in A. Bottoms, S. Rex and G. Robinson (eds) *Alternatives to Prison: Options for an Insecure Society*, Cullompton: Willan.

Rumgay, J. (2007) 'Partnerships in probation', in L. Gelsthorpe and R. Morgan (eds) *Handbook of Probation*, Cullompton: Willan.

Rutherford, A. (1993) *Criminal Justice and the Pursuit of Decency*, Oxford: Oxford University Press.

Sandel, M. (1998) *What Money Can't Buy: The Moral Limits of Markets*. Available online at: http://www.tannerlectures.utah.edu/lectures/documents/sandel00.pdf.

Sandel, M. (2009) *Justice: What's the Right Thing to Do?* London: Penguin.

Sandham, J. and Octigan, M. (2007) 'Motivational interviewing', in DPOM.

Scott, P. (1977) 'Assessing dangerousness in criminals', *British Journal of Psychiatry*, 131: 127–142.

Selby, P. (2007) 'Address at Westminster Abbey 11 June 2007'. Available online at: http://www.ws3.prisonreform.web.baigent.net/subsection.asp?id=916.

Sentencing Guidelines Council (2009) *Magistrates' Court Sentencing Guidelines*. Available online at: http://www.sentencingcouncil.org.uk/guidelines/guidelines-to-download.htm.

Shapland, J. (1988) 'Fiefs and peasants: accomplishing change for victims in the criminal justice system', in M. Maguire and J. Pointing (eds) *Victims of Crime: A New Deal?*, Milton Keynes: Open University Press.

Shapland, J., Atkinson, A., Atkinson, H., Dignan, J., Edwards, L., Hibbert, J., Howes, M., Johnstone, J., Robinson, G. and Sorsby, A. (2008) *Does Restorative Justice Affect Reconviction? The Fourth Report from the Evaluation of Three Schemes*, Ministry of Justice Research Series 10 /08. Available online at: http://www.justice.gov.uk/restorative-justice-report_06-08.pdf.

Sharpe, J. (1990) *Judicial Punishment in England*, London: Faber.

Shaw, M. and Hannah-Moffat, K. (2000) 'Gender, diversity and risk assessment in Canadian corrections', *Probation Journal*, 47 (3): 163–172.

Shaw, M. and Hannah-Moffat, K. (2004) 'How cognitive skills forgot about gender and diversity', in G. Mair (ed.) *What Matters in Probation*, Cullompton: Willan.

Sheffield Pathways Out of Crime Study (n.d). Available online at: http://www.scopic.ac.uk/StudiesSPooCS.html#top

Sherman, L. (2009) 'Evidence and liberty: the promise of experimental criminology', *Criminology & Criminal Justice*, 9 (1): 5–28.

Silver, E. and Miller, L. (2002) 'A cautionary note on the use of actuarial risk assessment tools for social control', *Crime and Delinquency*, 48 (1): 138–161.

Skidmore, D. (2007a) 'Conciliation', in DPOM.

Skidmore, D. (2007b) 'Drugs intervention programme', in DPOM.

Skidmore, D. (2007c) 'Offender management as seen by other agencies', in DPOM.

Skinner, B. (1973) *Beyond Freedom and Dignity*, Harmondsworth: Penguin.

Smart, C. (1976) *Women, Crime and Criminology: A Feminist Critique*, London: Routledge & Kegan Paul.

Smith, D. (1998) 'Social work with offenders: the practice of exclusion and the potential for inclusion', in M. Barry and C. Hallett (eds) *Social Exclusion and Social Work: Issues of Theory, Policy and Practice*, Lyme Regis: Russell House.

Smith, D. (2004) *The Links Between Victimization and Offending*, Centre for Law and Society, University of Edinburgh. Available online at: http://www.law.ed.ac.uk/cls/esytc/findings/digest5.pdf.

Smith, D. (2005) 'Probation and social work', *British Journal of Social Work*, 35, 621–637.

Smith, D. (2006) 'Making sense of psychoanalysis in criminological theory and probation practice', *Probation Journal* 53 (4): 361–376.

Smith, D. and Vanstone, M. (2002) 'Probation and social justice', *British Journal of Social Work*, 32 (6): 815–830.

Smith, K. (1989) *Inside Time,* London: Harrap.

Snacken, S. (2010) 'Resisting punitiveness in Europe?', *Theoretical Criminology* 14 (3): 273–292.

Snowden, A. (2007) 'Sex Offender Treatment Programmes (SOTPs)', in DPOM.

Social Exclusion Unit (2002) *Reducing Re-offending by Ex-prisoners*, Office of the Deputy Prime Minister. Available online at: www.gos.gov.uk/497296/docs/219643/431872/468960/SEU_Report.pdf.

Solomon, E. and Silvestri, A. (2008) *Community Sentences Digest* (2nd edn), London: Centre for Crime and Justice Studies. Available online at: http://www.crimeandjustice.org.uk/communitysentencesdigest2008.html.

Spalek, B. (2003) 'Victim work in the probation service: perpetuating notions of an "ideal victim"', in W. H. Chui and M. Nellis (eds) *Moving Probation Forward: Evidence, Arguments and Practice*, Harlow: Pearson Education.

Stanley, S. (2009) 'What works in 2009: progress or stagnation?', *Probation Journal* 56 (2): 153–174.

Stephens, K. and Brown, I. (2001) 'OGRS2 in practice: an elastic ruler?', *Probation Journal*, 48 (3): 179–187.

Stern, V. (1999) *Alternatives to Prison in Developing Countries*, London: International Centre for Prison Studies and Penal Reform International.

Stout, B. (2007) 'Diversity', in DPOM.

Straw, J. (2009) *Probation and Community Punishment*, speech at Probation Study School, University of Portsmouth 4 February 2009. Available online at: http://www.justice.gov.uk/news/sp040209.htm.

Stylianou, S. (2003) 'Measuring crime seriousness perceptions: what have we learned and what else do we want to know', *Journal of Criminal Justice* 31: 37–56.

Sutton, C. (2007) 'ASPIRE', in DPOM.

Sykes, G. and Matza, D. (1957) 'Techniques of neutralization: a theory of delinquency', *American Sociological Review*, 22, 664–670.

Talbot, J. (2008) *No One Knows. Prisoners' Voices: Experiences of the Criminal Justice System by Prisoners with Learning Disabilities and Difficulties*, Prison Reform Trust. Available online at: http://www.prisonreformtrust.org.uk/uploads/documents/No%20One%20Knows%20report-2.pdf.

Tata, C., Burns, N., Halliday, S., Hutton, N. and McNeill, F. (2008) 'Assisting and advising the sentencing decision process: the pursuit of "quality" in pre-sentence reports', *British Journal of Criminology* 48 (6): 835–855.

Taylor, I. (1998) 'Crime, market-liberalism and the European idea', in V. Ruggiero, N. South and I. Taylor (eds) *The New European Criminology: Crime and Social Order in Europe*, London: Routledge.

Thompson, N. (2006) *Anti-Discriminatory Practice* (4th edn), Houndmills: Palgrave Macmillan.

Tilley, N. (ed.) (2006) *Handbook of Crime Prevention and Community Safety*, Cullompton: Willan.

Tilley, N. (2009) *Crime Prevention*, Cullompton: Willan.

The Times (2009) 'Red tape is taking up 75 per cent of probation officers' time (30 October). Available online at: http://www.timesonline.co.uk/tol/news/uk/crime/article6895829.ece.

Toch, H. (1972) *Violent Men*, Harmondsworth: Penguin.

Today's *Zaman* (2009) 'Probation becomes an effective instrument for forestation'. Available online at: http://www.todayszaman.com/tz-web/detaylar.do?load=print&link=178653&yazarAd=.

Tombs, S. and Whyte, D. (2008) *A Crisis of Enforcement: The Decriminalisation of Death and Injury at Work*, London: Centre for Crime and Justice Studies. Available online at: http://www.crimeandjustice.org.uk/acrisisofenforcement.html.

Tonry, M. (1994) 'Proportionality, parsimony and interchangeability of punishments', in A. Duff and D. Garland (eds) *A Reader on Punishment*, Oxford: Oxford University Press.

Tonry, M. (1998) 'Intermediate sanctions', in M. Tonry (ed.) *The Handbook of Crime and Punishment*, New York: Oxford University Press.

Tonry, M. (2004) *Punishment and Politics: Evidence and Emulation in the Making of English Crime Control Policy*, Cullompton: Willan Publishing.

Trotter, C (1999) *Working with Involuntary Clients: A Guide to Practice*, London: Sage.

Tuddenham, R. (2000) 'Beyond defensible decision-making: towards reflexive assessment of risk and dangerousness', *Probation Journal*, 47 (3): 173–183.

Tyler, T. (2003) 'Procedural justice, legitimacy and the effective rules of law', *Crime and Justice* 30: 431–505.

Underdown, A. (1998) *Strategies for Effective Supervision: Report of the HMIP What Works Project*, London: HM Inspectorate of Probation.

van Kalmthout, A. and Derks, J. (eds) (2000) *Probation and Probation Services – A European Perspective*, Nijmegen, The Netherlands: Wolf Legal Publishers.

van Kalmthout, A. and Durnescu, I. (eds) (2008) *Probation in Europe* (2nd edn), Nijmegen: Wolf Legal Publishers.

van Zyl Smit, D. and Ashworth, A. (2004) 'Disproportionate sentences as human rights violations', *Modern Law Review*, 67 (4): 541–560.

Vanstone, M. (2000) 'Cognitive-behavioural work with offenders in the UK: a history of influential endeavour', *Howard Journal* 39 (2): 171–183.

Vanstone, M. (2004a) 'Mission control: the origins and early history of probation', *Probation Journal*, 51 (1): 34–47.

Vanstone, M. (2004b) *Supervising Offenders in the Community: A History of Probation Theory and Practice*, Aldershot: Ashgate.

Vanstone, M. (2008) 'The international origins and initial development of probation: an early example of policy transfer', *British Journal of Criminology* 48 (6): 735–755.

Vaughan, B. (2007) 'The internal narrative of desistance', *British Journal of Criminology*, 47 (3): 390–404.

von Hirsch, A. (1996) *Censure and Sanctions*, Oxford: Oxford University Press.

Victim Support (2007) *Hoodie or Goodie? The Link between Violent Victimisation and Offending in Young People.* Available online at: http://www.victimsupport.org.uk/About %20us/Publications/~/media/Files/Publications/ResearchReports/hoodie-or-goodie-report.

Walker, A. (1993) *Possessing the Secret of Joy*, London: Vintage.

Walker, H. and Beaumont, B. (1981) *Probation Work: Critical Theory and Socialist Practice*, Oxford: Blackwell.

Walker, N. (1980) *Punishment, Danger and Stigma: The Morality of Criminal Justice*, Oxford: Blackwell.

Walker, N. (1991) *Why Punish?* Oxford: Oxford University Press.

Walker, N. (ed.) (1996) *Dangerous People*, London: Blackstone.

Walker, N. (1999) *Aggravation, Mitigation and Mercy in English Criminal Justice*, London: Blackstone.

Walklate, S. (ed.) (2007) *Handbook of Victims and Victimology*, Cullompton: Willan.

Walmsley, R. (2009) World Prison Population List (8th edn), London: ICPS. Available online at: http://www.kcl.ac.uk/depsta/law/research/icps/downloads.php?searchtitle= world+prison&type=0&month=0&year=0&lang=0&author=&search=Search.

Walters, J. (2003) 'Trends and Issues in probation in Europe' – paper delivered to PACCOA Conference, Hobart, Tasmania, 1 September 2003. Available online at: http://www. paccoa.com.au/PDF%20files/John%20Walters.pdf.

Ward, T. and Brown, M. (2004) 'The good lives model and conceptual issues in offender rehabilitation', *Psychology, Crime & Law*, 10 (3): 243–257.

Ward, T. and Maruna, S. (2007) *Rehabilitation*, London: Routledge.

Wargent, M. (2002) 'The new governance of probation', *Howard Journal* 41 (2): 182–200.

Weaver, B. and McNeill, F. (2007) 'Desistance', in DPOM.

Wedge, P. (2007) 'Children and families of offenders', in DPOM.

Wham, C. (2007) 'Correctional Services Accreditation Panel', in DPOM.

Whitehead, P. (2008) 'The probation service reporting for duty', *British Journal of Community Justice*, 6 (3): 86–96.

Whitehead, P. (2010) 'Social theory and probation: exploring organisational complexity within a modernising context', *Social and Public Policy Review*, 4 (2): 15–33.

Whitehead, P. and Statham, R. (2006) *The history of probation: politics, power and cultural change 1876–2005*, Crayford: Shaw and Sons.

Whitfield, D. (2001) *Introduction to the Probation Service* (2nd edn), Winchester: Waterside.

Whyte, B. (2007) 'Scottish courts and sanctions', in DPOM.

Williams, B. (ed.), *Reparation and Victim-Focused Social Work*, London: Jessica Kingsley.

Williams, B. (2007) 'Victims', in DPOM.

Williams, B. (2008) 'The changing face of probation in prisons', in J. Bennett, B. Crewe and A. Wahidin (eds) *Understanding Prison Staff*, Cullompton: Willan.

Williams, B. and Goodman, H. (2007) 'Working for and with victims of crime', in L. Gelsthorpe and R. Morgan (eds) *Handbook of Probation*, Cullompton: Willan.

Willis, A. (1977) 'Community service as an alternative to imprisonment: a cautionary view', *Probation Journal*, 24 (4): 120–125.

Woolf, Lord Justice (1991) *Prison Disturbances April 1990: Report of an Inquiry by the Rt. Hon. Lord Justice Woolf (Part I and II) and His Honour Judge Stephen Tumin (Part II)*, Cm. 1456, London: HMSO.

Wootton, B. (1978) *Crime and Penal Policy: Reflections on Fifty Years' Experience*, London: George Allen and Unwin.

Worrall, A. and Hoy, C. (2005) *Punishment in the Community: Managing offenders, making choices* (2nd edn), Cullompton: Willan.

Wright, M. (2008) *Making Good: Prisons, Punishment and Beyond* (2nd edn), Winchester: Waterside Press.

Wright, M. (2010) *Towards a Restorative Society: A Problem-solving Approach to Harm.* Available online at: http://makejusticework.org.uk/wp-content/uploads/2010/04/Martin-Wright-_-Towards-a-Restorative-Society.pdf.

Zedner, L. (2004) *Criminal Justice*, Oxford: Oxford University Press.

Index